Global Purchasing:
Reaching for the World

VNR MATERIALS MANAGEMENT/LOGISTICS SERIES
Eugene L. Magad, Series Editor

Global Purchasing:
Reaching for the World

Victor H. Pooler C.P.M.

Foreword by Harold Fearon, Ph.D., C.P.M.

VNR VAN NOSTRAND REINHOLD
_____ New York

Library of Congress Catalog Card Number 91-38975
ISBN 0-442-00711-6

Printed in the United States of America

Van Nostrand Reinhold
115 Fifth Avenue
New York, New York 10003

Chapman and Hall
2-6 Boundary Row
London, SE 1 8HN, England

Thomas Nelson Australia
102 Dodds Street
South Melbourne 3205
Victoria, Australia

Nelson Canada
1120 Birchmount Road
Scarborough, Ontario M1K 5G4, Canada

16 15 14 13 12 11 10 9 8 7 6 5 4 3 2 1

Library of Congress Cataloging-in-Publication Data

Pooler, Victor H.
    Global purchasing: reaching for the world/Victor H. Pooler.
        p.   cm.
    Includes bibliographical references and index.
    ISBN 0-442-00711-6
    1. Purchasing. 2. Foreign trade regulation   I. Title.
    II. Title: Global purchasing.
    HF5437.P63   1991
        658.7′2—dc20   91-38975
                                                                    CIP

To the memory of our beloved son, creator of this bookcover sketch, "Reaching for the World," and one of the finest persons who ever lived—

Thomas John Pooler
1959 to 1985

Contents

Foreword

In his book, *Global Purchasing: Reaching for the World*, Victor Pooler has stripped the supposed maze of complexity and misunderstanding from international commerce. This book provides extensive background materials for both the purchasing/materials practitioner and the academic who wishes to use it as a text.

The author's extensive international experience lends credibility. Of special interest are the global supplier sourcing strategies.

The basics of good offshore buying are universal and of great importance to America. There is a need to analyze and investigate global supplier capabilities. On-the-job buyers need global techniques they can apply. Import prices are destined to rise, and it will take better buying strategies to deal with the multi-billions of dollars of purchases made outside the United States.

This book brings together in great detail the full spectrum of benefits available to the global buyer. He or she has an opportunity to view the global economy and understand its financial implications. It contains a working knowledge of import regulations, customs tariffs, currency translation issues, hedging, cultural awareness applied to negotiations, and logistics—all covered in detail.

During the 1990s, the world of the global buyer will become a reality. Long neglected is the American buyer's study of other cultures and the techniques of dealing with suppliers outside our national boundaries. This book goes a long way in filling that knowledge void.

> Harold Fearon, Ph.D., C.P.M
> Director, Center for Advanced Purchasing Studies,
> and the National Association of
> Purchasing Management Professor Emeritus
> at Arizona State University

Preface

This book is a labor of love. My motivation has been twofold: to keep giving to my profession, but primarily as a means to honor my late son. Tom and I had talked about his illustrating a management and sports bookcover. He envisioned a quarterback drifting back to throw a pass to a businessperson sitting at a desk. It was not to be.

After Tom's death, I found his pencil sketch, "Reaching for the World," depicting his hand stretched toward the globe. Hence, the birth of this bookcover and title: "Global Purchasing: Reaching for the World."

The information in this book comes largely from my more than 40 years of experience as a licensed engineer, buyer, senior buyer, manager, director, president, and consultant. Presenting offshore seminars for the last seven years provided the discipline and feedback to improve this work. At the World Trade Institute, in New York City, I increased my working understanding about customs, import regulations, tariffs, currency translation issues, and logistics.

Teaching purchasing as an adjunct professor at Syracuse University helped me to appreciate the need for practical educational material. Foreign government officials attended the International School of Management, where I lectured, bringing me contacts with cultural diversity. Conducting on-site negotiations, facilities capability surveys, and lectures, and travelling to 30 countries has increased my cultural awareness and international business understanding.

For about the past ten years, U.S. companies have urged American buyers to buy offshore. While imports continue today to good advantage, the pendulum of costs has shifted. U.S. labor costs have dropped, compared to those of offshore suppliers. American labor costs are now in fifth place globally.

The buyer has far more economic leverage than many buyers themselves sense. The sales function legitimately seeks to cut out competition. Yet the essence of buying is to *create and use competition* among sellers!

I've long sought to explain the scope of the buying job, which is unusual in business. Often, when making specific purchases, the buyer must control and coordinate other actions, such as engineering requirements, quality standards, and production timing. Yet seldom does the buyer have any direct authority over any of the people or departments having influence.

In 1964 I wrote the American Management Association's "The Purchasing Man and His Job." Typical of the times, this first purchasing management book did not recognize the impending contributions of women in the profession. Nonetheless, it filled a void. Translated into several languages, the book sold in Japan for 20 years. Hopefully this current work will fill an offshore void in the body of knowledge, much as my earliest publication did.

Authors know it's not as simple as sitting down to write a book. When I began POOLER & ASSOCIATES consultant business in 1986, I documented every purchasing, materials management, and importing topic. Using a personal computer and Wordperfect software, it took five years to set down the "nuts and bolts."

Special thanks go to several people who advised, reviewed, and helped with this manuscript. Many suggestions were followed, others were not, and the opinions expressed are mine. I was fortunate to have help from true professionals. They included:

- Dr. Harold Fearon, former chairman of the Department of Management at Arizona State University, and the National Association of Purchasing Management Professor. My thanks to my longtime friend who wrote the Foreword for this book.

Dr. Fearon unknowingly planted the seed for this book. In an interview[1] about the need for educational teaching materials, he asked, "Should there be a formal course in international purchasing?" Assuming a "Yes" response, Dr Fearon continued, "If there should be, are there teaching materials available to do it?...Who's going to teach it?...They're interesting questions, and ones which we have to come to grips with."

- David J. Pooler, former Director of Corporate Purchasing and Subcontracts for General Dynamics. David, my oldest son, has the skills and insights to remove wordiness. His global travels as a skilled practitioner updated me where needed.
  Among those that edited certain chapters were:
- George Yarusavage, Corporate Manager, Transportation, GTE Service Corporation made suggestions on logistics reflecting deregulation.
- Dr. LeRoy H. Graw, Adjunct professor at the University of Texas at Arlington, was a latecomer to the review team. He helpfully volunteered and shaped several chapters on the buying routines.
- Tomas R. Serrano of Associated Technical Services prepared my special graphics.

---

[1]*New England Purchase Magazine.* December 1985. p. 16

- Dr. Joseph L. Cavinato, Penn State University, author of West's *Purchasing and Materials Management*. I was that publisher's reviewer. By a strange twist of fate, the favor was returned when Van Nostrand Reinhold assigned this book to Professor Cavinato as their expert reviewer. Thanks to him for his contributions and early support.

While leading sales training sessions, it became clear to me that *the buying job has much inherent power*. Yet buyers often fail to use leverage because they do not understand their buying role. To gain competitive conditions, a company must put as much global leverage as is possible into the hands of its buyers. And the buyer must use it!

Today's buyer must conscientiously seek to expand their outlook toward global buying. When a young boy picks up a lump of coal, he sees a rock to throw. In the same lump of coal the engineer sees a source of heat energy, the BTUs to cook a meal. The nuclear scientist sees enough pent up power, if released by nuclear fission, to drive a ship to Europe. The lump of coal doesn't change.

The buying job itself may be like that rock. It may look the same to some, but global purchasing is an expansion of an already complex job. There are few limits to the variety and type of global buying arrangements that buyers can carry out. It's a matter of outlook. What do you *see* when you think of global purchasing?

During the 1990s, I believe we shall witness the further evolution of a buyer dealing in global markets with economic acumen. To negotiate and source well offshore, a buyer doesn't have to be a student of world affairs and geopolitics. He or she does have to be knowledgeable and well read! This book is part of the answer to advance a professional strategic overview of today's demanding global purchasing arena.

Global Purchasing:
Reaching for the World

1

Domestic Versus Offshore Sourcing: An Overview

World trade by definition is "To buy and sell worldwide." If a company sells worldwide, can it buy solely from domestic sources? Absolutely not! Unless, like the ostrich, we bury our heads in the sand.

Presidential candidate Wendall Wilkie proclaimed 50 years ago, "It's one world!" The phrase has stuck. Symbolic of today's world economy is the fact that you can buy Gucci bags, Sony Walkmans, and McDonald's hamburgers in almost any country, including the USSR. An American may drive in a Japanese car, shop in a British-owned boutique, and buy clothes imported from China, paying by a check drawn on the Marine Midland Bank, owned by Hong Kong interests.

A one-world economy is evolving. Businesspersons have found that the lowest cost of manufacture can result by taking advantage of native competencies. American companies have forged new business partnerships, joint-ventures, and other international arrangements to share the costs and growth opportunity. Making this possible is rapid communication, computerized information, and better transportation, along with international business acumen.

Europe, the United States, and Japan make up almost 70 percent of the free world's gross national product. Europe's pending consolidation in 1992, to the point of a single currency, is now being resisted in part primarily by the United Kingdom. Today it is speculated that the world economy is integrated by 50 percent. Projecting ahead, perhaps 75 percent integration will take place within 20 years.

The three trading blocks are compared in Table 1-1. The United States has the world's largest national economy. With a gross national product (GNP) at $5,200 billion, the United States is number one in both imports and exports. Its foreign trade alone, at $837 billion, ranks as the world's fifth largest economy. Some American states' economies are larger than many nations'. California's economy

1

TABLE 1-1.   How the great trading blocks stack up in 1990.

	EEC	USA	Japan
Population (millions)	325	249	123
Gross Domestic Product (Billion U.S. $)	4,856	5,201	2,834
$ per Capita	14,942	20,887	23,040
Trade Balance (Billions U.S. $)	-7.58	-114.98	+76.92
Inflation %	4.7	4.8	2.3

DATA SOURCE: Copyright DRI/McGraw-Hill. Reprinted with permission

is larger than Brazil's, and Texas's is more than the combined GNP of the Association of Southeast Asian Nations.

How large is current world trade between all nations? An estimate is $2,600 billion. Japan and Germany rank number two and three, respectively, in the free world, as seen in Table 1-2. Some fast-growing economies are omitted that may produce a far different list if compiled in the next ten years. With the world economy growing about 3 percent annually, there could be some surprises about the countries that may be contenders for future strong trade.

Brazil, with low wages and large labor resources, is a large producer of

TABLE 1-2.   GNP and international trade of major nations.

Gross national product in U.S. billions of dollars			
	GNP 1989	Int'l Trade	% World Trade
United States	5,201	837	32
USSR	2,400	52[a]	—
Japan	2,834	432	15
Germany, West	1,203	493	19
East	135	60	2
Combined	1,338	553	21
France	956	296	11
Italy	866	197	8
United Kingdom	834	240	9
Canada	550	190	7

Total All International Trade = $2,600 Billion

DATA SOURCE: Copyright DRI/McGraw-Hill. Reprinted with permission.
[a]Value understated by barter.

agriculture products as well as major arms seller. From 1950 through 1980, Brazil's growth rate was about 8 percent. South Korea, also growing 7 to 8 percent annually, has a work force that works harder than even the Japanese. Americans know how diligently the Japanese work, but some Koreans refer to them as lazy. Cheap labor and government policies are supporting growth, but labor unrest threatens to slow their future progress.

Mainland China is slowly developing and has yet to fully embrace the free market. China wants trade growth after witnessing Taiwan's progress and contemplating its own inheritance of Hong Kong at the end of this century. Their GNP is growing at 3 to 4 percent per year, and is expected to step up to about 5 percent per year. India may be the sleeper in the developing nations. Somewhat backward in economic development, India has been growing since 1979 at a rate of almost 6 percent. India has a highly educated professional work force.

American trade has developed heavily with our friends in Europe and Japan, but Americans often underestimate the extent of our trade with Canada. Canada is the United States's largest trading partnership, with about $175 billion of trade flowing across our border last year. Together, we make up the largest trading partnership in the world.

Japan is number 2 and closing rapidly. Mexico is a distant number three among America's trading partners, with $33 billion, 70 percent of their total trade. However, Mexican reforms to their economy is making Mexico attractive for trade and investment.

As the economic leader of the free world, Americans champion "free trade." We deal with 35 major trading countries. The brand of free trade that made America successful was by obliterating state barriers. This was possible under our one government. Trade is so important to the United States that there is consideration to create a cabinet-level committee to assess strategic implications for the nation.

INTERNATIONAL TRADE ENVIRONMENT

The American economy, beginning early in the 1980s, found that some domestic companies were unable to compete in world markets. This had a major impact on both buyers and sellers. They were caught in the squeeze of trying to stay competitive while still satisfying customers who were themselves striving to meet the flood of foreign competition. Foreign components and supplies upset some older secure channels of supply, as buyers were sometimes assigned target percentages of offshore purchases.

Globalization of production has reshaped and reduced the U.S. manufacturing base. Economics of the early 1980s adversely affected the United States, as high production costs made American products non-competitive in world markets. An old story that bears repeating is how the American baseball glove was 95-percent replaced by gloves from Japan, Taiwan, or South Korea. And gloves and clothes were just the start. The American-invented radio is 100-percent produced abroad, as are black-and-white TV sets. Few companies assemble color TV sets in the United States, and those that do rely heavily on imported components. Japan and South Korea make most videocassette recorders (VCRs).

Japan produces much of our high fidelity audio equipment and machine tools, as well as most hand-held calculators. VCR products sold with an RCA label are a private brand purchase from Hitachi.

Today, 98 percent of the cameras Americans use are imported, as are 85 percent of women's shoes, 65 percent of our luggage, seven of every ten calculators sold, and three of every ten cars. Even six of ten personal computers are imported, and some of IBM's models reveal a "Made in Japan" label on their keyboard.

Our basic industries producing steel, copper tubing, and textiles have suffered large losses and layoffs of employees. Seeing inroads into their markets, American firms struck back and bought into foreign operations. Or they put their manufacturing facilities in other countries. "Technological insertion" was their term to teach others how to do the job. These new ventures in turn competed with their American plants to determine where they would make their products.

COUNTERTRADE BECOMES A REALITY

Other countries, particularly developing countries, those behind the former Soviet Iron Curtain, and China, want part of the trading action. Trade has lagged with these state-controlled economies. It is difficult for American businessmen or women to sell to or buy from them. American buyers often must deal with governments in these managed economies.

In the 1960s Far Eastern countries began to seek access to America's technology, but they lacked dollars. So, in effect, they said, "We'll buy from you, but you should buy from us. Of course, you pay us in dollars." To make sales, you must go by their rules. Why? *They've built it into their contracts!*

These types of activities have existed for years in Germany, France, and Austria, but are new in the United States. About 120 countries today insist on countertrade arrangements. Perhaps as much as 20 percent of today's world trade involves countertrade. Some believe it may rise to about 50 percent. Among solely American companies, such activity is described as *reciprocity*, which is illegal. Among international partners, such practice is legal and often a required activity.

Probably half of all trade is under some sort of restriction. You can't export or import anything to Brazil if it's already made there. For example, if a manufacturer in Brazil wants to use a pump they make themselves outside the country, the company must use a competitor's pump if it is made in Brazil.

Other examples of restrictions reported are:

- Indonesia requires that any exporter selling more than $750,000 of goods to the state must buy an equal amount of local goods.

- Saudi Arabia wants their oil partners to buy their rock bits and tools in their country. So does Brazil, India, and Nigeria.[1]
- Mexico requires that 50 percent of every car be made from native parts.
- Canada, Australia, and most European and Far Eastern countries use offset to increase their exports, when purchasing from the United States.

Types of Countertrade

Countertrade can be defined as "any transaction involving an exchange of goods or services for something of equal value." Sometimes cash is used to pay for any value differences. Types of countertrade are barter, counterpurchases, buyback, offset, and joint venture.

Barter is a direct swap of materials or goods without funds. In exchange for $2 billion worth of soda, Pepsi got 10 ships and $1 billion worth of vodka from the USSR. An American ice cream firm sells Russian matroiska dolls along with walnuts and honey. And a magazine publisher sells a Soviet edition for output from a sausage factory and ad revenues in the United States.[2]

"Counterpurchases" occur when the seller agrees to buy partial value of an initial sale from the buyer. Of all countertrades, 26 percent are this type of arrangement, in which the sale of a company's product is tied into a separate agreement. The seller agrees to buy, from the country to which the sale was made, part or full value of the sale. These obligations can be assigned to a third party by prior agreement.

In "compensation payback" the seller agrees to buy back production from a plant or technology sold in the original transaction. Europeans use the term "compensation payback," and Americans use "buy-back."

Offset is most common of all, with about 43 percent of countertrade volume. Offset is when a seller is obliged to offset from the purchaser a percentage of the sales value, to compensate the buying country. Offset can take the form of purchases or other actions that include:

- Direct offset—Those purchases of items or technologies directly relating to the sale of goods. An example would be the sale of F16 fighter planes being offset by a purchase of items or materials that go into those planes.
- Indirect offset—Those items not directly linked to the sale. For example:

  a. Purchase of Turkish rugs,
  b. Provision for export development assistance to the buying country in areas they designate, and
  c. Assistance, including investments in the buying country in areas of the country's expressed need.

---

[1]Rethinking global corporate strategy. *Wall Street Journal.* April 29, 1985.
[2]*Forbes.* June 1990. p. 9.

Offset creditable transactions are subject to the priorities requested by the buying country and the creativity of the seller in coming up with projects that meet those priorities. In making this kind of deal, a sales contract binds the seller to buy, from the buying nation, a percentage of the value of the sale. Part of the sales value is offset by purchases to be made by the seller.

True-life offsets made by equipment manufacturers have actually included buys of panty hose, vacation excursions, and wine. Other stories are told of Polish hams and Romanian nails, and other exotic combinations. Some deals, recently reported in the *Wall Street Journal*[3] help show us what is going on:

- Control Data sold a computer to Russia by agreeing that they would buy Soviet Christmas cards. Religious customers did not buy the "Made in the USSR" label.
- Coca-Cola found itself stuck with bathtubs from Eastern Europe, along with substandard Chinese honey. Coca-Cola also built a tomato-paste factory in Turkey and helped build a whey-protein plant in the Soviet Union.
- Goodyear traded "tires for minerals, textiles, agriculture products, almost anything."
- General Electric and Northrup sold aircraft engines and aircraft to Switzerland while agreeing to a 50-percent purchase of Swiss tools.
- Boeing and Rolls-Royce concluded a $1 billion swap of ten 747s for Saudi Arabian oil.

The above examples show the relationships that are part of today's business arrangements. These deals allow foreign countries to develop specific industries, achieve technological advances, improve foreign exchange, and manage large external debts. How much countertrade do most countries expect? The percentage compensation varies with each transaction. Some may be as low as 10 percent, while others require full compensation, or more than 100 percent.

A *joint venture* is a coproduction effort to manufacture in a host country that might supply land, raw materials, brick and mortar, and labor. The U.S. partner often provides technology, some production machinery, and perhaps finance. Output is shared by the partners.

Globally, under the U.S. "Free Trade" policy, the U.S. companies have more freedom to compete. This is an area where purchasing and marketing can work together. Reasons for fostering countertrade activities are that it:

- Promotes and increases the certainty for future sales of the company's products overseas;
- Meets foreigners' demands that sales to them be matched by purchases from them in some way;

---

[3]1985. Selling tool: countertrading Rises as Nations seek aid with exports. *Wall Street Journal.* March 13.

- Supplies the domestic company's needs for real industrial products, not exotic handicrafts; and
- Is the only way to make sales to poorer countries where import financing isn't available

Countertrade Impacts Buying

Does countertrade actually affect importers and buyers? You bet it does! These newer trade tactics affect your buying and managing job. Of those responding to a survey by *Purchasing* magazine, 51 percent said their company made such deals in the past year. Another survey showed that 83 percent of buyer respondents are partners in countertrade activities. In 34 percent of the responses, the purchasing function is responsible to find internal uses for countertrade goods. Fifty percent reported they can use 100 percent of accepted goods within their firms. The other half had to search for a way to use alternative parts, sheet metal, grain, and even vacation cruises.

Often large, long-term military sales are made this way. A report from the International Trade Commission (ITC) said the United States has been making billions of dollars in military sales under agreements that, in return, require U.S. companies to buy heavily from allies in Europe, the Middle East, and Asia.

Those purchasing managers that need to start a countertrade program will want to review this strategy below. Countertrade literally puts American buyers on the foreign supplier's payroll. They travel around the globe to find what they can buy to follow marketing's effort to sell abroad. Buyers must push within their companies for increased purchases overseas.

Starting A Countertrade Program

The Trade Act of 1982 enables the United States to set up Export Trading Companies and countertrading cooperatives, to jointly help absorb a variety of required countertrade purchases. To start up a countertrade program, these guidelines may help:

- Take an inventory of all purchases corporate-wide.
- Test foreign sourcing with countertrade possibilities.
- Search out other U.S. companies and countertrade co-operatives to see if any collective options exist.
- When a match is found, pursue it.

How your company organizes for countertrade depends on your needs. With a large potential, you may want a specialist. At least have someone accountable to be responsible to handle the internal communications.

Foreign Export Trading Companies (ETCs) match international buyers with sellers. Credits may be sold or bought by a third party with bank approval. Switch trading is the term used to describe the use of clearing account credits or debits under trade agreements. By joining a co-op, smaller and medium sized firms can participate in countertrade-type activities. Most trading co-ops are divisions of major corporations. Examples are Caterpillar World Trading Co., Coca-Cola, General Electric, Combustion Engineering, Control Data, Rockwell International, and Honeywell High Tech Trading, Inc. These co-ops welcome inquiries from any company with interest. Westinghouse Trading Company offers a total approach, including global sourcing, import, and transportation services.

These ETCs were hailed as being a step toward a U.S. trade revival, but few domestic companies report making much money. Some companies were reported as having losses. Sears announced in 1986 that, after four years of losses, its World Trade Inc. was being phased out. So far, U.S. trading companies haven't made much headway versus the Japanese, who control at least 10 percent of U.S. export trade. The Japanese point out that it took them almost 100 years of persistence to develop to their current dominance.

In the meantime there's a moral for buyers considering the use of a U.S. (or indeed any) trading company: check the finances of such intermediaries as carefully as you would those of any important supplier.

Some caveats to overcome problems with countertrade are:

- Be wary of product dumping or getting stuck with unwanted or low-quality goods to complete a sale.
- In the agreement itself, get the broadest definition with leeway in qualifying for the offset. Also, secure the longest length of time to fulfill the conditions without penalties.
- Expect that complex and extensive negotiations will be required.
- May limit more helpful buying options.

EMERGENCE OF THE GLOBAL CORPORATION

Consider how joint ventures and the quest for world trade growth have led to the emergence of the "global corporation." Global companies have integrated production economies while the world is still fragmented by politics. Perhaps the automobile industry typifies the global corporation. Facing tough domestic and foreign competition, U.S. automakers closed down plants, laid off employees, and fought to survive. As each American assembler closed, the loss of business hurt hundreds of smaller suppliers of parts. Now, many foreign parts suppliers are moving their production into America.

American automakers build cars in Canada, Brazil, Australia, Mexico, and many other countries. American auto companies at first decried the foreign invasion of autos and sought the imposition of quotas. Japan again invoked their "voluntary quotas" to forestall imposition of formal quotas. We've seen that that action hasn't slowed their export success.

The trend to increased offshore sourcing is expanding. Imported cars make up 31 percent of the U.S. auto market and sell for prices ranging from a low $5,000, for the Yugo GV, to the $198,000 Rolls-Royce Limousine.

America's companies have stepped up sales of foreign-made cars under their own name. American companies have pushed to join forces and share technology. The idea has been to keep home base production, or control it by overseas manufacture through a joint-venture partnership.

Each of the Big 3 automakers has joined forces with a Japanese producer. Chrysler owns part of dominant partner Mitsubishi Corporation. Chrysler will build in the United States, but on a Mazda chassis. In turn, Mitsubishi Corporation is a 15 percent owner of Korea's Hyundai. General Motors and Toyota have similar arrangements. Isn't it interesting to watch the complexity of relationships in today's global reality?

Imports have affected America's electronics and appliance industries also. Though developments are not as dramatic as in autos, the air conditioning industry and others are affected by global markets. The total of all imports to the United States is about $500 billion. An estimated 15 percent, or almost $75 billion of American imports, is by U.S. multinational companies.

There are significant differences between international and domestic commerce. Political reality of foreign trade is important. Sovereign countries promote policies to protect their economic growth, increase employment, and maintain price stability. A summary of some developments affecting trade includes the following:

- World markets are more complex, but provide new market opportunities.
- Increased worldwide competition is a fact.
- Emergence of bilateral trade agreements aimed at improving world supply by dropping trade barriers.
- Countertrade in purchasing becomes a necessity.
- There is ongoing redeployment of capital and human resources on a global scale.
- Today we are seeing continuous company reorganization with fewer people and a new flexibility.

The global corporation is serving global markets as part of complex interwoven global relationships. Equity ownership is global. International boundaries are no longer a barrier to financial money transfer as the global corporation operates. Some executives tell of close business relationships that are a natural growth of national economies melding into one global economy. The business leader of today needs a global outlook. The purchasing manager and the buyer's vision can no longer stop at the national border. The marketplace is global, customers are global, and competition is global.

CHANGING PURCHASING ROLE

Basic purchasing function objectives are to:

- Control expenditures;
- Assure economic supply; and
- Contribute to profits.

Although these objectives remain the same, the scope of the procurement buying process is broadened and improved by a global buying perspective. Believing that buying overseas is too complicated, some buyers hesitate to try it. Others mistakenly figure that it's little different from buying locally. Procedures for doing business abroad are much the same as doing business in town. The procurement process is shown in Figure 1-1. However, use of added forms and details come into play.

Look at it this way. If you live in New York (or your home town), buying from California isn't quite as easy as buying locally. When offshore sourcing, to buy from Korea, Japan, or Germany, it gets much more difficult.

If an item can't be found in one part of the world, the American buyer can buy it in another. And the buyer may want to buy it from a third country and ship it elsewhere. For example, if it's more helpful, buy from Singapore and ship to China, with the arrangements controlled from the United States. There is no limit to the variety and type of global buying agreements that are possible.

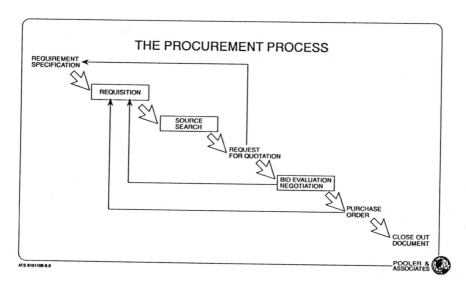

FIGURE 1-1.   The procurement process.

Some known examples show the involvement. A buyer found China's low labor rates attractive, but the Chinese government's allocation system for materials inefficient. Schedule reliability was poor. So, total costs were not always as economic as expected. Hong Kong is a source for low tech electronics and mechanical work. Major American electronics companies buy parts for shipment into Hong Kong and then via rail to China for assembly. Hong Kong performs the testing and packaging before exporting to the United States.

It's not enough to make goods in just the native country alone. If these products are sold elsewhere, they must be globally competitive.

You could compare the role of the purchasing manager (PM) with the production manager. The production manager works within the center of the sphere defined as manufacturing. The buyer is on the fringe of this production sphere, but also on the fringe of a sphere of global suppliers. So, the buyer is in conflict between two worlds.

Using the global marketplace, the buyer gains leverage to keep domestic suppliers' prices competitive. What incentives exist to buy in worldwide markets? When surveyed by *Purchasing* magazine[4] about reasons for offshore buys, the following were reported (percentage of managers giving that reason is in parenthesis):

1. *Price* (74 percent)—The major reason for going off shore. About 7 percent of all components come from overseas sources. Buyers report price advantages yield savings of 20 to 30 percent. A few report up to 40 percent.
2. *Quality* (46 percent)—Comes in second (though companies claim it is number one).
3. *Uniqueness* (41 percent)—The item is unavailable in the United States.
4. *Increased number of suppliers* (35 percent)—Where there is inadequate domestic supply (better deliveries).
5. *Worldwide technology exposure* (23 percent).
6. To become *globally competitive* (21 percent).
7. Meeting supplier's *"offset"* requirements (5 percent).

Exports provide capital and jobs for natives, while imports provide capital and jobs for offshore suppliers. Getting goods abroad at a lower price and better quality increases U.S. consumers' buying power. As a result, real income rises, giving a higher standard of living.

What Differs When We Buy Offshore?

When buying globally, buyers have to consider the differences that affect buying offshore. Routing shipments through foreign countries, clearing through customs, and paying the proper duty are examples of procedures not required for purely

---

[4]1987. The why, how, and what of overseas purchasing. *Purchasing*. June 25, p. 54.

domestic buying. While cryptic, the following compiled listing came from many discussions about this subject.

To study the offshore marketplace, ask ourselves and explore, "What are the differences between domestic and international buying?"

Function	Domestic	International
Determine need	Sales, production	Longer forecast
Inventory impact	Asset dollars	Usually larger, longer supply lines
Specifications	Quality impact	More specific
Information sources	Accurate data	Not as available
Communications	One language	Translation problems
Dispute settlement	Negotiations	Arbitration
Negotiation	Key activity	Multiple cultures and customs
Political/government	Seldom involved	Often more vital
Business environment	Stable rules	Multiple environments, diverse and changing
Sourcing	Homogenous market	Fragmented markets, much more complex
Legalities	U.S. Law, UCC	GATT and treaties
Scope of buying job	Broad	Far more expansive
Supplier relations	Important	More demanding, time consuming
Countertrade	Illegal	Part of marketing strategy
Placing PO	Routine	Added clauses
Documentation	Standard	New forms to execute
Payment	Open account	Letter of credit, etc.
Currency	Single	Varied value and stability
Exchange restrictions	None	Translation risks
Tariffs	None	Customs regulations
Distribution	Air, rail, truck	Plus ocean transport
Insurance	Blanket	Marine

International Versus Global Buyer

What is the distinction between an international and a global buyer? The first time a buyer imports from a foreign source, he is an international buyer. An exchange of goods taking place across a nation's boundaries is international buying. The international buyer seeks mainly his own advantage.

An example of global buying follows. A company that has divisions in 15 countries seeks to get maximum value. In deciding sources, the buyer doesn't solely use others' volumes to enhance its own purchase. The global buyer uses competitive advantage when the minimum total landed costs are achieved for all buying operations, worldwide. Global buyers want to increase economic leverage to benefit all. Products produced for shipment elsewhere must be globally competitive.

In summary, America is still striving to revitalize its manufacturing in order to reassert economic leadership in the free world. We need to strategically orient ourselves globally, not solely in marketing but in procurement as well. Buyers should apply the leverage that global supply brings to affect the cost of products purchased.

Because of the high impact of material costs, purchasing pushed aggressively to use global supply to attain "worldwide cost leadership." A strategic emphasis was to maintain market share, which resulted in an increased emphasis on procurement as part of an integrated global corporation's strategic management.

Today's purchasing manager has to have and use knowledge of the "ins and outs" of foreign sourcing. The American buyer is rising to the challenge. Offshore purchases make it possible for many American companies to better compete and sell abroad.

Manufacturing, cost of product, and quality have become focal points of corporate strategy. Those companies that can deliver a product anywhere at the lowest possible cost will survive and grow, as others fall aside. International competition can be healthy! This is a new global game.

Will importing cool down? No way! Improvements in data collection, communication, and transport have forged a one-world economic climate. Partnerships have spawned today's global corporation, which mandates that buying be global as well as international in scope for long-term survival.

Some Buyers Are Reluctant to Source Offshore

Despite the overwhelming evidence of advantages, many purchasing managers find it difficult to get their buyers to act. Probably nobody has surveyed why buyers don't source offshore. Many buyers find it is easier to buy what they bought locally the last time. There are advantages and disadvantages in worldwide buying and selling. What's wrong with local buying? Nothing, provided good value results, but you won't know unless you've tried!

DISINCENTIVES—ROADBLOCKS TO OVERCOME

Experience has shown that some disincentives or *roadblocks* to successfully source offshore are:

- Language barrier;
- Nationalism—local source preference;

- Lack of knowledge of foreign supplier's culture;
- Customs regulations and duties;
- Currency exchange rate confusion; and
- Lack of buying strategies.
  These disincentives should be addressed when starting our program.

Language Barrier

Language is often the first and most important barrier. Offshore supplier's person-nel speak much less English than Americans think. Because they nod and say, "Yes," trying to be friendly, doesn't mean they always understand.

Within some countries, several languages are spoken. India has 16 languages with hundreds of dialects. Indian businessmen acknowledge that, with the English language, they can run their country. Even a tiny country, such as Switzerland, has three separate languages—French, German, and Italian. Two languages are spoken in Belgium and Canada. In Toronto, even a mundane traffic ticket has 7 languages printed on it.

In such an environment, the need is clear to speak slowly and avoid local slang. Horror stories have been known to occur! Pepsi once advertised on Taiwanese billboards, "Come alive with the Pepsi generation." Or so they thought. People interpreted it to mean, "Pepsi will bring your ancestors back from the dead."

The good news is that English is the language of international business in most areas of the globe. While you may not know many foreign languages (most American businessmen know only their own), it pays to greet the host or guest in their native tongue.

Nationalism—Local Source Preference

Nationalism does get in the way—universally, most buyers prefer to buy locally. "Buying Europe" is now becoming common in that region. Many buyers have a home country bias when deciding sourcing. "Buy America, Born in the USA" are a way of life getting renewed interest since the Gulf War surge of patriotism.

Protectionist sentiment has solid support among Americans. Offshore competi-tion has hurt many workers by causing plant closings and job losses. At one time, Congress had an estimated 300 bills bottled up in committee. They all called for increased tariffs that translate into higher prices for consumers. Most American consumers won't buy just American if it costs them money. Loyalty isn't too strong when it hurts the pocketbook.

Subconsciously, many buyers are local-buying oriented, and are more comfortable buying domestically. Perhaps they are driven by human nature to buy in town, in state, or in the United States, rather than foreign. The Japanese find it culturally difficult to buy foreign goods. For many reasons they manage to loyally buy Japanese.

A *USA Today* poll[5] reports that 54 percent of Americans strongly prefer to buy domestic goods. As expected, those people over age 65 are more likely to buy American than those age 18 to 25 (67 percent versus 25 percent). What about the preference of buyers in other countries? Citizens from other industrialized nations deliberately try to buy their own nation's goods. Of Spaniards polled by the Atlantic Institute for International Affairs, 87 percent agreed that they buy domestic-made products to boost their country's economic health. So do 70 percent of Italians, followed by the British and French at 65 percent. So, American buyers are not the only ones to have a "buy local" behavior.

Other buyers are just the opposite. They believe that all foreign goods are superior. "When in Rome...," "We can't buy good quality in town," or "The grass is always greener..." This type of buyer subconsciously feels we have to abandon our background culture and adapt to the foreign sellers' local culture and business practices. Simply getting a local seller to match a better price from a foreign source is a common though sometimes shortsighted practice.

Lack of Knowledge of Foreign Supplier's Culture

Lack of knowledge of the foreign supplier's culture has long been a weakness of American negotiators. Too often, the American buyer is seen as too direct and impersonal. In a hurry to conclude an agreement, his or her impersonal approach often offends the sensitivities of foreign businessmen. This result is clearly unintentional. A better understanding of others' culture and practices through study, travel, and experience all help overcome this roadblock.

Customs Regulations and Duties

High customs duties can wipe out a favorably quoted price. An unexpected change in duty rates based upon location of manufacture can change sourcing decisions. Many benefits available to importing buyers are not used. Chapters 8 and 9 covers these subjects in detail.

Currency Exchange Rate Confusion

Concerning financial considerations, importing buyers must work with and understand exchange rates thoroughly! The key is to decide whether to buy in U.S. dollars or in the foreign currency *before* placing the order. Also, when you buy in another currency, the possibility of translation losses affecting profitability concerns management.

---

[5] *USA Today* poll published June 11, 1984.

An attitude often expressed by buyers is, "I let finance take care of that." These buyers don't recognize that, while finance can act, only they know about the buying transactions. Without a sound grasp of these issues, buyers can't hope to take the action to allow finance to do its job.

Lack of Buying Strategies

This last roadblock is the most important. We might debate whether the economy is "one-world," but it's clear we must have an integrated global purchasing and materials strategy to world trade. Global purchasing is now a must. That being the case, buyers must conscientiously expand their outlook overcoming these road-blocks. By starting an offshore global buying program, buyers will be in a better position to help their companies complete globally.

2

Starting an Offshore Global Buying Program

A first priority should be to adopt a strategy to *start* an offshore global buying program. Should the purchasing chief appoint someone responsible or assume that role? A purchasing manager starting foreign sourcing faces two options:

1. Start with the available buyers and learn offshore know-how; or
2. Locate and hire experienced foreign sourcing buyers.

Can we isolate international from domestic buying? Yes, but we shouldn't. The reliance on the domestic buyer appears as the logical option. We should use our domestic expertise and expand purchasing outlook into global strategic procurement planning to gain offshore experience. The present buyers can become global buying experts with practice.

One essential is to provide education and exposure to offshore experience. Share with others that *purchasing is a multifunctional process*, and it will take both time and effort to expand globally. We must support worldwide sourcing within the business strategic planning of the company to assure support and resources.

Some foreign suppliers will arrange local stocks. Many foreign suppliers require lead times of six months to one year. Loss of flexibility to change can be the result. As an example, many Japanese firms will only change a schedule before they firm it to their plants.

Longer supply lines, loss of local stocking arrangements, and increased inventories may result from offshore sourcing. Allow four weeks in-transit shipping time from Europe, and five to six weeks from the Far East.

STRATEGY #1. IMPLEMENTATION STEPS
TO GLOBAL SOURCING

Let's assume you are just starting to source overseas. One of America's finest champion high jumpers always stood and nodded his head before his leap upward. He explained that he pictures each step. While the final takeoff step made the big difference, he had to see *each* step before starting. Some of these offshore steps are readily known by experienced buyers, yet each is part of the process. Don't skip any of them.

The following implementation steps will provide a useful offshore checklist:

Step #1. Commit Yourself To Study The Marketplace

Test your resolve to go through with foreign buying. This may sound like strange advice. However, purchasing managers who have started offshore sourcing know that some domestic buyers are prejudiced against buying foreign. Some buyers just go through the motions of getting offshore quotes, convinced that they don't want to buy overseas. Perhaps there is a sound reason for local sourcing only; but until the choices are explored, you can't be sure.

Step #2. Set *Your* Global Sourcing Strategies

Before a buyer makes an inquiry, certain issues should be considered. For example, should you buy in dollars or foreign currency? What affect does duty cost have on your buying decision? Simply making an inquiry may lock in your buying channel. So important is this strategy step, it is reserved for expanded coverage in Chapter 3.

Step #3. Expand the Knowledge Base—Sources
of Information

For domestic buys, the buyer has available the Thomas Register, Dun & Bradstreet, Sweet's catalogue, and so forth. How about offshore? The following suggestions list the best sources of global information.

Credit reporting firms issue guides on importing.

Encyclopedia—World Marketing Guide. Annual international directory by Dun and Bradstreet, 99 Church St., NYC 10007. This international directory lists principal international financial and business information for about 50,000 companies in 133 countries. Companies are located by S.I.C. number and listed alphabetically by country.

Similar to Thomas' Register are the following English edition directories of sources in Europe—use both:

Bottin International, 1 Rue Sebastian Bottin, Paris 7, France.
Wer Liefert Was, 2 Hamburg 11, Post Fach 140, Germany.

There are many places to get information such as the international yellow pages by country, city, and product. An 800 number found in your local phone directory can get yellow pages and white pages from anywhere around the world. An example is AT&T's "Italian Yellow Pages for the U.S." Directory (Issued annually in English). Free upon request or by writing to AT&T, 412 Mt. Kemble Ave., Morristown, NJ 07960-1995. Contains target industries, suppliers, and so forth.

U.S. Department of Commerce

The Department of Commerce, in Washington, D.C., has many area trade specialists in its International Trade Administration, (ITA). The department's (ITA) has local field offices. Export and import licenses are obtainable within 60 days at no charge.

Personnel are often returned foreign service commercial officers, available for counselling. The ITA's main thrust is to increase exports. Appointments are required. There is an East-West Trade Assistance group (BEWT) and another for the Near East (CAGNE).

Now that communist walls are falling in Eastern Europe, the ITA supports phone contacts through Soviet Desk (202) 377-4655, Polish Desk (202) 377-2645, and the Hungarian Desk (202) 377- 2645. Information on trade can be secured from the Eastern European Information Center (EEIC), Washington, D.C. Also, the USSR Trade Representation is in Washington, D.C.

In New York City are the U.S.–USSR Trade & Economics Board, Armtog Trading Corp. (Soviet firm), Polish Trade Office (212) 370-5300, and the Hungarian Trade Office (212) 752-3060.

"International Business Publications from ITA" lists all Department of Commerce publications. This and other information is in this book's Bibliography.

Various state departments of commerce represent the many states that take an active interest in exporting its products and often publish trade directories, and so on, as well as give assistance involving importing. Most have a mailing list service that gives names of foreign organizations interested in exporting products, by country, industry, or product interest. Apply through local Commerce district offices.

The Small Business Administration often has college students from universities with a department of international trade who may be available to help on basic overseas information. The SBA's Export/Import Services (XIS) screens both export and import data that is maintained by the University of Georgia. Contact the SBA district office that serves your community.

Chambers of Commerce

The U.S. Chamber of Commerce has contacts with overseas association memberships. A listing, "World Directory of Chambers of Commerce," gives foreign trade services available and is obtained from the Chamber of Commerce, Washington, D.C.

Visiting American Chambers of Commerce abroad provide aid for overcoming local barriers, such as language, customs, laws, and regulations.

The International Chamber of Commerce (ICC) is a grouping of national committees in 58 countries, with ties to members in 50 others. It has 7,000 member companies and business associations that believe in self-regulation of business. The U.S. Chamber of Commerce is an affiliate.

The ICC's role is to coordinate and consult within the United Nations, EEC, and others, to assist in practical services to business. ICC publishes a wide variety of books and pamphlets listed in the Bibliography. Their *Business World* has four issues per year of information on international business, and is available for about a $15 subscription.

Foreign chambers of commerce may be contacted to help identify local trade directories, and so forth. For example, the Hong Kong General Chamber of Commerce (22nd floor, United Centre, 95 Queensway, Hong Kong. Tel: (5) 299229. Telex: 83535 TRIND HX) assists with Hong Kong trade and joint ventures. They handle trade inquiries, arbitration cases, issue Certificates of Origin, and will arrange trade missions.

Purchasing Associations

Contact other buyers who buy offshore, through the National Association of Purchasing Management's Info Center (special kits on selected subjects with over 850 books available). Write NAPM, 2055 East Centennial Circle, PO Box 22160, Tempe, AZ 85282. Tel: (602) 752-6276, Fax: (602) 752-7890.

Join NAPM's International Group, one of 16 special groups that has 300 members who are interested in sharing and working together. They hold meetings and issue a newsletter of upcoming events that have international trade as a topic.

Contact with foreign Buyers can be made through the International Federation of Purchasing and Material Management. The IFPMM identifies specific members offering assistance in most countries. Also, attend some of their international meetings held in major cities. Write IFPMM—International Management Institute, PO Box CH—5001, Aarau, Switzerland. Tel: (064) 247131, Telex: 981293.

Trading Bureaus, Associations, and Others

Ports of entry or U.S. Customs district offices can be most helpful in supply pamphlets or offering advice as requested. Contact your nearest office. Port authorities often publish general information on export/import related subjects and maintain overseas offices. A separate listing of U.S. Ports is available.

The World Trade Institute (WTI), One World Trade Center, N.Y.C., 10048, runs evening courses and various seminars and conferences on world trade. They teach popular foreign languages and offer interpretation. The WTI sponsors an International Business Development Group (IBDP) that does project work for individual clients. XPORT—The Port Authority Trading Company fosters increased export and import trade.

Commercial banks assist by providing brochures and telling what they know about the reliability of local manufacturers. The Manufacturers Hanover Bank has a World Trade Group that works out trade alliances, particularly for exports. If a deal is too big for a company, the bank will buy and sell products for about a 2-percent fee. They provide countertrade advice and services for "switch trading" and "clearing dollars," and so on. They advise on credit information, foreign exchange and currency options and are headquartered at 270 Park Avenue, New York, NY 10017.

Other banks, such as Chemical Bank, Marine Midland, and others, have economic data available. Barclays of London supplies excellent data on all foreign countries' economics.

The American Association of Exporters and Importers (AAEI) has, since 1921, promoted fair and open trade among nations. With over 1,200 member U.S. firms, this association represents both U.S. exporters and importers before Congress, the Executive branch, and U.S. Customs. They provides assistance in technical areas such as customs regulations, procedures and policy, general system of preference, licensing, and trade publications.

Trading bureaus and associations represent many countries. Some examples follow. Commercial attaches of foreign countries will, upon request, furnish data on that country's industries. Try the Brazilian Government Trade Bureau, Consulate General of Brazil, 551 Fifth Ave., NY 10176. Another is the Electronic Industries Association of Korea, Room 1101, World Trade Center Building, 1—1, 2-ka, Hoehyun-Dong, Chung-ku, C.P.O. Box 5650, Seoul, Korea. Tel: 778-0913 Telex: KTANEWS K24208/EIAK.

The Federation of Hong Kong Industries, Hankow Road, Tsimshatsui, Kowloon, Hong Kong (Tel: (3) 7230818 Telex: 84652. HKIND HX) houses the Design & Packaging Centre and operates the Hong Kong Standards & Testing Centre. They take trade inquires, and issue certificates of origin.

Specialists in seminars and training for importation, materials management, and purchasing, and who issue Buying and Negotiation Guides, are POOLER AND ASSOCIATES, One North Ridge, Syracuse, NY 13214 Tel: (315) 446-4412.

Information services sell their database. For example, CompuServe, Inc., Columbus, Ohio, has 325,000 subscribers worldwide who can gain access to their data base network through personal computers. The subscriber is billed for time spent using its system. Others are G.E. Information Services and Dialog Information Services.

These are but a sampling of the wealth of informational sources available. Use this book's Appendixes and Bibliography for on-the-job reference and guidance.

STEP #4. Decide *What* to Source Offshore.

Start with simpler, noncritical items, as early efforts need to be successful. Protectionist sentiment exists among fellow employees. If the first shipment is rejected, employees often react negatively, making it more difficult to grow your program.

As an example, before buying from Brazil, make sure the Brazilian company can import any needed materials. For instance, a capacitor manufacturer needs to import special polystyrene sheeting.

Some of the prime product characteristics to consider would include:

Product acceptance
Functions and features
Quality
Manufacturing costs
Resources and materials required
Producibility and cost to adapt
Availability
Competitive offerings
Maintenance and service
Method of usage
Packaging
Physical form (shape, size, or color)

On the job, buyers will want to think of specific items they buy! Whether purchasing services, MRO, commodities, components, or all these, only you can decide *what* to buy!

Step #5. Pursue Suppliers with Low Cost Productive Labor

The American short-term goal of profitability encourages the option of either buying offshore or producing there to take advantage of lower labor costs. Global companies continue to source high labor content items from these low labor cost countries.

Low foreign labor rates are seen as a problem to maintaining our American industrial base. But they also represent an opportunity for manufacturing savings. Followers of the textile industry know how those plants migrated from New England to Appalachia. They then moved to Japan, Korea, Taiwan, and finally into Indonesia, the Philippines, India, and Sri Lanka.

As labor costs rise, industries become more inclined to pull up and move, a process taking about five years per move. As an example, a watch manufacturing plant manager explained that he had originally supervised Rhode Island women. He moved with the plant to Arkansas and then to Scotland. Shortly thereafter, the plant was moved to Taiwan, where watches were made when the author inspected that operation. Parts shipped in from Scotland were assembled into completed watches in Taiwan. Then the case was removed and shipped to the U.S. Virgin Islands, where the case and guts were reassembled and shipped into the United States.

Let's look at the hourly compensation for manufacturing in industrial nations shown in Table 2-1. Japan's wages, which were half in 1985, are up to 89 percent of the U.S. production worker's wages by 1990. Now, Japanese companies are shifting some component production to South Korea, whose workers earn $3.57/hour today.

Recent U.S. wage gains are at a lesser rate. The almost 10-percent yearly wage gains in the early 1980s has dropped to about 4 percent currently. And there have even been some reductions. Average hourly pay in manufacturing rose from $13.85/hour to $14.31 in 1989. Yet it has fallen into fifth place worldwide. This compares with number one German labor cost of $21. Perhaps surprisingly, number four is Canada at $14.71.

However, it should be noted that this relative lowering of American labor cost is not solely because of smaller U.S. wage increases. Where a foreign currency, such as the Mark, has risen, German labor costs rise versus American. Translating foreign currency into dollars for comparison to U.S. wages causes much of the change.

TABLE 2-1.   Hourly compensation costs in industrialized nations

Manufacturing production workers

	1988		1989		
	$/Hour	Percent	$/Hour	Percent	Rank
United States	13.85	100%	14.31	100%	5
Japan	12.86	93	12.68	89	8
Germany					
West	18.45	133	21.00	146	1
East	—		5.40	38	
Canada	13.54	98	14.71	103	4
United Kingdom	10.46	76	10.48	73	9
France	12.96	94	12.75	89	7
Italy	12.87	93	13.20	92	6
Sweeden	16.82	121	17.48	122	3
Switzerland	17.46	126	18.12	127	2

DATA SOURCE: Copyright DRI/McGraw-Hill. Reprinted with permission.

Notice the developing countries' much lower wages, as shown in Table 2-2. Mexican workers, mostly women, now earn $1.79/hour, falling to $0.81 at the Maquiladora border plants. Study the favorable rates for the "Four Tigers" (Hong Kong, South Korea, Taiwan, and Singapore).

Perhaps the last haven for followers of low cost labor are Malaysia, Indonesia, Thailand, People's Republic of China, and the Philippines. All are at about 0.46/Hour, or 3 percent of U.S. labor rates. With labor costs one-quarter or less than the highly industrial countries, the less developed countries have a formidable advantage.

Now obviously the United States can't possibly match those rates! Nor would we want to. If labor costs were reduced drastically, Americans wouldn't be able to consume as well. And the world depends greatly on America as a buyer.

Table 2-3 shows some of the Eastern European rates now of interest as they become more inclined to free trade. Over the course of time, labor differentials will mean less, because automation and robotics are reducing the labor content. In the meantime, though, labor differentials will remain a critical factor affecting the source selection process.

Step #6. Forecast Needs and Set Target Prices

Determine your quantity need pattern. Domestic suppliers can ship within the normal 13-week lead times of most materials requirement planning, or MRP system. Most foreign suppliers usually work with a minimum one-year forecast. Seasonality is important. For example, manufacturers assemble window air conditioners in late winter and early spring. Sales are heaviest in the heat of summer.

TABLE 2-2. Hourly compensation costs in developing countries

Manufacturing production workers	1988 $/Hour	1989 $/Hour	Percent of U.S.
Brazil	1.50	1.86	13
Greece	5.22	5.38	38
Hong Kong	2.44	2.85	20
Israel	5.19	n/a	36
Mexico	1.72	1.79	13
Foreign owned		0.81	6
South Korea	2.50	3.57	25
Singapore	2.67	3.09	22
Taiwan	2.72	3.43	24
Venezuela	4.74	n/a	33

DATA SOURCE: Copyright DRI/McGraw-Hill. Reprinted with permission.

TABLE 2-3. Hourly compensation costs in Eastern Europe

Manufacturing workers including benefits

Poland	$1.35
Hungary	1.70
USSR	1.84
Czechoslovakia	2.05

DATA SOURCE: Copyright DRI/McGraw-Hill. Reprinted with permission.

Inventory control is simply answering, "*how much* to buy, and *when* is it needed?" In most companies, 20 percent of the items will amount to more than 80 percent of the dollars spent. Decide on a target percentage of annual usage to source abroad. Consider the use of a domestic backup source, at least initially.

A good rule of thumb, when setting an offshore "target price," is the price should be 15 to 20 percent under current cost, including freight. That's roughly the point where offshore buying becomes helpful. That target may vary, based on other possible company strategies. It probably isn't worth your while to buy offshore for less than a 15 percent expected price reduction.

Also, set a total dollar volume target. Reducing a price, say 80 percent, and saving $100 total is senseless if the purchase administration costs increased an extra $200. Setting a target price strikes a bogey for you to measure performance downstream.

Step #7. Identify and Locate Offshore Target Suppliers

Domestic salesmen are always reminding the buyer what their companies offer. When sourcing internationally, the buyer usually has to take the initiative to find better sources of supply. It is important to know about the political stability of a supplying country. What are its geographic characteristics, cultural attributes, market practices, and future growth opportunities?

The most difficult part of the search is identifying specific companies. Buyers should study what items are imported now by others. Products successfully imported include finished goods, machinery and equipment, sub-assemblies, electronic and mechanical parts, ferrous and nonferrous metals, cast iron and stainless castings, fasteners, bearings, valves, batteries, motors, glass, textiles, tires, selected chemicals, and plastic resins.

What countries should buyers look toward as potential suppliers? We readily think about the usual sources—Japan, the United Kingdom, Germany, and so on. What about the newcomers where labor cost advantage is such a factor?

Table 2-4, of the Origins of 1989 United States Imports, shows that import volumes continue to grow. By far, the largest volume of imports into the United States is from Japan, Canada, and Europe.

TABLE 2-4. Origins of 1989 U.S. imports

	Percent of U.S. Imports	$ millions
1. Pacific Rim		
Japan	19.7	96,938
Taiwan	5.2	25,627
South Korean	4.2	20,551
Hong Kong	2.1	10,237
Singapore	1.9	9,196
Australia	0.8	4,198
Indonesia	0.8	3,875
India	0.7	3,550
2. Americas		
Canada	18.3	90,202
Mexico	5.8	29,000
Brazil	1.8	8,716
3. Europe		
Germany	5.2	25,684
United Kingdom	3.8	18,909
France	2.7	13,530
Italy	2.6	12,725
Sweden	1.0	5,092
Netherlands	1.0	5,079
Switzerland	1.0	4,795
4. Middle East		
Saudi Arabia, etc.		n/a
Israel	0.7	3,323
5. All other countries (Oil imports here)	20.0	98,967
Total all imports	100%	$493,304

Compiled by: Pooler & Associates
DATA SOURCE: Copyright DRI/McGraw-Hill. Reprinted with permission.

Countries whose export volumes to the United States have been rising include Australia, Brazil, Canada, France, India, Indonesia, Italy, Israel, Japan, Mexico, Singapore, the United Kingdom, and Yugoslavia.

Below is a listing of potential target supplier countries for select industrial items:

Items	Possible source country
Capacitors	Brazil, Canada, Singapore
Castings and forgings	Austria, Brazil, China, England, Germany, Italy, Netherlands, South Korea, Spain

Components and hardware	England, France, Hungary, Italy, Japan, Taiwan, Singapore, Spain
Electronic assembles	Canada, England, Germany, Ireland, France, Hong Kong, Japan, Malaysia, Mexico Singapore, South Korea, Taiwan
Engines and parts	Austria, Belgium, England, Germany, Japan and South Korea
Machinery	Canada, England, Germany, Japan, Switzerland
Motors	Argentina, Australia, Brazil, Italy, Mexico
Inverters	Japan
Mechanical parts	Denmark, England, Germany, Italy, Netherlands, Sweden
Petrochemicals	Argentina, Algeria, Australia, Brazil, Mexico, Saudi Arabia, Venezuela
Raw materials	Africa, Canada, England, Finland, France, Mexico, Peru
Refrigerant	Japan
Sheet steel, galvanized	Canada, France, Germany, Japan, South Korea
Tools	Germany, Hong Kong, Japan, Taiwan, South Korea
Valves and accessories	Denmark, Germany, Italy, Japan, Mexico, Taiwan, South Korea, Switzerland

Note: Some companies allow buyers to spend 1.5 to 2 percent of the item's value to start up offshore sourcing.

Within your company, use requests for quotes (RFQ inquiries), correspondence, and buy record history. A database of likely offshore items to buy is good information to start your offshore source search. Typical commodity database headings that the buyer might use are the following:

COMMODITY SPECIFICATION   ANNUAL USAGE   USING PLANT   SOURCE COUNTRY   COMPANY ADDRESS   PRICE/UNIT   REMARKS

Buyers should get quotations for major items, considering the following:

Source Company	Regional, Country Characteristics
Profitability	Government regulations
Manufacturing costs	Political/legal
Production capability	Culture
Management interest	Economic development
Cost to adapt	Technological ability
Policies	Expectations and preferences
Organization	Nontariff barriers
Resources	Climate and geography

Identifying specific target companies results from studying available data. The World Trade Center's "Network" program will, upon request, print out available sources it has recorded. A weakness is that they list only foreign sources that pay for their listing.

Step #8. Communicate Within Your Company

Develop top management support. Talk personally with in-company personnel in such functions as quality control, inspection, engineering, production, and finance. Get them into the act. Overseas buys are going to mean increased difficulties for them, at least in the beginning. Develop contacts abroad carefully, and prepare others for the task.

Meeting with QC and other people who do the job helps your company personnel gain confidence in the offshore supplier's integrity and commitment to quality. Take a good look at the prospective supplier's processes and examine their production methods and equipment. Share your vision and explain the "big picture" and what you expect from your offshore venture. Ask for their input. Share the responsibility and success. Praise the team for their contributions. Don't go it alone.

Step #9. *Prepare* Yourself and Your Buying Team for Negotiation

Before having discussions and negotiations, there is no substitute for planning. Where does the buyer find out what he or she needs to know? There is lots of help for the asking.

It helps to:

- Find and develop early buying successes as examples.
- Ask those buyers and managers who source internationally now—those who are working with the marketplace today.
- Attend a seminar, a shortcut refresher or cram course on what's going on. Meet other buyers and managers whom you can phone occasionally. What results have they had?
- Do your homework—study literature, foreign business methods, and culture. Reading this book is a progressive step.
- Travel overseas and hopefully attend a trade fair.

Examples of some trade shows of interest are the Machine Tool & Electronic's Exhibitions in Paris, and the Hanover Fair, the Leipzig Fair, and the Munich Electronics Trade Show, all in Germany. Japan has an electronics show in Osaka. International exhibition trade shows are held in Bucharest, Hungary, Poland, Romania, and Yugoslavia. And there are many others.

Step #10. Making the Sourcing Decision

From our initial target search in Step 6, you've identified several potential suppliers. We now screen our candidates based on some considerations affecting the sourcing decision.

Before you buy anything, it makes sense to qualify any new supplier. When placing a trial order, it's wise to do a source-located inspection before the first major shipment. Highly sophisticated companies prefer to prequalify suppliers well in advance of buying.

Qualifying parts or products is the direct responsibility of the design engineering organization. The economic and supply considerations are introduced by purchasing early in the source selection process.

Purchasing must represent supplier input, such as pricing, availability, and so on. With a global viewpoint, buyers search out and screen new potential world-class suppliers. The mission is to have available such information in advance, so it can be quickly fed to engineering as needed. Purchasing should provide a window as to new global components or materials suppliers. The term "World Class Supplier" has come to mean those suppliers that can deliver their goods anywhere globally, at competitive cost in all marketing arenas.

This case, taken from a real-life situation, brings out sourcing issues to ponder before tackling other buying strategies in the next chapter.

CASE HISTORY: SETTING A GLOBAL SUPPLIER SOURCING STRATEGY

Thomas Manufacturing Inc. (TMI), Scranton, PA. makes air purifiers. Purchasing manager David, and buyer Steven.

Industria S. A., Sao Paulo, Brazil. Joint-venture partner with TMI, also makes purifiers. Director Carlos.

Electronica S.A., Sao Paulo. Makes capacitors. Vice president Sales Luis.

Thomas Manufacturing (TMI) wanted to become the global marketing leader for air purifiers. To do this, TMI formed a partnership with Industria, maker of the same products in Brazil. Industria also provided sales access to a now closed Brazilian market. A program to standardize on a global purifier design was started.

One-third of TMI's sales are exports. Yet only 2 percent of their assembled product was purchased from abroad. Management had, on several occasions, said that purchasing should aggressively pursue global options. David, a 20-year veteran manager, wanted to improve their supplier selection process.

David believed that foreign buyers are sometimes at an advantage learning to deal globally. David's strategy was stated by repeatedly urging his buyers to search overseas. He wanted the buyers to expand their buying horizons and qualify a greater number of lower cost foreign suppliers. David's policy was to take the first trip into each new country to explore buying opportunities. He then advised his buyers to follow up.

This past spring, David visited Brazil to meet new joint-venture partner Carlos. David arranged to inspect several high potential component suppliers. He was most interested in capacitors manufactured by Electronica. TMI purchases $8 million of capacitors annually for four different U.S. plants. David believed that the new partnership's combined capacitor volume could help make their costs more competitive. Together, they could reach the corporate goal to become number one in America, Brazil, and possibly worldwide.

The Plot Thickens

David's education began when partner Carlos expressed his pleasure, "Finally, my U.S. partners are about to begin buying components through me." This had never been discussed with TMI's management. It came as a complete surprise to David, looking to put the buying power of the two companies together to get mutually lower cost capacitors.

Brazilian law restricts anything from importation if a similar item is already produced there. For example, if his company needed a pump they made in the United States, he must buy his competitors'. Or they could make their own in Brazil. This policy of local content is to build the country's industrial bases.

David learned how a Brazilian purchasing manager makes an offshore buy. Because of extreme debt, Brazilian law prevents a company from making foreign payment for one year. If buying equipment, companies have to stretch payment out over 5 years. Suppliers will not wait that long. So, what does the purchasing manager do?

As an example, here is how a French pump is bought. The purchasing manager visits an American bank and borrows $100,000 at 10 percent interest. He sends his purchase order to the French manufacturer. The supplier ships in 6 months and tends his draft for payment to his bank. The U.S. bank transfers the money to Yugoslavia. Where did they come in?

A Yugoslavian-Brazilian bilateral agreement helps Yugoslavia get increased cash flow of dollars. The Yugoslavian bank pays the French company on time. One year from the date of shipment, the Brazilian company pays off the U.S. loan.

While negotiating, David found suppliers wanted to know, "What does the price have to be? We can work it out." This mirrored what David was told, "In Brazil, there is a way to do anything." But there were other surprises too.

Brazilian economics allow a company to sell abroad at prices below it's production cost and still make money. How can that be? Partner Carlos explained to David that, with a Bifiex agreement with the Brazilian government, the following benefits accrue:

16-percent value added tax is waived.
16 percent of another tax is also dropped.
Money may be borrowed at 10 percent interest (versus 450 percent inflation).
$2 of goods can be imported, not normally permitted, for every $3 of goods exported.

In short, almost a dollar is recoverable for each export sales dollar, because of government concessions designed to encourage exports. David thought, *"That's a lot of creative maneuvering our American buyer doesn't get."*

Partner Carlos's idea was to also export, in addition to finished products, components made by other Brazilian companies. Carlos figured he could export them to U.S. partner TMI by acting as export agent. Carlos's negotiating hand with supplier Luis was strengthened, as his Industria was Brazil's largest buyer of capacitors.

Before David's trip to Brazil, Carlos had contacted Luis and told him of his plans to export capacitors to TMI. Luis knew that if he tied in exclusively with Carlos, he might lose the total U.S. market potential that a U.S. distributor might deliver. So, he quietly began dealing with a U.S. distributor.

As an inducement, this distributor offered TMI a price 10 percent below the U.S. market. Further, they agreed to set up a local Scranton stocking program. No U.S. supplier would consider this service. Using this information, buyer Steven had negotiated U.S. manufacturer's prices down 10 percent. Steven had been commended for this $800,000 savings by the company president, upon purchasing manager David's recommendation.

Carlos, upon learning about the distributor, angrily bawled out supplier Luis! He threatened to pull his buys away from them. Luis expressed privately to David, "Carlos should be satisfied with exporting his purifiers. He should leave the small capacitors to us so we can live, too. We need export credits to import more metallized polypropolene film from Germany." Recall that David did not learn about these involvements until his trip.

The two Brazilian managers remained at loggerheads. Partner Carlos was stubbornly angry. Luis didn't want to deny his distribution agreement and tried to be conciliatory. Luis's sales strategy was to show that his capacitors were the technological leader. They made dry capacitors, compared to the U.S. supplier's use of PCB oil, which was an environmental hazard. This, plus an extra 5-percent lower price he now offered David, made this foreign sourcing most attractive.

Meeting to Resolve Differences

With all the parties in Sao Paulo, Luis, trying reconciliation, arranged a breakfast meeting before his capacitor plant tour. However, an angry Carlos refused, making it clear that *his plans* for control of all exports were to be followed. David felt somewhat bound to support his partner, although he wanted his department to control its own purchases.

David struck an understanding with Luis. TMI uses capacitors in other U.S. plants and would continue to buy from Luis. However, half the export credit (or equal value) had to go to partner Carlos. Luis expressed belief that it could be done as David stressed, "Half a loaf is better than none." The deal was set!

Upon return home, an elated David invited Steven to lunch to discuss the increased savings potential. The new 5-percent reduction, added to the 10-percent previous saving, would produce profit of $1.2 million. Buyer Steven, an engineer, expressed interest in the design breakthrough. But, he said, "I'm worried about backup supply and my relationship with the U.S. suppliers." Steven pointed out his present supplier's price concession, along with the longtime fine delivery job. "My suppliers assumed they will keep the business based on their concessions."

Saying he understood the importance of making a good offshore sourcing decision, Steven agreed to increase Brazil import orders to 10 percent of needs. Though appearing reluctant when asked by David, "Can't we buy more?", Steven never voiced objection to the arrangement.

Several weeks later, Steven proudly announced that his U.S. suppliers had met the latest Brazilian prices. Further, they would have a new dry design within a year. So it wasn't necessary to wait for shipments from a distant supply source. Soon thereafter, TMI announced the Scranton production move to Brazil. During the next trip to the United States, Luis advised David, "I had to break our sales agency." Buyer Steven agreed to use up the local distributor inventory. David was left to ponder his strategy for improved offshore sourcing.

First surmise the goals of each of the cast:

Cast member	List their objectives below

1. Purchasing manager David
2. Buyer Steven
3. Joint-partner Carlos
4. Capacitor supplier Luis

Please answer these questions:

1. From a purchasing viewpoint of getting the lowest cost for his company (savings of $1.2 million were made), should buyer Steven receive a merit raise? Or should he be fired?
2. What were the results, from the position of:
   a. Joint partner, director Carlos?
   b. Capacitor manufacturer Luis?

3. What about the results from TMI's management strategic position on becoming a global company?
4. From purchasing manager David's position of improving the selection process, what were the results?

Sometimes your sourcing choice is clear and you've selected the supplier quickly. For important volume purchases, you've got to consider the upcoming negotiations and the issues presented throughout this book before the selection process is completed.

3

Set Your Global Sourcing Strategies

Offshore sourcing provides buyers with multiple strategic options. A global corporation buys in highly competitive worldwide markets, but how do we get global source development? We must come to grips with strategic guidelines.

To ensure management support and resources, worldwide sourcing must be included within the business or strategic planning of the company. Purchasing planning should mesh with company goals, with emphasis on purchasing integration and contribution.

Purchasing has to figure out what it can buy to support marketing's effort to sell abroad. A "strategy" is a *plan* to reach our goals. Purchasing strategy should adjust to the supply market and production systems, as well as marketing strategies and company objectives.

The purchasing department should:

- Support company strategic objectives;
- Know interlocking supply relationships, such as joint ventures and licensees; and
- Integrate with the business strategies through better communications.

To identify strategies for your purchasing department, make a list of your strategic planning ideas, considering the following:

- Focus on buyer's intrinsic buying power—use leverage to improve your company's competitive market position.
- Integrate commodity productivity projects with new product development projects.
- Manage performance related strategies:
  a. Control department expenses;

   b. Foster product cost reductions with engineering (i.e., provide cost data to engineering on future pricing trends)

   c. Upgrade product quality through quality and reliability efforts.

- Measure purchasing productivity and interpret results.
- Conduct minority/small business program.
- Put all program elements into priority by importance.

You should set your strategies based on *your* situation. In the meantime, having decided to pursue Strategy #1, to start a global sourcing plan in the previous chapter, here are some other valid strategies to pursue:

- Use procurement plans stemming from company goals.
- Maintain a strong Total Quality Management (TQM) System.
- Compare total landed cost of acquisition.
- Seek assurance of supply (multiple sources of supply).
- Strive to source through the best buying channel.
- Use available purchasing techniques.
- Consider the need for an international buying office.
- Develop supplier partnering.

STRATEGY #2. USE PROCUREMENT PLANS STEMMING FROM COMPANY GOALS

Strategic procurement planning is made possible by using a "Procurement Plan" as the basis for action. A combined engineering, manufacturing, and purchasing strategy should be formulated. The documented procurement plan becomes the blueprint used by each manufacturing location as it sources its requirements.

There should exist an action plan for the year. At a minimum, the plan should include (1) targets for the number of new teams to add, (2) savings targets for each, (3) steps to take to coordinate with engineering, (4) efforts to reduce sole source, and (5) steps to improve *make* versus *buy* approaches, and so on. Fig. 3-1 shows the three components of a procurement plan: *history, commodity overview*, and the *strategic plan* itself.

A written plan controlled by the headquarters commodity manager is agreed to and executed by the team. Once in place, this team is quickly activated by phone, under stress of impending price increase, product trouble or deliveries, or whatever the need.

Some areas that purchasing can contribute to a company's success are:

- Tracking and managing supply availability;
- Interpreting the strategic implications of global supply for the company;

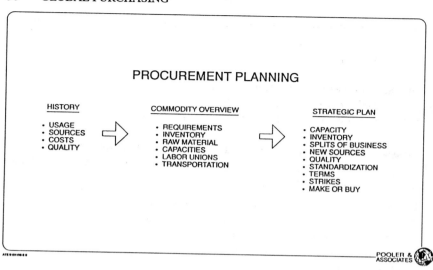

FIGURE 3-1.   Procurement process.

- Identifying future supply needs and services; and
- Developing global supply alternatives.

Make offshore sourcing part of your procurement plan. Some examples of procurement planning tactics to use are to:

1. Evaluate and obtain participation in decision making and procedure planning of offshore purchases.
2. Identify global source availability.
3. Set up and implement integrated materials measurements.
4. Initiate and/or participate in make versus buy studies.
5. Set material standards for special inventory investment, planning to avoid outages of critical supply items.
6. Manage cost reduction and materials profit improvement programs.
7. Create material systems studies about information systems and techniques.
8. Work on special materials projects.
9. Assist in the integration of materials policies.
10. Study short- and long-range material prices.
11. Search out new materials development and availability.
12. Evaluate consolidation of shipments, and so forth, in cooperation with traffic.

STRATEGY #3. MAINTAIN A STRONG TOTAL QUALITY MANAGEMENT (TQM) SYSTEM

TQM starts with management commitment to a formal goal setting, quality system analysis, and measurements system. Specific quality strategies used by professional purchasing departments are:

• Enhance Statistical Process Control;
• Set supplier quality programs—Consider Zero Defect concept;
• Know your cost of quality;
• Raise quality levels of products; and
• Increase automation and reduce variability.

Statistical Process Control (SPC) involves charting key dimensional tolerances, and so forth. Its use by a supplier is indicative of potential for world-class performance. This term, "world-class," has come to mean those suppliers who can deliver their goods anywhere globally at competitive cost in all marketing arenas.

Don't underestimate the importance of knowing precisely the quality needed. Explore global buying opportunities, study foreign business practices and culture, and meld engineering/purchasing efforts. Examples of information needed are specifications, drawings, and samples. This step requires engineering/purchasing cooperation to achieve proper complete specifications. How does this differ from domestic?

More details need to be given. A local supplier knows quality standards by experience—what is okay and what is not. Such details must be explained to the new foreign source.

Copies of ASME or UL codes may have to be provided, along with any special tests to which parts will be subjected. Local suppliers know these facts from experience. A foreign supplier may be searching without guidance, hesitant to admit it since he or she wants to please. Buyers must be sure the foreign source can meet these special technical requirements.

Quality can be described in a number of ways in our purchase order by: 1. brand, 2. grade, 3. sample, 4. physical and chemical constituents, 5. method of manufacture or production, 6. materials used, and 7. performance. But, quality is relative to other factors too.

Prequalification

It makes sense to qualify any new supplier before anything is bought. Buyers can spearhead a "prequalification" effort to identify new global sources and, also, new processes or methods of production.

Source qualification can range from simple to quite complex for high-tech state-of-the-art hardware. When placing a trial order, it is wise to perform an inspection at the supplier's facility before the first major shipment. Meeting with your supplier's quality department and others who do the job helps you to gain confidence in their integrity and a commitment to quality.

Older Military Standard 105D spelled out requirements of sampling plans and a method of statistical quality control. An Acceptable Quality Limit, or AQL, was often set around 1 or 2 percent. But, currently, working to Mil-Q-9858A, the AQL concept is not accepted. Commercial companies also consider this AQL unacceptable today, in light of Japanese standards of "parts per million."

Purchasing and quality control working together can improve acquisition by concentrating on 1. design 2. manufacture, and 3. purchase. Control of the "cost of ownership" begins in the design phase by choosing suppliers who can meet the required quality levels. Focus on design by doing the following:

- Keep routine contact between buyers and key engineering sections;
- Maintain dialogue with supplier's engineers;
- Achieve design integration by being part of the design team process;
- Attend key engineering design meetings;
- Spearhead standardization efforts;
- Search for less costly substitutes of equal or better value;
- Analyze product development projects and time to go into production; and
- Arrange test procedures to analyze supplier failures that can be reduced and, in turn, might allow elimination of any incoming inspection.

Among items that may be checked for quality are the processes being used, the techniques and controls on the finished product, plus test methods and test data that support the product ratings. Any allowances for deviations or substitutions should be clarified. Any penalties for failing to meet quality standards should be spelled out.

To check the quality of potential European suppliers, find out if they've gotten ISO 9000 certification. The International Organization for Standardization issued its ISO 9000 series of five international standards for quality management and assurance. They define minimum requirements for a quality system. This has been adopted within the United States as the ANSI/ASQC Q90 series. Though not well known domestically, about 10,000 companies from about 30 nations have been registered.

Early Supplier Involvement

About 70 percent of production savings occur from improvement in design. Begin by using some of these tactics:

Tactics:	Results Tracked:
Parts per million (PPM)	Higher quality reports
Train people	Quality and SPC awareness
Improve quality	Cost of quality reduced
Purchased	
Fabricated	
Quality circles operating	Number of circles
Buyer/supplier programs	Programs ongoing
Certify suppliers for results	Suppliers certified
Use of personal computers	Failure analysis
Quality task force teams	Team reports

Review suppliers performance in giving technical support to solve problems. Evaluate their capabilities to provide technical leadership. Coordinate engineering/purchasing/supplier meetings.

But when it comes to the real world, in industry, the more expensive a product, the better quality must be. You get what you pay for, right? Wrong! Price is what you pay, quality is what you receive. It is not always an issue of pricing versus quality. For example, compare a beautiful gold tie clip versus a paper clip. They will both do the same job, but one is much more attractive, though expensive. "Suitability for a purpose" means you can't isolate quality alone. *Quality* cannot be divorced from the intended *end-use* and *cost*!

STRATEGY #4. COMPARE TOTAL LANDED COST OF ACQUISITION

If some American buyers recognized all costs incurred by their purchases, they might *not* source some items they now buy and import. That's because it's not easy for busy buyers to gather the cost pieces in various financial data, to realize the extent of the extra costs for some offshore buys.

Picture this scenario. Purchasing manager Amanda Kay urges her buyers to "outsource" to increase purchased materials savings. "Use offshore sources that are at least 10 percent cheaper," she tells them.

Hoping to make a "quick kill," buyer Steven tells a domestic electrical salesman how his management wants him to source offshore. The salesman says, "We'll sell you a generator made in France at a 20 percent savings versus what you're paying now."

Engineering judged the quality as okay and completely interchangeable. "Great!" responds Steve, who tells the supplier, "Here's my new order now."

Steven fills out the first outsourcing savings report, but boss Amanda rejects it, saying, "No, you're buying domestically a foreign-produced item that someone else is importing."

Later, Steven submits a new savings report for a $3,000 savings. He claimed a generator buy was "outsourced at price 20 percent below previous domestic price paid."

Amanda noted that Steve included freight costs, but didn't itemize specifics on duty, brokerage fee, or marine insurance. She decided to check it out herself.

Below is Amanda's analysis of Steven's savings, taken from a real-life example:

Generator price	$10,200.00
5% buying commission	500.00
Marine insurance	180.00
Customshouse broker	125.00
Certificate of inspection	375.00
International freight	2,200.00
Domestic freight	780.00
Invoice total	$14,360.00
Plus customs duty	300.00
Total landed cost	$14,660.00

Steve is called into Amanda's office and is surprised to hear, "Hey, you knucklehead! I expect you to pay less when you go offshore. Your offshore buy cost another $4,460, or 45 percent in 'extras' above the price paid. There's a net loss of 5 percent from this botched offshore sourcing attempt. Next time you better get with it and make sure what items truly cost. Not professional, in my opinion."

What is your response to the above scenario? Should Steven have bought offshore? Wasn't he, like many buyers, simply *unaware of all the extra costs* when offshore sourcing?

You know it's not enough to simply consider the price of what is bought. This example makes that crystal clear! And there are those "hidden costs" not accounted for in the above example. Isn't there extra clerical costs and longer delivery time in transport? Don't forget that *goods on the high seas are usually part of your inventory*!

Correcting warranty, scrap/repair, field trips, retrofits, and claims settlement expense are extra costs. Also, what about those added costs resulting from longer design cycle time, or excess labor costs due to poor quality information?

Import Pricing Checklist

As an aid to consider total landed cost, this checklist can help analyze cost factors in your offshore buy:

- Price in U.S. dollars.
- Export packing, marking, and container costs.
- Commissions to customs broker.
- Fees for consultants or inspectors.
- Terms of payment costs and finance charges:
  a. Letter of credit fee;
  b. Translation costs; and
  c. Exchange rate differentials.
- Marine insurance premium.
- Customs documentation charges.
- Import tariffs.
- Transportation costs, including:
  a. From manufacturer to port;
  b. Ocean freight;
  c. Freight costs from port to company plant;
  d Freight forwarder charges; and
  e. Port handling charges or warehouse costs.
- Foreign taxes imposed.
- Extra inventory itself, plus inventory carrying costs if, for example, the foreign purchase requires a larger company stock than for domestic supply.
- Extra manpower needed to buy overseas. More documentation paperwork.
- Increased costs of overseas business travel, international postage, telex, and FAX and telephone rates.
- Hidden costs, such as obsolescence, deterioration and spoilage, taxes, losses to damage and theft, and delivery longer time frames. Administrative costs for ordering are higher than for domestic purchase.

For about the past five years, U.S. companies have "outsourced" for imports that continue today to good advantage. But the pendulum of costs has shifted. Any decision to source overseas should be made based on the best ultimate value. It should be clear that price should be judged in perspective to the *total landed costs* incurred.

STRATEGY #5. SEEK ASSURANCE OF SUPPLY

Whether to use single or multiple sources is a controversial subject. Some buyers argue that multiple sources reduce risk while increasing costs. Without question, some American companies today are using fewer sources. The major thrust has been quality guru Edward Deming's advocacy for using just one supplier. He claims that you're lucky if you get one company who can make what you want. Also, some American automakers who sole source say the practice cuts down on component dimensional variability. With fewer suppliers, they claim to be able to work more closely in meeting design and quality requirements. They say it is easier to insist on a process for failure analysis when the supplier knows he or she has total responsibility.

Sometimes a distinction is made between sole or single source. Sole is said to mean that there is no one else qualified or available. Single means that the buyer chooses to use only one of several available sources. So, a sole source may be beyond the ability of the buyer to change.

Not all buyers have embraced the single source philosophy. Traditional reactions from buyers has been, "What if my supplier goes on strike, or burns down, or gets flooded out?" Those are still valid questions when offshore sourcing. They could add, "What if the ship sinks, or is rerouted?" Water damage is possible as well as a sudden dock labor stoppage. Whether to have a backup source or use a single source depends largely on whether you have time to recover from unexpected delivery delays or quality problems. Another factor is your trust in a source and your relationship with them.

If buying for a high volume assembly line, you'll need an alternative. If buying for resale, or if you can wait for new shipments, perhaps a single source is sufficient. Most experienced buyers prefer a backup. Most quality gurus might point out that if you back up source, each source will feel relief of responsibility. Single source puts 100 percent burden on the supplier partner. Once fully understood, the partner will step up to the challenge of true partnership.

If you use single sources, but still want backups, here's a thought. Divide the business, say castings, among two foundries. Give each half the total casting volume, but *all* of the volume of each pattern. This gives maximum item volume production to each supplier. Have an understanding that capacity will be made available on other sizes that each does not produce, in case of an act of God or dire problems.

There are economic reasons that should be considered. For example, with at least two sources, there is competition. Buyers note that airfares they pay for travel are always cheaper when there are several airlines vying for their business. Sales seeks to eliminate competition. Consider the fundamental that the buying job seeks to create competition!

For buyers to use international leverage to maintain costs, engineers must provide acceptable worldwide supply options of foreign sources. A major deterrent to using maximum economic leverage is when the marketplace contains a single seller, or buyers have not qualified a second source.

The act of considering offshore sourcing is seen as a threat to domestic suppliers' security and often causes a downward domestic price adjustment. That's in the long-term interest of a healthier American economy. Multiple sources prequalification of important suppliers provides an escape valve to reduce risk, so changes can be made without drastic quality affect. The buyer who has prequalified international suppliers doesn't wait for emergencies or troubles to develop.

For buyers to use global leverage, engineering must provide acceptable global supply options of foreign sources. The key is a joint effort in concert with engineering, to further reduce sole sources. Audits have proven the high cost of not exercising buying leverage.

Some talk about the Japanese method of working with only one supplier (they usually have alternates), but the ability to reward or punish a supplier by using your economic leverage is hard to surpass. The author admits to a bias favoring use of competition, only possible by having multiple sources. A stated policy to use only one source removes much economic leverage. Why leave your most important weapons at home when negotiating abroad? The choice should be the buyer's.

Since this position flies in the face of much current thinking, the summation is left to a younger purchasing manager, whose opinion is respected. When queried, David Pooler wrote, "In general, I concur with the current thinking and would be reluctant to abandon the single source philosophy as a whole. However, I believe that certain 'higher risk' environments not only justify, but support, a multiple sourcing strategy. Each commodity or item should be judged on its own."

STRATEGY #6. STRIVE TO SOURCE THROUGH THE BEST BUYING CHANNEL

Deciding through which channel to buy is a key strategy! The first offshore channel setup will likely endure. Should you wish to change them later, it may be difficult, if not impossible. An intermediary who has set up a strong relationship is hard to remove.

The need for a channel strategy stems from the need to properly define the marketplace. For example, a U.S. buyer learned that his company's German buyer was buying the same item he was from the same supplier, but paying a much higher price. His company was unable to negotiate a reduction in the German price paid, even though it was challenged as too high. This is an excellent example of the seller defining the marketplace. Had the buying family been strong enough to have redefined the marketplace (which is often possible), they might have gotten the reduction.

Whoever can select the marketplace channels and define the worldwide market basket will probably control price levels. As an example, here is how an items cost is escalated through international market channels.

Item manufactured offshore	$ 1.00
Transport cost	.15
Tariff	.20
Importer pays	1.35
Importer mark up (25%)	.34
Wholesaler pays	1.69
Wholesaler mark up (33.33%)	.56
Retailer pays	2.25
Retail markup (50%)	1.13
Consuming buyer pays	3.38

As seen above, if buying direct, the buyer pays $1.35 for the item. His costs increase until he buys within the United States at the going price of $3.38. Buyers should understand the marketplace so that they can select their buying channel.

The main buying channel options open to the buyer are shown in Figure 3-2 Channels of Distribution. They are as follows:

1. Direct from the foreign source;
2. Through local U.S. representative or distributor;
3. Trading organizations;
4. Specialized independent agents; and
5. Interdivision or joint-venture partner.

Other channel combinations, including government controlled sellers, are possibilities, but the above are the primary ones. Each buyer must determine the optimum buying channel and strive for it. Of the above five options, the one preferable for high volume purchase is buying directly from the foreign supplier.

1. Direct from the Foreign Source

Direct importing usually gives the greatest probability for favorable prices by eliminating middlemen profits. Communications complexity is reduced, while placing most of the burden and importing risks on the buyer. Those with competent, experienced importing specialists prefer this direct approach.

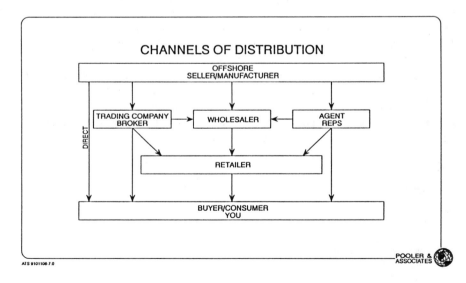

FIGURE 3-2. Channels of distribution.

Sometimes, buying channels may be influenced by factors over which the buyer has no control. This channel isn't always possible to achieve, nor is it desirable for all buyers.

2. Through Local U.S. Representatives or Distributor

This is indirect importing where the buyer knows he's using foreign supply, but buys it as a domestic purchase and is not in direct contact with the supplier. Indirect importing may cost more, but places those risks on the seller.

Many companies either can't afford or don't want costly overseas trips, so a domestic buying agent may help. Because of increased buying of castings, plastic parts, and specialized electronic components, there are a lot of middlemen. Buying specialists offer to source and import from a buying perspective.

Export management companies (EMC) are specialists that will do supplier surveys, cost analyses, sourcing, purchasing, inspection, engineering support, and other services. They offer to help purchasing managers with procedural compliance, letters of credit, foreign payment procedures, customs clearances, transoceanic buyer-supplier communications, offshore quality control, and foreign product delivery scheduling and expediting. They tend to specialize on high-tech items, such as precision castings or molded rubber parts.

When tooling is required, the buyer pays for half the price until the production samples are approved, much as in the United States. The agent is paid after the terms for the letter of credit are completed.

Fees for such importing specialists can be 10 to 15 percent of purchases for low volume, but usually are 3 to 5 percent. The commission can be built into part prices, or negotiated separately. Remember, keep any fee off the invoice. If the fee is in the part price, you're paying duty on it.

In effect, the buyer turns the buying over to the agent who should locate several potential sources and get several pricing proposals. They should produce contract prices in 2 to 4 weeks and production samples in another 60 days. They'll handle all arrangements from transport, delivery, and so forth. If the agent buys with his own PO and handles all details, you don't know what the agent is paying for the purchase.

3. Trading Organizations

Foreign trading companies (FTCs) match international buyers with sellers. They have operated successfully for many years around the globe.

The Japanese trading companies are perhaps best known, and include such names as such as Mitsui, Mitsubishi, and Murebena, to name a few. The Japan Trade Center, 230 North Michigan Ave., Chicago, IL 60601 will supply lists of trading companies, and sell "The Role of Trading Companies In International Commerce," JETRO Marketing Series II. The Israel Trade Center, 111 West 40th

St., New York, NY 10018 (212) 594-5215 and the Korean Trading Center, 111 East Wacker Drive, Suite 519, Chicago, IL 60601 (312) 644-4323 are typical of many country-sponsored groups of possible service.

Ministry of Foreign Economic Relations & Trade (MOFERT) is used for all aspects of trade with China. Trading companies under MOFERT contract with producers or end-users to advise on purchase, and so forth. Many of these MOFERT trading companies are collectively represented in the United States by China United Trading Co. of New York. Tianjin Foreign Trade Corp., 236 W. 18th St., New York, NY 10011 handles trading for that city.

The U.S. trading companies were reviewed in Chapter 1, under the section on setting up a trading co-op.

4. Specialized Independent Agents and Merchants

It is important to know whether a seller is an agent or merchant. Note that merchants take title and control of goods, agents do not! Agents can be found both overseas and in the United States. Bear in mind that the laws of various countries clarify the responsibilities of the parties and frequently discriminate against the foreigner (a U.S. firm, for example). To minimize risk, there is no substitute for selecting a good agent. Historically, many agent arrangements have not worked well because foreign laws protect their nationals, with escape clauses that exempt domestic principals from obligations that they place on foreigners.

In the United States, domestic agents can be of help—whether they're called brokers, traders, merchants, or supplier reps. These can help smaller buyers that may not have the expertise nor the time to buy globally without help. Some of these agents also concentrate on particular import-buying services. Others offer a virtually complete package and are typically known as EMCs.

A broker often buys and sells for his own account. If the buyer deals with a broker, who in turn buys from a foreign company, establishing responsibility for product liability and warranties may be difficult. One solution would be for the buyer to *make sure title passes to the agent or broker*. Then the Universal Commercial Code has jurisdiction.

Merchants are also known as wholesalers, export trading companies, distributor/dealers, import jobbers, or wholesaler/retailers. A distributor buys in his own name, carries inventory, and provides parts support and may offer other services such as repairs. He may be franchised, but beware: if chosen to receive a buyer's initial purchase order, there is seldom a way around this channel later should the buyer now wish to deal directly with the supplier.

To locate an overseas agent or representative, check with other buyers. Also consult the Commerce department that maintains the Export Mailing List Service (EMLS). For a fee, they provide this EMLS list of overseas firms along with names of representatives.

5. InterDivision or Joint-Venture Partner

A company may call upon a division in another country to negotiate for them. Joint-venture partners with global contacts can be helpful. Usually, the agreement will be confirmed with the U.S. company's purchase order.

The option to use this channel depends on one's corporation structure. Within larger corporations, there are many opportunities for good results by working with these partners.

STRATEGY #7. USE AVAILABLE PURCHASING TECHNIQUES

Buyers can strive to achieve strategic global competitiveness of their company, using some currently available tools and techniques:

- Stockless purchasing;
- Blanket contracts;
- Forward buying versus hedging;
- Strong long-range source development; and
- Team buying: local, national, and global.

Some analytical techniques used by buyers include:

- Make or buy analysis;
- Standardization and simplification;
- Cost and price analysis;
- Statistical and graphic analysis;
- Value and cost analysis;
- Lease versus buy; and
- Learning curve.

Getting into all the above is beyond the scope of this book. But offshore buyers sometimes forget the simple technique of cost and price analysis to reduce high prices, based on examining the various elements of cost that make up a price. The challenge is to determine when a price is fair. While difficult, foreign suppliers may provide cost factors to enable useful analysis if they are convinced it will help them. Try to get as much information as possible from the supplier.

Use the simple pricing formula:

Price = Material + Labor + Labor Burden + General
       Administrative costs, plus profit.

Material includes that which goes directly into the product. Labor is that which directly fabricates, assembles, and finishes the product. Material and direct labor make up the direct costs. The indirect costs are the overhead and all else. Overhead includes handlers, depreciation, repairs, and the factory costs.

Manufacturing Costs = Material + Labor + Labor Burden

Tooling and engineering costs may also be itemized, if a large part of expenditure. It is important to know whether a material burden is used. In an actual dispute, a buyer agreed that the supplier would invoice at cost. Both parties felt it a fair settlement until two weeks later when an invoice called out "costs" as including a 50-percent material burden. In the eyes of the buyer, material burdens were unheard of, whereas, the seller claimed that, since he had little labor, he always used a large burden on material. Be careful of all facts early in the game!

Such analysis forms the basis from which the buyer can question and probe to find economies. When monitoring price increases, it can be seen that a 5-percent increase in labor costs cannot justify a 5-percent increase in product price when material costs are holding steady.

The important point is that techniques that work domestically will probably work offshore. Use them.

STRATEGY #8. CONSIDER NEED FOR AN INTERNATIONAL BUYING OFFICE

While not an urgent priority, sooner or later, purchasing managers should consider whether to set up an international purchasing group or a foreign buying office. You can buy from a foreign source either through an offshore buying office. or from your own home office location. A prime reason to locate a buying organization in a host country is that lower procurement costs will usually result. Being near the supplier's doorstep tightens up the supply loop. Also, product availability and your ability to troubleshoot on the spot comes into play. To cost justify having an office, most with one say you should be spending about $4 million annually and saving 20 percent of that amount.

Some large companies such as Kodak, Xerox, IBM, NCR, GTE, and others have established resident international buying offices. Negotiations and details are better controlled within the supplying country. Paying the markups, fees, and other hidden costs are reduced. Local expediting can replace overseas trips costing thousands of dollars.

A foreign office may be staffed with foreign nationals who communicate easily with their native language. They can advise on exposure to foreign politics and any foreign taxes. While the office is often started by an American, it is difficult to staff a foreign office. Native nationals understand the rules of their game. They can negotiate better with an understanding of the local language and business customs.

Prime locations are Tokyo, Singapore, and Hong Kong for the Pacific Rim.

Tokyo and Osaka for Japan are expensive. Seoul, South Korea, Taipei, Taiwan, and Singapore for Malaysia are sometimes used. Hong Kong can be used as a central base for all Asia. Amsterdam and Brussels are good European locations. London is the most convenient to cover all of Europe.

On the other hand, there are legal reasons to buy directly from your home office location. Some claim the use of the phone, telex, or FAX keeps the expediting costs reasonable. Even companies with overseas offices may use them primarily to do the scouting, negotiating, and expediting. However, the purchase order itself will be issued from the U.S. home base. One reason is that the U.S. legal system is invoked and provides recourse to restitution.

If the purchase order is issued from the foreign territory, the transaction may be strictly a foreign transaction from a legal standpoint, a situation with which your company may be uncomfortable.

4

Negotiations Dealing with Foreign Cultures

If we had to agree on only one key personal trait that a professional buyer must possess, it would be the ability to negotiate. Most of us underestimate our ability to influence others. The buyer has far more economic leverage than he or she believes when they use persuasion to negotiate.

Many buyers think that for them to win the negotiation, the other party must lose. Not so! Most successful negotiations are "win-win." The buyer gets a measure of what he or she wants and so does the seller, though maybe neither got everything they'd like. Recall that a *negotiation is a mutual bargaining discussion, to arrive at terms agreeable to both parties.*

A powerful leverage effect is available to keep domestic suppliers competitive when the buyer uses the international marketplace. Negotiations in buying change depending on their purpose listed below:

- Set a specific contract price;
- Revise existing prices either upward or downward;
- Change prices to meet adverse costs or operating changes;
- Get agreement in advance on terms and conditions; and
- Settle various commercial problems not foreseen.

Note that most buying negotiations involve prices! The following approaches to price, while offered with tongue in check, give an insight into true pricing methods.[1]

- "Tag-along" studies all his competitors' price sheets and matches them exactly.
- "Ratio specialist" believes established percentage profits are valid, so everything has to get the same multipliers.

---

[1]Adapted from Victor H. Pooler. 1964. *Purchasing Man and His Job.* New York: American Management Association.

- "The mathematician" creates charts and trend lines, weights averages and standard deviations. Prices are precisely where the lines intersect.
- "Psychologist" figures, "If I do this, this will happen, then the probability is this will result. So, I'll start by asking for this price."
- Quick change artist" reacts to all competition and suggestions without much forethought. A better price exists across town? Prices shift to meet the moment.
- "Novelist" doesn't believe in worrying about price structure. He quickly comes out with any "safe" price. He expects to haggle over discounts, just enough to get the sale.

These humorous methods are close to the mark domestically. Do you suspect they're different internationally? It's helpful to study how sellers set prices. Salespeople want buyers to believe that their prices are based on costs. However, other matters, such as demand, availability, competition, and marketplace price levels affect price as well. Proving the case is the question, "If costs determined prices, why do so many companies lose money?" And why is it that prices change from time to time, place to place, and customer to customer?

Ask yourself why profit margins for products within a company vary so much. Experienced domestic buyers know well about price flexibility. Also, they've learned that suppliers don't always know their costs—at least accurately. That may be even more so, internationally.

While negotiation techniques may be used worldwide, the major challenge is to *apply them with an understanding of the cultural and business practices* of the other party. Cultural understanding has long been considered an American short-coming.

Americans often make blunders without their knowledge. When you meet someone, do you touch their shoulder or grab their arms? Europeans or Orientals feel ill at ease when touched, other than when shaking hands. Do you pass food with your left hand? That's highly offensive in India and the Orient where the left hand is used for bodily functions, leaving the right solely for eating.

American buyers talking to Arabians find them right in their face. Americans back up as the Arabs follow closely across the room. Never ask a Saudi about his wife. He may have several and will usually ignore you anyway. However, if talking to an African visitor, you must inquire about his wife, or he'll feel you're socially aloof. The trouble is, we are often ignorant of little deeds that may offend, and of course the foreigner won't mention it.

Americans give gifts of sets of 4, 6, or 8 wine goblets, but in Japan sets are 3 or 5, as 4 is an unlucky number. "Aren't they peculiar," some might say? Cultural variations are not right or wrong—simply different.

What do we mean by "culture" and how does it affect dealing with foreigners from a global perspective. *The American Heritage Dictionary's* definition of culture is "a style of social and artistic expression peculiar to a society."

Elements of culture include language, education, religion, attitudes, social organization, and political life. Individual sellers, as well as buyers, have differences in personalities and styles. Yet there are culture similarities and differences that have been documented and studied. These facetious rules of thumb may help:

In Britain, you can do it, provided it's not forbidden.
In Germany, you can do it if it's allowed.
In France, you can do it even if it's forbidden.
In Russia, you can't do it even if it's allowed. (Changing?)
In Switzerland, if it isn't forbidden, it's compulsory.
In Brazil, you can do it, even if it's impossible.
In Japan, you can do it, if they say they can.
In the United States, you can do it... *Do it over again!*

One seeming weakness is our American cultural tendency to make too many errors—be it the wrong size, color, part number, and so forth. Not only labor, it's in the office force. Compared to the Japanese, who are meticulous and careful, Americans are often perceived as loose with details. Many American managers don't take notes around the conference table, while foreigners often keep extensive records that are later compared. Industry is working through quality programs to "do it right the first time!"

American culture is often a puzzle to foreigners. We have such a diversity of ethnic cultures that borrows from all races and nations. U.S. culture is unique. We do business first, then build a relationship. Business people in every other culture in the world build relationships before doing business.

A world culture doesn't exist. Rather, there are many subcultures and individual distinctions. We can't hope to know all cultures, but *to understand others we should first understand ourselves*!

HOW DO AMERICANS SEE THEMSELVES?

Many Americans believe they have boundless opportunity. There is nothing we can't do—if we want to! We have much confidence. A naivety that perhaps comes along with our openness, usual sincerity, and directness stemming from our early pilgrim heritage. We believe in fairness and "playing by the rules." There is a tendency for "one-upmanship" and a "win/lose" value system. If he wins, then I must lose.

Americans love competition! Our competitive skills are honed not only in our sports, but our businesses. Children naturally "keep score." "Who has the most marbles?" "Who's the strongest, tallest, quickest?" It's natural in our culture. Japan's beating us productively bothers our sense of competitiveness.

A pioneering spirit exists. It wasn't a fluke that Americans got to the moon first.

We pride ourselves on being number one. The Syracuse Orangemen are number one! Put the TV camera in front of the worst sports team in America and their fans still proclaim *their* team is the true number one.

Sometimes we forget we're a product of a revolution. We have been tested in a Civil War. We're idealists and romanticists. We believe in the American dream— anyone can come here and make it. People can, through hard work, earn a living, get a home, and raise a family here better than anywhere else on earth. Isn't that true?

And we're moralists! We like to tell other nations how they should act. Our way is best, of course. We like to preach to others on the virtues of the "American way." Others don't have the high ethics and morals we use in business. We alone have the right answers.

We are self-centered. Our tendency not to study other cultures or nations as others do us is now a *major disadvantage in dealing internationally.* Foreigners, sometimes educated in our school systems, understand not only their own ways, but ours also.

FOREIGNERS VIEWPOINT OF THE AMERICAN BUYER AS NEGOTIATOR

To perceive ourselves as others might, how do offshore suppliers see you—the American buyer as negotiator? Foreigners are told Americans have a macho, cowboy, *"I'm in charge" style*, referred to as "John Wayne" negotiators. Take it or leave it![2] Some Americans' idea of a tough negotiation is seen from trying on shoes. Upon finding the first pair that fits, they say, "Wrap 'em up. How much are the damages?"

Those who study us say that, based on American culture, we usually have a problem dealing with: 1. pace, 2. communication, 3. conduct, 4. relationships, and 5. use of power. Let's briefly review these 5 areas.

1. Pace

Americans want people to get to the point. We are in a greater hurry. Foreigners are repeatedly told to plunge right into the subject. Advice to Americans is to "count to ten" when waiting for replies to questions. If there was time for only one piece of advice in dealing with foreigners, it would be *"be patient!"*

Do any time constraints exist? If you must buy, and do it quickly, you are at a distinct disadvantage. We have to be prepared for negotiations to take longer. As

---

[2]Though this chapter was written well before the Gulf War, wasn't this exactly President Bush's stance with Iraqis?

Table 4-1 shows, if it takes one hour, day, or week to negotiate with Americans, it will take two times that with Europeans, and about six times with the Japanese. It is possible to conclude a contract in three days, but only if most of the details are settled well in advance. Major agreements may take four, five, or more rounds of thorough discussion.

Be sensitive and tolerant to the time needed to reach consensus decisions—not just the Orientals, but the Germans also. The American may perceive vacillation while consensus is being reached.

2. Communication

Shockingly, many Americans upon travel abroad find that, despite much progress in recent years, many foreign people still speak foreign languages. Seriously though, the prime problem for most negotiators worldwide is almost always communication.

Americans got many of our business practices from the British. However, because we historically share a common language and heritage does not mean we're alike. Remember, the *"British just don't speak American."* In England if a play "bombs," it's a hit show. In America, it's a dud—an outright flop! "Knock me up at 7 in the morning" is a perfectly good way for the British businessperson to leave a morning wake-up call. To an American, of course, it means to get someone pregnant. So you see that, even with the same language, different cultures often interpret meanings differently.

Words have different meanings. A cosmetic firm reportedly was about to introduce Country Mist in Germany. At the last minute they switched to Country Moist, upon learning that mist meant manure in German. An exchange student, wishing to thank his host for sponsorship during the school year, wanted to say, "May heaven preserve you." Not confident of the word "preserve," he properly looked it up in the dictionary, and wrote, "And may heaven pickle you."

Say, "How cool you look tonight" and your wife is flattered. But you better not try telling her, "You don't look so hot." Southern fried chicken makes the mouth water, but how about technically-as-accurate dead chicken fried? These all make a point that even with our "American" language, communication is far from simple.

TABLE 4-1. Factors when dealing with foreigners

	Americans	Europeans	Japanese
Time to negotiate	1	2X	6X
Product costs	Thinks he knows	May not know	Detailed analysis
Pricing	6 methods	What the market will bear	To get job

While you may not be expected to know many foreign languages (most American businessmen know only their own), it pays to greet the host or guest in their native tongue. If you don't know how, ask for the proper way to say pleasantries, as most people are proud of their language and heritage.

We're blessed that English is the language of international business. When a Japanese firm negotiates a deal in Europe, it will be in English. German firms don't put labels "Fabriziert in Deutschland," but "Made in Germany" on their exports. Some Italian, Dutch, and even French international companies have adopted English as their official language.

It is trite but true that you should talk somewhat slower than normal, if others haven't a good command of English. After all, we're important (and perhaps arrogant?) enough that the foreigner usually has to speak our language.

Small talk is not wasting time in the Orient. We must discuss the pleasantries before getting down to details of business. Talk of family, sports, or their local events of interest if you expect a friendly relationship.

Sales are made with emotions, not solely logic. The study of emotions leads to the study of body language. Some experts claim that 90 percent of communicating is by other than word meanings. Someone may say something he does not mean and his mannerisms will give him away. Body language is an overlooked part of communications. It can be broken down into various categories: facial expressions, eye contact, posture, movement, speech, tone of voice, and attitude.

- Facial expression. We tend to like someone with a ready smile. But, not at the wrong time! Frowns show disapproval or distaste.
- Eye contact. We rely on our perceptions of others, whether accurate or not. Many of us believe that someone is more honest if they maintain eye contact. Mother says, "Look me in the eye and tell me you didn't eat those cookies." Americans tend to mistrust someone who is "shifty-eyed." Not true when dealing with Mexicans! They're taught to look away when talking with strangers. Isn't that one of the cultural problems between Black Americans and Koreans in New York City, since Koreans avoid eye contact when handing back change at their stores?
- Posture. Someone who leans forward is seen as interested, compared to someone laid back and relaxed with legs crossed. Crossed folded arms sometimes tell us a person is unfriendly or closed to change or suggestion.
- Movement. Drumming your fingers, fiddling with rings, and tapping your foot all are distractions that give others a feeling of impatience or of little interest in their ideas.

In Bombay, Indians wobble their head sideways. They're not indicating "No." It means, "I'm with you." So, use of an interpreter means more than simply understanding words.

- Speech pattern. Rate, volume, or clarity of speech affects how your message is received. Advanced preparation allows you to speak comfortably. People can listen at 400 words per minute, yet we speak at about 200. Listeners have "free time" to notice many little distractions, while speakers think about what to say next.
- Tone of voice. What you say is often lost in how you said it. Tone of voice conveys more meaning than words. Nervous people raise their voice. You need to be confident to convey a positive upbeat tone.

Long silence can mean disapproval, but short silence is habitual, a time to think between speaking. Japanese frequently will remain silent. Americans feel they have to "keep the party going." Silence is a form of communication—accept it!

Adjust presentations to the foreign audience. "Have you heard this one?" Jokes can be dangerous or backfire during business discussions. A speaker talking at a European meeting wanted to tell a story about a buyer. Speaking in English, interpreters relayed the talk in French and German. The Germans were stoic and expressionless, while the French roared with laughter. Afterward, the speaker made a point of telling the interpreter what a good job she had done, especially with his joke. The interpreter, slightly flustered blurted out, "Monsieur, I didn't understand you, so I just told them a joke of my own."

Being too candid is an American characteristic that is often misconstrued. It is not always seen as a virtue. The Chinese believe if you admit a weakness, you probably have many other facts to cover up.

Watch Out for Symbols

We need to watch out for symbols and gestures. They may not be what we think! Simply waving your hand to a Greek can be misunderstood. Almost any hand signal has different meanings in different cultures. In Yugoslavia, when a person searches for good luck, they clench fist with thumb within the fingers. We cross our first and second fingers for either good luck or before telling a fib.

The "V" for victory is usually recognized, but not all other symbols. Be wary of using hand signals, for they may not be what you think. Tapping the side of the head in Europe means something is crazy. An exception is Holland where "How clever or smart" is conveyed.

In ancient Rome, the thumbs-down symbol said it all! Hitchhiking with a fist and the thumb is an obscene gesture in Australia. The thumbs-up symbol, given with a quick clockwise jerk of the right hand, is a Brazilian's way of showing approval. To an Iranian, it is the filthy sign.

The hand symbol of "0" with three fingers means "OK" in the United States, "zero" in France, and "money" in Japan, while in Germany and Brazil its meaning is an obscene reference. This is a true story about the dedication of an American company's new Brazilian operation. The government officials were present along with local plant officials, their wives, and families. Public relations, wanting to be dramatic, decided to have their CEO whisked away in a helicopter from the assembled crowd after the dedication ceremonies.

The helicopter hovered above as the excited crowd below watched with impressed interest. The chairman leaned toward the window and with a big grin, gave the Brazilians the infamous hand symbol.

Color has a small but important role to play in symbols communication. Western cultures readily identify the *Red* Cross as a symbol for help. Moslem countries prefer a Red Crescent symbol. Blue has a good luck connotation to an Arab. White means pure in Europe and America, but in Asia it means death.

Language Translation

In most foreign countries, English is common. However, some countries' businesspersons do not understand it well, and they prefer their local language. Some suppliers who use interpreters understand English quite well, just as Iraq's Saddam Hussein uses interpretation. He corrects some English words his interpreter chooses. Interpretation allows suppliers time to think and a chance to play dumb when it is to their advantage.

Individuals and private firms offer translation service in their local telephone directories. AD-EX Worldwide of Menlo Park, California, lists a toll free phone— (800) 223-7753. They and others are members of the American Translators Association. It's best not to wait until overseas to hire a translator. Among sources for help on interpreters are the U.S. embassies and foreign consulates. They can arrange translation, especially on initial visits.

Finally, *listen, listen, and listen more.* None of us do enough.

3. Conduct—How We Relate!

Americans usually put out the bottom line first. French put out their arguments first. Americans often seek form over substance. For example, we'll make a flip chart presentation, with the speaker marking up the data with dramatic overstatement and flair. It doesn't always impress. Foreigners may feel you didn't bother to prepare.

In some societies, frequent interruptions occur. Examples are Saudi Arabia and other Gulf countries. Businessmen take phone calls and stop to talk to others while negotiating with you. Break your pitch into short segments that can be delayed and picked up later. When presenting in the West, it's more comfortable to operate from the left side because people read left to right. However, stand on the right side of the visual as you talk when addressing people who read from right to left.

Offshore suppliers expect to do what we call "haggling," or "horse trading." The Chinese love to negotiate, seeing it as an act of "friendship and honesty." Americans call it an "auction," when a buyer gets supplier "A" to go below supplier "B" 's price and then asks B to do better—keeping this up for some time.

An American's directness, impatience, and forcefulness, so productive in Europe, now become liabilities in the Orient. We may appear arrogant and lacking of humility, having too much pride in ourselves and our companies. The "ugly American" syndrome is still alive.

If you're resenting some of these comments, you're being quite American. The author was cut off by a buyer in his seminar who said, "Yeah, but we're the customer— so what"! And that's true, we can get away with a lot when we're the customer. But, what if we don't have that much economic clout or where leverage is neutral?

4. Relationships

Does trust exist? Ask yourself if you believe there is a basis for negotiation. Does the supplier have something to give? If there's no room for give and take, the negotiation may be a waste of time. Both sides must want an agreement.

In most cultures, business is conducted with friends. It pays to work for a trusting and open relationship. You must meet the right people. If people don't know you, it doesn't matter what the proposal or price. Individual relationships, once established, replace any cultural caveat. So you must first set good relationships that are built slowly over years of trust.

The higher in the seller organization you get, the better. Orientals greet visitors with like rank. So, if you have a vice president in your party, you'll be received usually by higher rank than if you have a manager. If your president is present, you'll receive the highest turn out. Usually, your first acquaintance will be the level in the organization you're stuck with.

Social activities are an integral part of business negotiations. Dinner and perhaps barhopping are all opportunities to see how you behave with them. It's as true whether you're drinking schnapps in Germany or enjoying sake in Japan.

Orientals value friendships and frequently refer to their acquaintances as "family." Newcomers are at the bottom. Example: The author visited a major Japanese corporation and was refused admission as a competitor. Then, with a headquarter team led by another division that was a joint partner of the Japanese, we held a meeting. Their chairman welcomed us as, "our family."

Their CEO was told that he was to receive a pin that was identical to that worn by the U.S. Secretary of State Alexander Haig (our former company president) when seen on Japanese TV. The author will always recall the emotion as that simple, inexpensive pin was received. Aides propped up their shaking CEO while the emblem was pinned to him. To an American it would have been a simple gesture. To that Japanese manager, it was an honor transcending value.

Europeans are much more title conscious than Americans. Word of a German or Italian Doktur is unquestionable. Use of designations of your degree (BSME), Professional Engineer (P.E.), or Certified Purchasing Manager (C.P.M.), and so on, impresses foreigners and should be used.

We also have to be slow to criticize and not offend or insult any visitor or host. "Loss of face" is not just an issue for Orientals.

5. Use of Power

Suppliers usually dislike power plays of any kind. The upper hand, from a personal power position, often rests with the home negotiator. That's why a buyer is usually better off negotiating at home, behind his own desk. Internationally, however, the buyer frequently must negotiate on foreign territory, often with foreign rituals where he's not too comfortable.

Global cultures can be divided into North, Central, and South American, European, Middle East, and the Orient. Buyers must deal with differing cultural norms on the major three business continents:

1. Oriental mutually cooperative relationships;
2. American adversary buy/sell relationships; and
3. European national partnering relationships.

Be aware of restrictions on foreign sellers' authority. Can they sign or negotiate agreements without approval? Ask them! Sense the relative power of the parties— who is the boss? More important, *who makes the pricing decision?*

What are the social backgrounds of the negotiators? Their status in the parent organization? Answers may give clues to the tendency to take risks, wing it, or play safe. Often, foreigners may put image over substance. Is there a tolerance for ambiguity or not?

Scandinavians design flat organizations with few levels of management—good for overhead, but it thwarts the Americans psychological desire to achieve promotion. The individual versus group. We Americans believe we're individualists. Americans consider the Japanese so regimented with their military uniforms with hash marks. The paradox is that it is we Americans who spell out rigid details for our laborers.

OFFSHORE NEGOTIATIONS AND TACTICS

Having stressed cultural issues, let's now apply them to our negotiations. Most effective negotiators work on what you *need to have*—not stated *wants*. For example, someone says, "I want an apple." You don't have one. His stated position is that he *wants* an apple, but his *need* is that he's hungry. Your bargaining chips are that you have a sandwich and banana. Offering either will fulfill his need to overcome being hungry.

Another example: two woman both want an orange, but you have only one. Based on their *wants*, you can't win. Upon exploring their *needs*, you find one needs an orange for juice while the other needs grated rind for pie flavoring. Applying that to the job, a salesperson tells you, "I *want* a higher price. She *needs* greater profit! Offering greater volume or lower manufacturing costs may satisfy that need.

The art of negotiation can be stated in five steps:

1. Preparation for negotiations.
2. Define *your position limits.*
3. Develop a strategic plan.
4. Control the climate or behavior.
5. Address alterative solutions to seek "win-win" results.

Negotiations offshore, compared to domestic practices, are not too different. The basic tools and techniques while conducting an actual negotiation are similar (for example, the attitude of the negotiators, the need to set goals, determining when and what to negotiate, preparation). Yet there are differences to explore.

To achieve good negotiations, buyers must use persuasion and arguments, both emotional and logical. Our challenge is to find an answer to, "How do we put economic leverage on an international bargaining table?" Not an exact science, nor does any formula exist.

1. Preparation for Negotiations

Leave lawyers out of negotiations. Consult them at home, follow their advice, but don't take them when negotiating an overseas purchase. Having a lawyer present may be seen as a threat to sue and that you're not confident of the negotiation outcome. Some lawyers sometimes make simple business arrangements too complex. The introduction of a lawyer makes parties having difficulties communicating tend to mistrust each other.

Plan the agenda ahead to your advantage. Brief team members beforehand so that none of them tips your hand or gives up a point before you do. Make sure your team agrees on the overall strategy to follow. Who shall talk? Who keeps minutes for distribution, and so on? How will you handle disagreement among your team members? Who has authority to make final decisions?

Select Location of Meeting

British managers will try to avoid your meetings. European managers work by themselves and hold few meetings. You must make sure, before visiting, who will meet with you. And decide on the best place to hold your meeting. It is not always desirable to negotiate in your host's office.

Set the meeting to begin at a time that will allow for a relaxing lunch at a proper time. People are always more agreeable, though sometimes drowsy, after eating.

Allow extra time to agree. Opening a meeting with a statement, "We have to be out of this room by 2 P.M.," may mean the agreement is thwarted. Or if you rush now, you may not get a satisfactory result.

2. Define Your Position Limits

Set targets and goals as a team. Commitments must not be given before the resolution of major negotiation goals are met. Is there a basis for negotiation? Does the other party have something to give? Know what you can expect to gain by negotiating.

Have reasonable goals and expectations—usually a minimum and maximum position. Don't set price targets and goals too low. If seller makes his early quotes high, based on the feeling that you will be satisfied, it will be more difficult to drop the prices later. Better to "be tough" early so that the supplier's first proposal is a realistic offer from which to negotiate.

3. Develop a Strategic Plan

Buyers should have a strategic plan, and then use effective buying tactics to carry it out. "Strategic planning" is *how* to win the war! (Strategic or long range takes one year or longer to complete.) Tactical is how to *win the battle*! (Tactical is short-range, more day-to-day action that is concluded in less than one year).

First, size up your opponent. Some like to look at the attributes of a good negotiator. An interesting verbal sketch is that we are all born with, or soon acquire, a pair of "sunglasses." Americans have yellow, Japanese blue. When we study the Japanese and try to see their blue, what do we get? Green!

Most buyers are not born with either sunglasses or negotiation skills, though some people have more natural ability than others. We all negotiate in daily living. Personal attributes of negotiators include knowledge, attitude, skill, analytical ability, good communications, patient, and even tempered. Also, a dose of courage and sense of humor may help.

Remember that personal values of the negotiator are nonnegotiable. Successful negotiations are the result of a dedicated effort to improve by following proven techniques. So, we'll look at some negotiation techniques that experienced negotiators use.

Decide whether to take the initiative or hold off. Should your position be revealed? What information is to be given? These things should be settled in advance.

Psychologists tell us that if you have a choice, take a chair where there is no barrier, such as a desk, between you and the other party. That tells buyers that sitting behind your own desk helps make you somewhat superior and gain you more respect. If you must sit opposite the other party's desk, shift to his or her left, so he or she talks to you from his left rather than head on. The author set his desk to the right side of his office, so he looked ahead or to the left for discussions with visitors. Note that the visitors also looked left also. It does make most of us feel more relaxed and is easier to converse.

4. Control the Climate or Behavior

Those who deal with the Japanese notice how polite they are. The Japanese treat presenting the business card as sort of a drinking tea ceremony to observe proper etiquette. Americans may casually hand or toss theirs out while stretching across a table, but a Japanese will try to use both hands and bow politely.

Business cards are not just for ceremony. Take plenty of them. They're cheap. Place supplier's cards in front of you as reminders of the people positioned around the table during negotiations. With the cards displayed in front, there is no need to guess who is speaking.

In the negotiation environment itself, most foreigners take time for proper decorum. Japanese maneuver seating arrangements. They put the most important negotiators at the center of the room and arrange their counterparts directly opposite. The seat we take at the negotiation table may prejudice the outcome.

Watch Out for These Social Slights
Be wary of age differentials. Westerners are often annoyed when Koreans ask their age. Respect is shown for age and position in their society. The eldest Oriental is most often the ranking member, and they expect high ranking executives to be seniors. They will suspect that a young, bright American is a lower level person sent to deal with them. Because a westerner's age is difficult to judge, their way to be socially correct is simply to ask, "How old are you?"

Failing to recognize cultural differences may cause needless friction:

- Surnames are used in most countries. Mr. Etienne Michael from Paris should not be called "Etienne" upon first meeting him.
- Informality is often associated with poor upbringing.
- Respect rank, degree, or titles.
- Remain silent at times! Often, greater concessions result from a seller's fear of losing business. Suppliers may talk themselves into a better settlement than the buyer expected. (Foreigners have identified this trait as a weakness of American selling.)

Some Other Negotiation Tactics
Tactics of buying change, depending on whether it's a buying or selling market. In a seller's market, it may take a more friendly type personality to succeed—one with

better interpersonal skills and the ability to establish trusting relationships and who is politically adept at being well-liked.

The buyer must often "sell" to get the goods instead of someone else. Greater shrewdness is needed to get better prices. The buyer must be a skilled negotiator to perform in tough global markets. A hard-nosed purchasing manager may not be seen as "with it" by his management. So, to be truly effective, our buyer should adapt his style to suit.

Of course, the buyer can't, like the chameleon, change colors as every market changes, but he has to moderate away from extreme positions and be flexible enough to understand his environment.

Finally, this time-tested tactics checklist[3] will give you some thoughts before a session:

DO's

- Find out if the seller is interested in making a deal. There is a time when negotiation is fruitless, especially when one side isn't interested in settling or agreeing.
- Negotiate at home when possible.
- Be patient! Patience is one of the highest attributes of the offshore (domestic also) negotiator. Few successful global negotiators plunge in and try to wrap everything up too quickly. The author has been in negotiations when it looked hopeless. By patiently waiting for others to find a way out a deadlock, it usually will be done.
- Enlist the aid of team specialists in manufacturing, finance, and engineering to help evaluate tooling and other special costs. Purchasing research will help supply basic data necessary for negotiating in depth.
- Use techniques, such as cost and value analysis, that provide grist for discussion on how to reduce prices.
- Negotiate for the long pull—not the short-sighted advantage that may backfire at the first turn of economic conditions.

DON'Ts

- Tip your hand too easily!
- Accept the first thing or idea tossed out. When acknowledging the other side's point of view, the buyer doesn't have to agree with it.
- Get so bogged down in details that the overall objectives are lost. Many a session occurs where there is agreement, only to have someone keep negotiating and lose it.
- Use information you know is wrong or weak that strains your credibility as you are forced to acknowledge the facts.

---

[3]First published in the late 1960s when the author wrote the American Management Association's Bulletin #50, "Developing the Negotiating Skills of the Buyer."

- Try to prove the supplier is wrong! You may succeed in embarrassing him and winning your point, but you've damaged your relationship.

5. Address Alternative Solutions to Gain Concessions

When making a concession, don't give it too quickly or easily! Also, "Quid pro quo"— *ask* for something in return. Also, when conceding, do so graciously without haggling. Some negotiators probably think if they act hurt when they compromise, they won't have to give more. Recall, when it's all done, *both parties should be reasonably satisfied about the deal.*

Negotiate with those who can make concessions. Often, a seller has a range of prices to submit. They can drop prices, say 5 percent without prior management approval. It is useless to negotiate with a seller if the offshore home office has set a firm price list. With a positive attitude, expect and ask for concessions!

Use many questions when probing for information and giving alternative options. Questions are better than provocative or controversial statements that may offend. They allow a touchy point to be put on the table in an inoffensive manner.

"Why?" and "Why not?" can be effective. Here are other simple questions to use. "What if we:

Give you a one- or five- year contract?
Drop your warranty?
Allow you to make during off-season?
Supply you with technological help?
Change your contract to blanket order?
Make progress payments?
Change our specs to what you'd make?
Provide the materials and components?
Buy a higher quality?
Double our order?
Buy all your output?"

Perhaps you can think of many others. All these questions give the supplier alternates that make it easier to perform.

Asking questions is a sound technique. But don't ask a negative question of an Oriental, for you will get the wrong answer. Example, "Aren't you going to quote us in dollars?" The answer may be "Yes." The meaning is, "Yes, we aren't going to quote you in dollars."

Negotiations Hit a Snag

Despite the best of planning and intentions, a negotiation may reach an impasse. Sometimes, Americans have to learn not to plunge ahead without slowing down.

You might liken it to driving a motor boat through seaweed. Gradually, the motor propeller fouls and turns ever slower as forward propulsion slows to a crawl. You can't get out of the weeds by racing full speed ahead. By reversing, the propeller casts the debris off. Then you can resume full speed. In business, sometimes the negotiator makes no progress heading straight at the problem. Turn around and go into reverse until the hazard clears. Then go ahead once again toward your target.

Divert attention if the negotiation hits your weak points. Shift to minor points that you may choose to concede later. When you can't resolve an issue, pass it over for a while. Arrange for a lunch or coffee break. Set a pattern of solving easier issues first. Give the other party a chance to back down. Caucus for cause, and compromise graciously when necessary.

How to Blow a Negotiation

We can learn from negative ideas too. Save some bargaining chips to use to get rid of a stumbling block, especially if parties begin to change previously agreed issues. Members of a team can provide unknowing stumbling blocks to successful negotiations. For example, here is a list of stumbling blocks guaranteed to blow any negotiation:

- Letting the supplier know there is no other source. Someone leaking that there is no other source or that they want the supplier regardless. (Somewhat at odds with supplier partnering, if single sourcing is practiced.)
- Boasting how much money you will make on your deal. Supplier will figure he or she has a good share of that coming. Better to stress how competitive your marketplace is and your concern that the supplier must help you meet that market.
- Divulging authority limitations. Making a statement, such as "I've got to clear it with the boss" weakens your negotiation power. Also, it may cause the seller to visit the boss.
- Not knowing what you want. Letting the supplier do the selecting can be okay in some instances. However, it usually allows the seller to get the best deal for himself. As in a store, you won't often get the best buy unless you know exactly what you want and go after it.
- Waiting until the last minute to spring a major issue. Better to outline it early.
- Giving up information on the seller's competition. Casual statements over lunch, "They can't furnish the plastic models we want," "They quoted us at $10 each," ensures you'll get prices just a small amount lower.

PUT IT IN WRITING!

Regardless of the culture or nationality, when agreement is reached, always reduce business discussions to writing. Your record keeper should be accurate. Simple language should be used with short sentences for clarity. Joint memos of understanding, prepared while negotiating, can be signed by both parties. This prevents arriving back in the United States and getting a written agreement totally different than you thought you concluded. By jointly agreeing to the final wording, it becomes part of the negotiation process. Loose ends are tied together.

In summary, American buyers need to learn:

- It is desirable to "get to the point," but not too abruptly.
- Develop strong personal ties and understanding with negotiators, if possible.
- Be more sensitive of the seller's "culture." Show an interest in *their* local events—the sumo wrestling or soccer. Recall how our forefathers learned to smoke the peace pipe.
- Plan ahead and expect to gain success.
- *Always be fair!*

And finally, regardless of outcome, even if a failure, remember to part on friendly terms. There's always another day and another buy. It always pays to be friendly. A smile covers many a misunderstanding. Be courteous and thoughtful of others' time and effort. Thank them frequently.

International negotiations can only be addressed based on a specific nationality. As the global corporations mature, cross-cultural issues can become quite confusing. On the job, the author has been in meetings where five or six nationalities worked for his company. We'd have a Frenchman and Japanese on the U.S. side. We've had sessions involving Americans, Brazilians, and Japanese at the same time.

Usually, most negotiations are between Americans and one other nationality. In a global corporation, there are many combinations possible, and ultimately we'll have a true global cultural marketplace.

Negotiations continues to be the heart of the purchasing job. It is a never-ending task. How well it is done determines to a large extent the difference between a paper-placing function and a profit-oriented arm of management.

5

Business Customs and Cultural Nuances

Here is an all-too-familiar scenario of our American failure to understand another culture. Buyer Michael wants an agreement with a Japanese company, so he arranges a hasty trip to Japan. He sets meeting for 8 A.M. Monday, after arriving late the evening before.

Michael opens the meeting by saying, "I have to be in London Wednesday and want to settle here today!" Deciding to lay his cards on the table, Michael asks their head man Morita-San, "Can't we get right to the point! I've studied your prices and can live with them. Isn't it possible for you to reach an agreement with me today?" Upon being told, "Yes," Mike plunges into the full details quickly.

Michael tells the supplier exactly what he wants, adding, "But we need these delivered in four months, not six as now promised. You can do it, I know you can." Japanese negotiator Morita draws breath through his teeth, then says, "It's very difficult." Mike doesn't give up and is gratified to hear Morita proclaim loudly, "Hai, Hai!" However, he knows it will take several months of thorough planning.

Michael again asks for reassurance, "Aren't you going to meet our deliveries?" He's told, "Yes," along with a nod of the head. "If there's any loose ends, we can have our lawyers settle," Michael says, bringing the meeting to a close. So, an enthusiastic Michael shakes hands with everyone and bids farewell.

"No problem," he tells his manufacturing vice president of his success upon returning home. "They'll do the job and can meet our schedule as requested."

Four months later, an upset boss, strides into Michael's office, saying, "No sign of even samples from that Japanese outfit! Better get a local source in a big hurry. We don't want to miss the coming season. And you only have 60 days to get this stuff pronto! How could you have misjudged this supplier so badly?" What would you advise Michael to do now? Update his resume? A buyer with experience dealing with the Japanese would recognize several blunders. Recall, in our chapter on negotiations, Michael should have learned he will get the wrong answer if he asks negative questions. For example, if a buyer asks, "Aren't you going to quote us in dollars?", the answer will be "Yes," meaning "Yes, we aren't going to quote you in dollars." The answer to Michael's query was, "Yes" (we *can't* reach an agreement).

Japanese tend to tell you what you want to hear. Because they often say an emphatic "Hai," they give the impression that they're always agreeing with you. "Hai" means "I hear" or understand what you say.

Suggesting a lawyer would be taken as questioning their Japanese integrity. Because Michael did not hear "No", does not mean he had an agreement. When the Japanese mean "No," they may say something like, "That's very difficult to do" or "We're studying it."—although the latter may also be a legitimate way of requesting time for consensus back home. Finally, by drawing air through his teeth, with a hissing sound and saying, "It's very difficult," Michael got almost an absolute "No!"

As we study below, other boners become evident. There are cultural differences in important trading societies. The point is that before negotiating with any offshore supplier, buyers must focus on their specific culture.

CULTURES OF THE ORIENT

The major cultures of the Orient are Japan, South Korea, Taiwan, China, and Hong Kong. With the balance of trade tilted to the Pacific, Americans find themselves dealing with about 34 countries with hundreds of languages and dialects. And each has its own cultural heritage.

Japanese Culture

Japanese cultural drive to be the "number one" economic leader is powerful! The people strive to do whatever they believe is necessary to achieve it. That's why most willingly put their job, company, and country ahead of their family and themselves.

The Japanese have long striven to emulate Western culture, even in their dress code. Yet, they have retained their own culture within their homes. People share a common heritage and language that is said to allow communication by tacit understanding. Japanese don't like arguments and place much importance in achieving harmony (Wa) with others. They are uncomfortable solving conflicts.

Japanese use three type bows, a 15-degree bow is used upon first meeting a colleague in a hallway. The 30-degree is the standard greeting for customers. Finally, the deep, 45-degree stooped-over, humble bow is for special occasions. In response, Americans find themselves bowing somewhat automatically. A rule of thumb is to match by bowing as low and long as the host—you can't go wrong.

People are addressed by their last name, with the added suffix "San." A guest becomes not "Mr. Pooler," but "Pooler-San." Japanese will not use first names, though some modern ones like to put American names on their business card, calling themselves, for example, George or Harry. Pass out plenty of business cards to everyone. Have your card printed in Japanese on the reverse side.

While President Reagan was pictured with his arm around President Nakasone's shoulder at the May 1986 Tokyo Economic Summit, the author learned long ago that Japanese don't like anyone to put their arm around them or pat them on the back. They prefer to stand their distance. Japanese, while stiff and quite formal by American norms, can be friendly and exceedingly courteous. Care is needed not to embarrass your Japanese visitor or host. They're very sensitive to appearances that offend. "Loss of face" is not just an expression. They try hard to be accurate and accommodating. One buyer told how the Japanese skillfully maneuvered him and his wife into a car's back seat. After being seated, it occurred to him it was *his* car.

Japanese use teams in negotiation. Don't rush discussions. Allow time to consider. Courtesy and interest should be maintained with the utmost integrity. Until the Japanese get to know and trust you, they will be innately cautious and not give much information.

Usually, your first acquaintance will be the level in the organization you're stuck with. Channels are locked in. Japanese share information by nature, just as they prefer to share their rooms, meals, and travel together. Also, in sharing all business decisions, no one individual is totally responsible for a mistake.

An agreement between buyer and seller is circulated in writing, for everyone's "chop" or seal—a buckslip termed "ringisho" (or Ringi). An upright seal signifies approval, a sideways seal simply notes but does not pass judgement. An upside down seal is a sign of objection, that may pigeonhole or kill the proposal.

Japanese ask lots of questions. When visiting, they'll go from office to office asking the same questions repeatedly. They're sorting out the facts and will discuss these matters later.

Japanese dislike power plays of any kind. They may shove and push to get on their trains, but rarely does it pay to rudely demand that they ship on time. Most Japanese businessmen from major suppliers are scrupulously honest. When they give their word, the buyer can depend on it. They are highly intelligent and group-oriented, always loyal to their organization.

Americans are sometimes surprised by Japanese who seem to laugh at inappropriate times. It is not due to an odd sense of humor; rather, it is their way of reacting to embarrassment.

During discussions, Japanese frequently will remain silent. Americans tend to feel they have an obligation "to keep the party going" by making lots of small talk. Long silence can mean disapproval, but short silence is habitual, a sort of time to think between speaking. Also, buyers will note that Japanese pronounce the letter "R" as "L."

Japanese are excellent at note taking and documentation. Because they do not want to lose face or be embarrassed, they will go to extremes to do what is required.

Japanese value friendships highly and frequently refer to their acquaintances as "family." Newcomers are at the bottom. Some companies have kept retired salesmen active in negotiations, just to keep up relationships with key American managers who work longer in life—age 65 versus 55 in Japan.

Style is important to the Japanese. How a meal looks and is served may be more important than how it tastes. The manner in which a negotiation is conducted may not be as important as the result, but the Japanese always put a lot of effort into proper decorum. When sitting down to negotiate or eat, the guests are always placed by the windows, with the host by the door. This tradition allows the host to symbolically protect guests from attack from the doorway.

If interpretation is necessary, hiring your own to represent you may be a good investment. Ask the interpreter to ask for answers to technical questions in Japanese.

Business entertaining is an expensive and integral part of Japanese business culture. If you're not in town, they're probably entertaining with fellow office managers. At a Japanese restaurant, where most entertaining will occur, the guest never sees the bill, which is discreetly handled away from the table.

Japanese will find an excuse for women guests not being included. Socially, they don't like to include their wives. This fact concerns many women buyers, who wonder how they will be treated on their first trip there. But lady buyers report that they are accepted as Japanese see more American women playing an important role in their negotiations.

Do try their customs. Sit at their low tables and use chopsticks. Shoes are removed in exchange for guest slippers. Warm sake (distilled wine from rice) will be served before dinner. It's traditional to fill each other's sake cups.

You can't meet or visit the Japanese without being an occasional recipient of a small gift. It will be well packaged and wrapped gaily in pastel colors, regardless of its value. Don't wrap anything in plain white, which signifies mourning.

Taiwanese Culture

The residents of the Republic of China (ROC) don't like to discuss the topic of mainland China. People are sternly anti-Communist. Because many top level executives or their parents came from mainland China during the revolution, many Chinese features of culture apply here. Chinese heritage managers speak good English. Lower level native management speak Taiwanese. The written language is classical Chinese characters. Mandarin is the official language of the island, but the Cantonese and Taiwanese dialects are spoken.

Use plenty of business cards printed in English and Chinese. Elder people are greeted first. A nod of the head upon meeting is normal and slight bows are considered a sign of much respect. Mr., Mrs., and Miss are used, followed by the single family name. Friendly relationships must be cultivated with great patience.

Taiwanese are characterized as soft sell, but, at the same time, they "buy hard." They are competitive bargainers who expect to "haggle," and so on. Taiwanese are highly inquisitive and more open than the Japanese. Still, don't be too abrupt. A subtle approach is always best in the Orient. Consistency that comes from a well-prepared agenda and approach is desirable.

Chinese expect to entertain the visitor in restaurants. Don't address business during entertaining time. Dinners consist of many courses, so be sure not to eat too much early. The host will serve his guests. Afterwards, he will characteristically apologize that the food was not good. Politeness calls for the visitor to maintain strongly how good it truly was.

Small gifts are common, but not necessary. Because of Chinese influence, many remarks on the Chinese culture apply in Taiwan as well.

Chinese Culture

The People's Republic of China, Mainland China, or Communist China are common Western terms denoting China, the world's oldest civilization and the third largest country in the world. Most Chinese businessmen speak the national "Standard Chinese," which is Mandarin, and perhaps one other dialect, such as Shanghai-ese or Cantonese. Usually, Chinese can read the different dialects, as the written forms are similar, though the meanings and pronunciations are quite different. A few words of greeting in their tongue will please the host.

Atheism is official endorsed by the Communist government. But religions are allowed, such as Buddhism, Taoism, and Christianity. Ancestor worship or folk religions such as Confucianism greatly influence family life!

Dealing with China, the buyer needs to be invited to trade. So it is usual to start by approaching a state trading corporation. This often means red tape and delay, but to trade, the system must be followed. There are two types of trading groups: those authorized by the Ministry of Foreign Economic Relations and Trade (MOFERT), and the others that are industrial-type corporations run directly by government agencies, such as the Ministry of Agriculture and the Ministry of Petroleum.

Shaking hands is done in business, but more commonly, a nod or slight bow is customary. Do not greet too casually, as introductions are quite formal. Mr. and Madame are usually used followed by the family name. So Yeh Zedong is addressed as "Mr. Yeh," while his wife would be "Madame Yeh."

Use business cards freely that are printed in both Chinese as well as English. Don't put your arm around or touch people, especially when talking with people of rank or importance. Chinese point with an open hand palm down. Avoid showing the soles of your feet, pointing your shoes toward others while sitting, or using the feet to move chairs, or hold a door open. Feet are considered unclean.

Visitors should avoid talking about politics or Chinese leaders. Discussing Taiwan has been considered off-limits. The Chinese refer to Taiwan not as the Republic of China, but as the "Formosa Province." This is changing as relations become better. Still, it is better not to discuss other countries, such as South Korea or Israel, that they don't recognize.

Chinese are the merchants of the Orient and are sometimes resented by other Asian nationalities. Chinese are punctual and usually arrive early for meetings. In negotiations, be certain that the person or trading organization has the authority to accept your offer to buy. One reason for not clearing matters promptly is the *inability* to determine who has the power or authority to negotiate.

A team concept of negotiations is followed by the Chinese. If you have three members, they may have 20. Their large buying teams are known to shock the seller by immediately requesting a price cut of about 30 percent. Conversely, sellers would be surprised if the American buyer suddenly just bought their initial offer.

Because of centralized control, some Americans may believe Chinese prices are uniform and not negotiable. Not so! They like to negotiate—"haggle" some people would call it. Dealing with the Chinese teaches us to immediately call for a large price reduction. If the buyer has no idea of an item's value, counter any offering price to sell, with about a 40 percent reduction request. The buyer can come up about 10 percent in price later as a concession. The term "auction" came from the experience of those dealing with the Chinese.

Not skilled in cost analysis, they often assure the buyer that, "Prices will be cheap." Prices will not be based on cost, rather what they think others would charge, regardless of their low labor costs. Sometimes this leaves Westerners feeling they are price gougers.

Some American negotiators assume that the Chinese display little interest in controlling either discussion or negotiations. Others observe that, as hosts, Chinese do relish taking control over the negotiations. First, they set an agenda in advance, and then open a negotiation with a statement to the effect, "Our custom is that guests are always allowed to speak first." This forces the guest to show their hand that is the starting point for concessions to be asked. And it is expected they are to get more concessions to keep the negotiations alive.

Chinese like to play one member of the foreign negotiating team against another, if they can create an issue. This splits the opposition. In dealing with Americans, they've learned to drop the hint quietly to one American that the negotiations may fail without agreement with what they want. Typically, our American friend immediately advises everyone that they must make more concessions.

Chinese keep good records of conversations. They use detailed Memorandums of Understanding (MOU). There is a deep-seated distrust of legalities, and China has not yet developed a system of commercial law. Mediation solves most Chinese disputes.

Chinese like to first have an MOU, loosely defining general principles, before negotiating the details. Chinese feel an agreement means that details will be worked out while each party continues to ask for their concessions. Later, they may say you are violating or not living up to the spirit of the agreed principles. The MOU will be used to prove their side of the understanding.

Keep notes and records visibly. Failure to do this may hint that you are not too serious. The Chinese usually will not speak English in negotiations. A widely used tactic is to use interpretation even when they may understand English. It allows time to think.

The Chinese seemingly have unlimited patience and are prepared to wait out an adversary to give concessions. Prepare to stay in China for a while. Learn to accept periods of silence, which don't mean disapproval. The process of discussion moves in a zig-zag fashion. Progress sometimes is rapid and then may slow down to a crawl. Discussions may circuitously move to an issue previously thought settled, or change to a new issue. If all goes well, a purchase will be concluded. Chinese are known to keep their commitments loyally once a final agreement is reached.

The buyer has to be prepared that, after days of negotiating and getting an agreement signed, the Chinese may reopen the negotiated issues. Chinese believe old friends, or even people from the same community, school, or company, should act as friends even if they don't know each other. Now that there is an agreement, their belief is they are now free to discuss such issues freely among "old friends." Chinese feel free now to ask lots of questions.

Though generally more aggressive and curious than the Japanese, like most Orientals, Chinese seldom say a firm "Yes" or "No." Agreement may take the form of, "Problems are not great," or, conversely, disagreement as, "Perhaps it's not convenient." The Chinese don't like open disagreement.

Chinese play their cards close to the table, while urging guests to come up with still more information. Small talk is avoided during negotiations. Sometimes Chinese appear totally hung up on a small point.

Those who deal with them feel that the Chinese don't appreciate the concepts of proprietary rights. Knowledge belongs to everyone, and you should share it with them even if it costs you lots to obtain it. The Chinese appear to have a deep suspicion that foreigners don't want them to know all the information they need. So flood them with lots of facts on the buyer's company, history, and so forth. The more details you provide, the more the Chinese are persuaded.

Chinese like to get the other party to assert and exaggerate its capabilities. Their response is to reserve the right to ask for more. They like to be in the negotiating position in which you are the superior, yet they maintain their dignity. People who are better off are supposed to always be generous. So you, the American, will usually be made out to be the more prosperous, and so on.

Many Chinese believe that most Americans are easily flattered, and are thus manipulated. They'll maintain elaborate courtesy and gestured humility, while being highly sensitive to any perceived insult.

The American executive who comes directly to the issues plays into the Chinese hands. Chinese have a way of manipulating a meeting so that the foreigner seems to be asking the Chinese for a favor or concession. This results in the foreigner often being in a defensive position.

Chinese believe that foreigners must "serve China" and do things their way. Chinese are demanding. They expect foreigners to pay the bill. General firmness on the buyer's part is respected. They take advantage of perceived hesitancy or weakness.

If you admit a weakness, you are probably covering up greater ones than those you've admitted. Frankness is not always seen as a virtue by the Chinese. The buyer must know and insist on performance and what is due. However, as guests, Americans should adjust to Chinese practices and not insist that ours is the only way. Smile when you say no.

One businessman always tells his host exactly how long he would stay to get agreement. If the Chinese, after much discussion, truly wanted to agree, and the deadline approached, they would announce that they had no concerns, though the issues that were stubbornly negotiated had not been settled.

Chinese food is important to them. Chinese prefer a Chinese breakfast and dinner wherever they are. They expect the visitor to eat their food, which fortunately is tasty to the American palette. Eat lightly as many courses are served, and you do not want to offend later by seemingly not liking the food. The host will signal when the meal is over, and everyone leaves shortly.

When eating popular catfish, Chinese never turn the fish upside down. Rather, they remove the spine and continue, because to invert the fish means the "ship has sunk" and your deal is dead.

Business is generally not discussed while eating, though an occasional tip or remark is made. During any formal type dinner, a ceremonious gift could be appropriate, but gifts are best not given. Chinese are sensitive and turned off by any hint of an excessive gift or bribe.

South Korean Culture

Chosen is the country's Korean name, and means "Land of the Morning Calm." While most Korean businessmen speak English, usually they get somewhat more than half the words correctly. Use of a local interpreter is recommended, if there are no local associates who can speak well.

Korean grammar and inflection is totally different from Chinese. Koreans have reputations as good listeners. One reason is that you must wait for the verb that is at the end of a sentence to get the proper meaning. Korean is one of only three languages that cannot be simultaneously translated. For example, one has to hear the last syllable to know if someone is going, will go, plans to go, didn't go, won't go, or wants to go.

Korean's religions are Buddhist (16 percent), with strong Confucian influence (14 percent), Christian (30 percent, with ¾ of those being Protestant), and Shamanist (26 percent), which believes in folk religions. It is suggested that businessmen never discuss Korean religion, politics, socialism, or communism.

Names are not used frequently as in the West. Koreans have three names: first is the family name (Kim, Lee, and Park make up 50 percent of the 200 different names), second is the generation name that all brothers (sisters if the family wants) share and has a lucky or prosperous meaning, and third is the given name. Greet people by title and family name. For example, Chun Doo Hwan is properly addressed as President Chun, but while a businessman he'd be Mr. Chun (the first name being the family name). Titles will proceed the family name, so the same person might be called Professor Park, Mr. Park, or Director Park.

As throughout the Orient, use plenty of business cards upon meeting. Bow slightly. Sometimes both hands are shook. Korean juniors bow lower than their seniors. Korean men sometimes hold hands in public, but strangers are not expected to touch them other than shaking hands in meeting.

Koreans often seem reluctant to give data when making proposals because they feel they're exposing their weaknesses. Many questions will be asked—some repeatedly. Be patient and politely respond to each.

Modesty is admired and courtesy expected. As with other Orientals, saving face and maintaining harmonious relationships are most important. They go to extremes to maintain harmony and avoid open conflicts. To refuse a friend a favor or request is an insult. A true Korean gentleman is reluctant to accept any honor and is extremely modest.

Koreans are more direct than Japanese and considered highly aggressive. While more direct, they don't like criticism or blunt forcefulness. As do the Japanese, they come well prepared to negotiate. And they're persistent.

After being shoved and by-passed while standing in Korean queuing lines while shopping, one would never suspect so fragile a business or social relationship exists. Koreans can't accept failure! Business bad news is never reported the first hour of the day. It's better to disclose at the end of the day or preferably week. This allows time to recover face, or Kibun.

A public reprimand in front of subordinates is most serious, as the image may be so damaged that the subordinate will no longer work for him. In business relationships, that should be maintained. American buyers must give the Koreans a way out if they can't fulfill their agreement or commitment. This is contrary to American procedure of "making them pay" or going to court.

Confucianism has no code for foreigners, who are "nonentities." No respect is due and none is expected. But, when a foreign businessman enters into a relationship, he receives the respect of his position.

Respect is shown for age and position in society. It may annoy Westerners to often be asked their age. Koreans have been taught to respect their elders. Usually, with age, position is also higher. Because a Westerner's age is difficult to judge, the way to be socially correct is to simply ask, "How old are you?" By finding out, they can give the respect due to you by their culture.

Koreans have a strong entrepreneurial spirit and you will be assured of their ability to perform. Buyers report that, only after they had placed an order, did the Koreans take action to erect facilities to produce. So, the advice is to go see the facility, just don't meet in hotel rooms.

Koreans are pleased to hear compliments about their economic progress, while at the same time they may be sensitive to hearing of the greatness of others. Once good communications exist, meeting procedures to get approval of required documents are easier than in the United States or Europe if you handle matters their way.

Don't use a red pen to sign your agreement, as the color red is a symbol of death. Another fetish is that their fourth floors will be marked "F," though the room numbers are 401, etc. The number 4 is an unlucky number, the same as our number 13.

Entertaining is an important aspect of business relationships. Tea, sweet coffee, or soft drinks will be served during business hours. Korean food is spicy. Popular are Pulgogo, which is a barbecued beef sliced thin, kimchi, which is a highly spicy, pickled cabbage, and dok, or pounded rice cake. Large amounts of fish and soups are popular. No desserts are served, though they may serve a fresh fruit in its place.

If invited to a home, remove your shoes and wait to enter until invited at least twice. Wives will usually not be included in entertainment outside the home. Bring flowers, fruit, wine, or a small gift. Gifts should not be opened at the time it is received.

Guests at dinner should start to eat first, and should never eat the last of any item. Custom is to refill any empty tray, and great embarrassment results if none is available. Food is passed with the right hand and the left usually supports the right forearm. Both hands are used when handing anything to a Korean.

Koreans talk little while eating, to signify that the food is good. Business should be reserved for later. Often, the guest is escorted outside without any good-bye. Everyone stands and leaves quite quickly.

Should a Westerner refuse a gift while honoring his ethical or company policy, he has to allow for much protest from his giver. One purchasing manager, after admiring a painting in a store, was distressed to see his host giving instructions to wrap a several hundred dollar painting. He hadn't realized that admiring an item may be seen as an invitation for a gift. Quickly, spotting a $15 picture, he declared how much he liked that one. His host immediately directed that the inexpensive picture be wrapped instead. This was an excellent tactic. While this purchasing manager would not accept gifts at home, he bent slightly, understanding the gift significance to the Korean. Yet he would not go beyond a reasonable, token value.

The proper social gift in Korea is money, placed in an envelope that is given at all special occasions, such as weddings. But it is not a proper Western business gift, as every American businessman knows.

Hong Kong Culture

The British colony of almost 6 million population was born during the Opium Wars in 1840. The United Kingdom is turning over this free colony of Hong Kong to the People's Republic of China by July 1, 1997. Though capitalism may not be legally abolished until late 2047, and despite China's assurance it won't be, many are anxious about the future of this vital business community.

Hong Kong lacks an indigenous culture and is caught between two contradictory cultures today—the British and the Chinese. Business customs are from English traditions, by a Chinese-cultured people.

Language is English and Chinese. Religion is Confucianism, though many also practice Buddhism and Taoism, and some Christianity.

Hong Kong businessmen have much experience dealing with Westerners and Americans. Considered easy to do business with, most foreign buyers use an agent or commissioned importer. Business suits are worn with casual attire in factories.

Like mainland Chinese, Hong Kong negotiators are meticulous in detail. Buyers should refer to the Chinese section of this chapter for greater insights. A main difference is that Hong Kong business people have long ago worked out the legalities and terminology to bridge East-West trade. You will be expected to be well prepared with specifications, quantities, shipping needs, and authority. Proof of your intentions to buy and ability to pay will be expected.

Joint ventures and licensing agreements are favored. Especially valued are those buys where the buyer provides new technology or product designs not now available in Hong Kong. It is important that buyers control their proprietary interests and rights to distribution. Hong Kong has been cited for using others' property. Buyers and importers may want to register new product designs with the Design Depository in the Hong Kong Design and Packaging Centre.

The Hong Kong/Chinese businessman likes to entertain in restaurants, as contrasted with the European native who prefers to have dinner parties held in their home. Guests should be on time. After dinner, guests often will rise to publicly thank the host in behalf of those invited.

CULTURES OF EUROPE

Traditionally, some American buyers have dealt with Europeans. Europe is considered as one European Economic Community (EEC), which at times can act as an economic unit.

Europeans are sensitive to suggestions that their productivity is lower than others. Setting a "target price" is often unacceptable and can be a turnoff to Europeans. But then, even knowing the hour to phone Europeans isn't simple. The Swiss often meet customers at 7 A.M. Norwegians have lunch at 11 A.M., Germans at noon, British at 1 P.M., and Spanish at 3 P.M.

In the United Kingdom, buyers arrive at their desk at 9:30 A.M. but hold calls until after 10. Greek businesspeople don't phone between 2 and 5 P.M. (their lunchtime), though they're trying to cut down on their three-hour lunches. And those friendly Italians are famous for disappearing after 2 P.M. Germans go home at 4 P.M. If you try for a dinner at 9 P.M. in Norway, you'll find the restaurant just closing.

While there are similarities within Europe, sort of like a diversified United States, there are still distinct contrasts in currency, tax regulation, company law, and accounting practices. Also, there are different languages and cultures that must be dealt with individually. Principal European trading partners' cultures that buyers will deal with are British, French, German, and Italian.

British Culture

Personal questions are offensive to the private nature of British people. They're not fond of being touched or grabbed by the arm as Americans like to do. Men like a soft handshake and not the pumping power grip.

Business practices are quite standard to Americans. Always be on time for business meetings. When giving facts, *understatement*, not boastfulness, is respected. Typical were the press briefings during the Gulf War. When asked if he thought the deserting Iraqis soldiers would be shot, the British officer replied, "Their government wouldn't look too kindly on their retreat." Conversation will be quite impersonal. Don't use a lot of emotional appeal or too much enthusiasm. Try not to talk too much and don't press for a fast agreement.

Status relationships are important. The British "Ole Boy Network" is well known. The British try to look you in both eyes, so you must stand back (6 feet). We think they're aloof and we're put down! The English shut off discussion when they look away. They think Americans are rude if we now interrupt while they're focused elsewhere.

French Culture

A handshake should be a quick single shake accompanied by slight pressure. American hand pumping is considered impolite. Address them as Monsieur, Madame, and Mademoiselle. Avoid talking politics, money, or personal matters. Be discreet. The French resent prying, personal questions.

They are proud of their cultural heritage. Prestige is revered, and one's status is important to business success. Individualism makes for compact meetings. The negotiator will be chosen based on his social class, school degrees, and even family ties. They will strive for a meeting of the minds.

Conservatism and status consciousness are seen as aloofness by many Americans upon first contact with their counterparts in France. Business is highly bureaucratic, with paperwork and procedures that must be followed. Also, the French government is often involved and has close ties with business. Decisions are highly centralized and reached after protracted discussion, so extra time must be expected. French connections, agents, or distributors are helpful.

Punctuality is expected, but decisions are made slowly. Detailed, legally binding contracts are preferred. Presentations should be subdued. The French tend toward logic and reasoning. They put forth their arguments first, before telling their final wants. The French love an exchange of ideas. It may appear as if they're debating. This often gives Americans the feeling that they take an antagonistic position, often seeming to disagree for the sake of discussion.

The French are not adverse to conflict, rather, it seems to stir their interest. And they respect those who state opposition. In contrast to the Oriental, who always avoids conflict, and the American, who can tolerate it, the French seem to "go for it."

It is difficult to impress the French, and they seem to resent someone who tries. Appealing to competition doesn't seem to work. They are relatively emotional, as compared to the German or British. However, it is sometimes difficult to tell if their emotionalism is for real or a tactic, as they love to play games.

French cuisine is world famous. Lunches and dinners last about two hours, allowing time to talk. Even with high level hosts, you may be invited to their small bistro where they dine frequently. Don't try to select wine as a gift; many Frenchmen like to choose their own. Flowers sent to their wives are preferred.

German Culture

Historically, Germans have a great fear of inflation because of memories of the runaway inflation in the early 1920s, when it cost millions of marks to mail a letter. Tales are still recalled about young men with suitcases loaded with marks on payday heading to pay bills or buy groceries.

Germans are quite formal and correct, especially with new acquaintances. In business, they often will give a firm handshake upon meeting and when leaving. German society is paternalistic.

Respect goes to those who dress the part neatly and who maintain proper decorum. First names are never used unless you are invited to do so. Always use the terms, Herr, Frau, or Fraulein with the last name. If in doubt about a woman's status, use Frau.

High value is placed on education. Those who have a degree or title use it, such as Herr Doktor Braun. At the university, he would be Herr Professor Braun. In business the "Doktor" title brings great prestige. Any comment or testimony by persons with that title carries great weight. About 80 percent of a major company's management may be college graduates, with 50 percent holding the respected doktor title.

There is a high regard for law and order. Keep to a set schedule. Punctuality is considered important. During negotiations, don't try to establish friendly relationships. The Germans are all business—straightforward, serious, and honest about doing business. But, after business is successfully conducted, they can be highly friendly and enjoyable.

Germans don't like to waste time with frivolities. Some feel German humor is hard to find. The author recollects a fine German couple who were his host at dinner. Sensitive to criticism, politics, and World War II, the wife was a former saleswoman who had lived in America. They could not understand why Americans thought The TV program "Hogan's Heros" was funny. It of course made the Germans out as "dumbkoffe." These people loved Americans, but just failed to see any humor or good in this spoof.

German managers are somewhat like their American counterparts, with a high entrepreneurial spirit as compared to other Europeans. They will be security minded and not likely to take high risks.

In negotiations, many decisions that Americans would consider routine must be approved by top management. Decisions are usually made by committees, so more time is needed to reach agreement than in the United States. So compromise is usually possible. That agreement should be well documented in detail.

Germans ask for breaks to caucus sometimes because they have to get approval. Before agreeing to it, make sure a specific time for regrouping is agreed to, for it's not always easy to break up their cloistered discussions among themselves.

Germans are technical and factual in negotiations. They usually take pride in their reputation for technical excellence, although the younger businessman is price conscious. They will not quickly approve engineering changes without thorough understanding. Lots of questions will be asked.

It is difficult to get information in Germany, as they tend to be secretive and withhold it. Because many negotiations include technical people, they may tend to be innately cautious and careful.

Negotiations are held with great attention to detail and order when conducting talks. Appointments are essential in advance. The German does not like interruptions or having to shift his plans. Avoid surprises, for they expect to be following an approved agenda and do not like to get sidetracked.

Germans have the habit of openly discussing in German their tactics, somehow forgetting that some Americans speak German. The author recalls several sessions where an American buyer would later tell exactly what the Germans would try to do. He understood German perfectly, having been raised there as a youth.

Some businesspersons, being aware of the German resentment of comparison with either the British or French, will use this tactic of competition from those countries. The German can be competitive, unlike the French.

By setting a negotiation session for a Friday afternoon, matters may be speeded up, as Germans look forward to their weekend activities. Neither do Germans take their work home, as do many Americans.

Germans pride themselves that, once they've given their word, they will live up to the agreement. A handshake binds the deal. However, written contracts should follow.

Many businessmen go home for their full meal at noon. The evening meal is simple yet wholesome, like an American luncheon—cold cuts, sandwiches, and so on. While eating, they traditionally keep the hands above the table as compared to our hands in the lap approach.

If invited to a home, candy, flowers, or wine may be presented or sent afterwards. "Thank you" notes are expected.

Italian Culture

How about those Italians? They're not just famous for disappearing from work after 2 P.M. Italians are quite flexible in compromise. Italy has been plagued by many labor strikes. But they're often quite orderly and planned.

The author once wanted to take a bus trip to Pompeii, but was told it was impossible, as there was to be a strike that Saturday. But the clerk said, "You can go on Sunday." Upon inquiring how, he was assured it would be okay. The strike would last just one day. It did. We had a great day, with our driver in high spirits after exercising his strike objections to his employer.

The author often recalls a statement by a professor at the University of Milan, saying, "Out of chaos comes great flexibility." Respect for that statement has been gained from observing that flexibility is critical. Often, a broken football play turns into a big gain. Eastern European events prove the point today. If you want change, make disruptions and cause confusion. When events are too pat, there's no reason to change.

Note the same flexibility when Italy lost its government over the Achille Lauro hijacking incident in 1985. Two weeks later, after the "crisis," the same people were back on the job, never having left. Italians have "lost" their government about 60 times during the last five years.

Italians can be gracious and friendly as a courtesy that is more than just interest in your business. You may need an Italian agent, and possibly local legal advice, for a major contract, because Italian business law is quite different than American.

Shake hands upon meeting and when leaving. Business cards are usually used. Close friends use first names and any title that applies. If any question, err on the side of granting status, such as "Dottore," which is highly flattering, assuming the host has a prestigious degree.

Don't talk business during social situations; rather, talk of family, sports, or events of interest. Don't tell jokes during negotiations or when business is being conducted. Get right to the heart of the meeting. Be well prepared to present your buying proposals, especially how it will be of benefit to them.

Employees can't be laid off in companies with 15 or fewer employees. One way around this is a company that will have many satellite small companies from which they buy. In truth, they own these "suppliers." As an example, the author visited a motor company that "buys" from about 30 small component or parts suppliers.

Each supplier has under 15 employees, exempting them from hiring or firing regulations. These small outfits each may have a piece of machinery in an "employees" garage. Parts are turned out as required and sold only to the motor company. None of this activity is part of the company's formal financial structure. Italians use imagination to get the job done.

CULTURES OF THE AMERICAS

In the Americas are the Brazilian, Canadian, and Mexican cultures.

Brazilian Culture

Brazil's use of the Portuguese language isolates them from the rest of South America. They are far removed from East-West tensions and free of American dominance. Sometimes they're sensitive to U.S. citizens calling themselves Americans. Brazilians tend to assume that they too come from the "Americas." Brazilians resent being referred to as Latin Americans by those who assume they speak Spanish. They are also sensitive to negative comments of a personal nature.

Family ties are strong, following a Catholic tradition of giving family priority over business. While they talk of a mixed racial society, Brazilians have an unspoken caste system. Cariocas are the fun-loving people in the Rio region who celebrate their famous Carnival before the Lenten season. The mighty "Engine of Brazil" is run by the industrious people of Sao Paulo, known as Paulistas. They are proud of their stylish Avenida Paulista Boulevard, not unlike New York's Fifth Avenue.

Brazilians love sports, especially volleyball and World Cup soccer. Huge soccer stadiums rock with flag-waving enthusiasts. They love to spend time on their beautiful beaches. Children play a form of soccer on the beach and everywhere in streets.

Perhaps Brazilians are more relaxed or casual than others in South America. They quickly call one another by their first name, but it's best for the foreigner to wait until it's suggested. While they're a warm and friendly people, the American "Hi" is perhaps too undignified for even this informal people.

Their last names can be confusing, as they're sometimes combinations of both mother and father's last names. So, when they show respect, they use first names and say Senhor Paulo, Evelyn Maria, and so on.

Quick to shake hands when greeting others, they use a compulsive "thumbs up" signal that is given with a flair. A sudden clockwise (from horizontal to vertical) jerk of the right hand that is given frequently in conversation. It is a signal that means, "Yes, I agree" or "I'm with you."

Crime is a problem, especially thievery. People driving cars are sometimes stopped by others and robbed in darkened alleys. Until 1985, there was no adequate federal social-welfare network, and many youths took to the streets in desperation.

The businessman is sometimes not safe unless with a group. Even then, stories are told, such as how a busload of invited foreign tourist agents on their way in from the Rio airport were stopped and robbed by people in police uniform. It is not uncommon to be accosted on the street by men dressed as women.

Business cards are a courtesy used upon first-time meetings. Business is best conducted on a personal basis. Maintaining a close friendship is more important than in America.

Brazilians do not seem to have a strict interpretation of ethical situations. Some Americans question the honesty of some employees there. One story told to the author was about a Brazilian manager who, upon being promoted out of purchasing, asked a consultant how to protect his kickback.

Many firms are government controlled. The state has a strong role that it plays in approving business ventures. The foreign businessman will need a local colleague to help him through government approvals and the bureaucracy that is inevitable when government plays a strong hand. If no English-speaking contact is available, a Portuguese interpreter will be necessary. Only well-traveled, top-level Brazilian businessmen will speak good English.

Throughout the day, businessmen have many "shots" of rich, black coffee served in demi-cups. 20 per day is not unusual. Business is conducted with more of a flair than in the United States, though at a slower pace. Don't rush or charge into presentations. It is best to wait for friendships to develop. Showmanship of a friendly type seems to please.

The strong influence of resident German managers, who are well organized and detailed, is imprinted on major operations. Brazilians expect and like to bargain. Be prepared to give and make concessions. Ask for more than you'll settle for. Even when matters are settled, you will have to push and expedite.

Time is not that important. Many Brazilians treat appointments as suggestions. One has to pin down a meeting precisely. If invited to a home, do not embarrass your host by arriving exactly on the time mentioned. Dinner is quite late and a business dinner might last 3 or 4 hours. Fashionably, arriving 15 to 30 minutes after the stated time is about right. But, for example, if attending the theatre following dinner, they might want to eat promptly. So, if you're expected on time for dinner or any other social event, they will say to arrive by "American time," meaning on time.

Noon lunches can be heavy meals. Brazilians eat many courses of different tasty barbecued meats in "churrascaria" or barbecue restaurants. It's a special favorite to provide to guests. You should take only small portions for there are many to sample. The waiters repeatedly place a long skewer on your plate while they slice off various wonderful barbecued meats.

A sentimental favorite is "feijoada," a dish of black beans and pork (originally entrails or parts of the pig's body that was fed to former slaves). This stew is a tradition that should be sampled at least once. It is tasty and nostalgic to Brazilians, just as pork and beans are to a New Englander.

Gifts are not expected, though every hostess enjoys candy or fruit. Sending flowers the next day is considered thoughtful.

Canadian Culture

Canadian culture is entwined with American because of geographical closeness and strong trading relationships. Coupled with the close contacts, the background of many Americans parallels the Canadian experiences. The same European powers played an important role in shaping the United States also.

Most Americans don't consider Canadians as foreigners. So they may believe there are no cultural differences. Americans have to be mindful that Canadians can be sensitive about French and English relationships.

"Canada" is an old Iroquois Indian name meaning "group of huts." Early French settlers moved to this area to escape the fierce Iroquois Indians to the south. Founding "New France." Canada's early settlers battled along with the British and French both vying for new territory. "New France" in the St. Lawrence valley and "New England" each encouraged settlement to maintain their claims. Though caught up in England and France's wars, since the War of 1812, the United States and Canada maintains what is regarded as the longest and friendliest open border in the world.

Following American Independence in 1776, many Americans, loyal to the Crown, moved into Canada. Some Canadians of French heritage moved into the United States. But most remained where they were, with divided loyalties.

Canada has two basic cultural heritages. About half of all Canadians are of British decent, and one-third are descendants of earlier French immigrants. French Canadians have kept their language and customs.

Strong cultural ties remain with Europe. Britons influenced Canada greatly, except in the Montreal and Quebec areas, which still speak French. Canadians here were strongly influenced by French traditions and heritage when they came into a virgin territory to colonize it for France. Other early settlers' cultures are the Scotch and Irish.

Two-thirds of Canadians live in the St. Lawrence and lower Great Lakes lowland regions. The French speaking Quebecois have in the past threatened to establish a separate nation. The Separatist movement is active and always present in Eastern Canada. Accommodations have been made to keep the country unified.

So, there are cultural differences that over the years have tended to meld into what some might call a North American culture. Some Canadians say they have picked up some of the best traits from their heritage from contacts with the British, French, and Americans. They mention leaving behind some of the negative aspects of these three societies.

Officially, Canada is bilingual: French and English. The exception is Quebec, where French is official. The religion is Christianity. The Roman Catholics are predominantly in the Quebec and Montreal area; and the Protestants, primarily Anglicans and Baptists, are located in Ottawa and the other major Canadian cities.

Use first names, but wait a bit with new acquaintances. They will invite you, too, when they detect you're being polite and friendly. Be wary of coming on as too overpowering. Canadians like a polite and perhaps slower pace getting into business details.

Canadians sometimes express a dislike at being talked down to. Americans are perceived for somewhat slight arrogance, often based on a lack of knowledge and appreciation of Canadian culture. In business, more appreciation by Americans about the importance of the strong relationship of trade with Canada might be welcome!

Government is committed to free-trade principles. The new U.S.-Canada Free Trade Agreement will gradually eliminate all restrictions between the two great trading partners. While now benefiting both nations, some Canadians express worry that being "too cozy" could result in the gradual loss of their cultural identity.

Certainly, negotiations would not be unlike in America. But, if dealing with a smaller French-speaking company, an interpreter might be necessary. And, lack of easy conversation would make for more formality. However, almost all companies have bilingual speaking employees. This shouldn't be a problem outside the French-speaking Quebec area.

Dinner is traditionally served early, between 5 and 7 P.M. Gifts are seldom expected. A polite "thank you" will suffice, the same as in the United States.

Mexican Culture

First names are not used unless there is a long, friendly relationship. "Senor," "Senora," and "Senorita" and used for "Mr.," "Mrs.," and "Miss," respectively. If there is a question of marital status, use Senorita.

Spanish influence affects cultural norms. However, unlike other Latins who say they are descendants of the Spanish, Mexicans say, "when we were conquered by the Spanish." Mexicans consider themselves as having an Aztec heritage.

Personal relations, as elsewhere, are important to business relationships. Protocol and social competence are admired. Shake hands upon meeting businessmen, but wait to see if women offer theirs. A slight bow usually suffices.

Direct contact within Mexico is preferred, and much business will be done through acquaintances, in place of official channels. Friendliness and courtesy, together with sensitivity to Mexican culture and independence, will help smooth relations.

The language spoken is Spanish and the predominant religion is Roman Catholic. Mexicans have strong feelings about their neighbors to the north, bordering on paranoia. As one explained, "When we look at a map, we always see the big United States sitting on our shoulders."

Unless there are previous contacts, there can be a suspicion about the Americans' motives. As is said, "We sleep with one eye open." Mexicans can be sensitive to comparisons and condescension. They don't like to be reminded of the U.S. border invasion by their countrymen. Proud of their independence, they sometimes complain when the word "America" is used exclusively for U.S. citizens.

Decisions are highly centralized. Managers decide without much consultation with lower levels. Prices can swing considerably. Negotiate them down!

The Mexican negotiator may be selected by his social standing and not technical talent. It may be more important that he have the proper family ties and political influence. Because of a lack of technical background, the Mexican negotiator may be thought to be lying. In truth, he may not have the answer but wants to give the impression he's knowledgeable. Mexicans appear to have macho-type traits. Yet trust and compatibility must be present, so Mexicans center on personal aspects heavily.

Deliberations are usually cautious and a margin for negotiation should be allowed. It will be expected that a better deal will be forthcoming. They may be overly dramatic, and appear emotional to the American. Mexicans see themselves as more reserved than brasher Americans. They prefer behind-the-scenes–type bargaining, and may see little value in direct negotiation exchanges.

Informational charts, samples, models, and so forth, are helpful and appreciated. Some Americans report that, after verbal arrangements were concluded, they were rescinded later. As elsewhere, there is no substitute for agreements to be in writing.

Some Americans feel that Mexicans are too relaxed in the use of time. You must allow for more time to conclude arrangements and be patient. Mexicans expect you to socialize with them before dealing. Also, business schedules should not preclude involvement with their family or friends.

Most businessmen take no siesta, but use the two-hour time for lunch and socializing. Between 2 and 5 P.M. is time for the main meal. Dinner is around 8:30, and it's not courteous to arrive early. The spouse is often invited.

In a restaurant you must ask for the check, "La cuento, por favor," or you'll not get one! If you go to the home, flowers for the hostess are always welcomed. A thank you and a phone call afterwards are standard.

Certainly, the above are sketchy ideas on complex cultural issues for the major cultures that American buyers will most likely engage. This review of specific cultures serves to point out cross-cultural frictions that Americans tend to overlook. Hopefully, the next time you deal with offshore suppliers, recalling some of these cultural issues will help you be a more professional global negotiator.

6

Complying with U.S. and International Legalities

Contract law originally was derived from English common law, and is a body of documented case precedents. Contract law is basically the same around the globe. Your contracts (purchase order) are implied (verbal) or, mostly, express (written). There must be an offer (to provide or do something) and an acceptance (signed acknowledgement to your international purchase order), plus consideration (normally the payment).

The purchase order becomes a binding contract upon acceptance or upon shipment of the goods. However, when a supplier sends in terms of sale, he or she in affect issues a counteroffer. The seller claims the buyer accepts the offer.

A strange happening takes place daily. Throughout the United States, thousands of purchase orders (POs) are prepared with carefully time-developed terms and conditions (T&Cs) of purchase. Methodically, supplying companies acknowledge these customer orders on *their* forms with conditions of sale.

If legal opinions were sought and then enforced, business would indeed grind to a halt. So what do we do? We go on mailing our POs, ignoring the supplier's terms, as the supplier does. Should a major difficulty arise, each party falls back on its terms and somehow reaches a settlement. Without the buyer's T&Cs, it would be difficult to build a logical negotiating argument, much less a legal case.

Satisfaction of the contract comes from performance. Nonperformance includes defective goods, rejection, and possibly damages. A party not complying with the contract commits a breach of contract.

Other key elements of every contract are:

- Manifestation of intent—both parties must agree to perform in some way.
- Reality of intent (issues of mistakes or, for example, use of duress when making contract).

87

- Capacity to act is required. Does the other party have the authority to commit his company?
- Legality of purpose—the contract is free of crimes or violation of licensing statutes.
- Compliance with statute of frauds.

If available, get your counsel to review areas where you need advice. Lawyers are most useful when protecting the company and buyer from unforeseen legal complications.

There are four degrees of competition in global economic systems. They are:

1. Perfect competition (many suppliers available);
2. Effective competition (several suppliers);
3. Imperfect competition—Oligopoly; and
4. Monopoly (sole source available, or only one close enough to supply).

Advocates of "free trade" prefer the first competition. There are few (if any) monopolist companies in the United States. U.S. laws forbid monopolies, but these laws may not apply when you deal offshore. Other countries with a different business policy have government-created or sanctioned monopolies.

Actions that restrict trade are potential hazards when dealing with foreign companies that are not covered by U.S. trade laws. Oligopoly, or "competition among the few," is sometimes met. Here, a few suppliers retaliate against competitors to hold price levels. A price increase is quickly followed by all.

INTERNATIONAL SELLER AND BUYER'S OBLIGATIONS

The seller incurs basic obligations in accepting an international purchase order. Unless otherwise agreed, the seller must:

- Supply the goods specified in the contract, and provide evidence of conformity as required by the contract.
- Bear all costs of checking quality, weight, quantity, packaging, and other expenses to assure that the goods are delivered at the right time.
- Give the buyer reasonable notice about arrival of the goods and when he or she can take possession.
- Assume risk and expense up to the point of change of ownership. This includes getting all documentation in the country of origin for shipment through intermediate countries, as required for import.
    The buyer assumes the following obligations and must:
- Take delivery of merchandise as soon as it is placed at his or her disposal.

- Bear all charges and risks from the time they are at his or her disposal or set aside as provided.
- Pay any customs duties and taxes levied (unless the contract makes this the seller's responsibility).
- Pay any extra costs (warehouse storage, etc.) should he or she fail to provide instructions in time to allow prompt shipment handling.
- Pay for all costs and charges incurred in securing documents, such as certificates of origin, export licenses, and consular fees (unless contract makes these the seller's responsibility).

Buyer's Authority

The buyer's job has a legal accountability derived from the law of agency. Your company's charter of incorporation transfers sole fiduciary responsibility to purchasing to commit for payment to suppliers. You must object to others committing your company to a purchase. If others do it routinely, suppliers are legally justified to take orders from them.

Agency law expects the agent (buyer) to follow instructions required by the principal. An agent gets the right to act for his or her principal through authority granted to him or her by the principal. Such authority can be actual or implied.

Loyalty is a necessity, as failure of the agent is cause to bring harm to the principal. The agent should have no personal interest in a contract negotiated for the principal. Buyers should not personally gain from, nor act for the other contracting party. The agent must not misuse confidential information about the principal.

Buyers are often warned to observe their authority limits to sign purchase orders. Internationally, it should be required that the party signing for the offshore supplier be a company officer, with authority to contract for his or her company. Many foreigners don't have such authority. In certain European countries, letters are signed by two people, showing a shared authority. This practice has also been followed by some South American companies.

The buyer often sees himself as a "shock trooper" on the line, holding prices steady and keeping increases reasonable or rolling them back. Supply and demand still affects prices under free trade, and this action often takes place at the buyer's desk. Legal issues arise from many commercial situations. Buyers should concern themselves with basic legalities.

UNIFORM COMMERCIAL CODE (UCC)

The federal government has authority to regulate business activity, as stated in Article 1, Section 8 of the U.S. Constitution. Congress is empowered "to regulate Commerce with foreign nations, among several States, and the Indian Tribes."

Within the United States, the buyer has the Uniform Commercial Code (UCC) as the legal standard. It is considered the most important regulation for U.S. commerce. The UCC is a set of commercial laws that prescribes legal guidelines and limits for business transactions. It consists of ten articles covering Terms of Purchase, Letters of Credit, Warehouse Receipts, Warranties, and so on. It is a living document that adapts as it is interpreted by the courts.

Under the UCC, title to goods and merchandise passes without the need for a document. In this respect, it is like buying groceries. The code trys to systematize procedures and simplify confusing, complex, and often contradictory rules derived from common law and statues from various states. Remember, though, the UCC is mainly of help in domestic transactions, unless agreed to by the foreign seller.

When a buyer buys from a foreign company through an independent U.S. based organization, the purchase is automatically under U.S. laws. Using a foreign buying office to place an order, however, raises a legal issue. Normally, in that case, the host country's laws take precedent. That is unless you get the supplier's acceptance of U.S. jurisdiction. Insert a clause to that effect. Note that even if a U.S. court decision is in your favor, unless the supplier has assets in the United States, the buyer may not get restitution.

Legalities of international buying are similar to those found in domestic buying. However, the scope of law expands to other areas, such as customs regulations, duties, import licenses, and so on.

IMPORT CUSTOMS LAWS AND REGULATIONS

Tariffs began with passage of the U.S. Tariff Act of 1789 by the first Congress to protect America's growing industry. All merchandise brought into the United States is subject to the U.S. Tariff Act of 1930, unless specially exempted by law.

Sometimes, other U.S. government agencies' regulations may apply to imports, such as the Occupation Safety Hazards Administration (OSHA), the Environmental Protection Agency (EPA), and the Federal Drug Administration (food and drug purchases). Also, the Department of Agriculture, Department of Commerce, State Department, and Internal Revenue Service all may provide the rules. However, their interests are enforced by the U.S. Customs Service.

U.S. Customs regulations are too detailed to list, with more than 180 miscellaneous tariff and trade bills approved. The American government has listed many foreign trade barriers that it will try to end. They are the subject of international trade negotiations. Regardless of the law covering disputes between foreign nationals, when importing into the United States, a buyer and his or her company are bound by all applicable U.S. laws and customs regulations on such imports.

Import and Export Licenses

A license or permit is needed to import alcoholic beverages, certain drugs, firearms, petroleum, plants, and vegetables. Watches and movements are licensed under the direction of the Department of Interior and Commerce. The Department of Agriculture licenses dairy products, such as butter and cheese.

While most industrial imports are unencumbered, different government regulations have to be met, but not all items require a formal license.

• The Toxic Substance Control Act of 1977 requires that hazardous substances be supervised by the Office of Hazardous Materials Transportation, Department of Transportation.
• Radioactive materials and reactors are controlled by the Nuclear Regulatory Commission.
• Radiation producing products, such as TV receivers, microwave ovens, x-ray machines, and laser products are covered by the Radiation Control for Health and Safety Act of 1968. To import these items, you must file Food and Drug entry notice Form FD 701. If radio frequencies are a factor, form FCC 740 is required.
• Narcotics and drug control are under the Department of Justice.
• Consumer products meet the Consumer Product Safety Act and also the Flammable Fabrics Act.
• Household appliances come under the Energy Policy and Conservation Act.

Arms and implements of war are licensed by the Treasury's Bureau of Alcohol, Tobacco and Firearms. Import Arms Licenses are sometimes required by Foreign Assets Control Regulations. For example, if buying goods from Cambodia, Cuba, Laos, Libya, Nicaragua, North Korea, Rhodesia, South Africa (Krugerrands and jewelry), and Vietnam. An import cannot be made from these countries until it is approved. If any question, specific inquiry is suggested. Write to: Office of Foreign Assets Control, Department of the Treasury, Washington, D.C. 20220.

A "validated export license" is needed if the buyer is sending out something that is listed as requiring a license to export. For example, say a buyer wanted to send the foreign manufacturer a duplicate electronic test stand. This would allow purchases to be tested at the supplier's plant.

The electronic testing equipment falls under the license class. Other items would be computer systems, numerically controlled machine tools, electronic instrumentation, telecommunications equipment, semiconductors, and so on.

Apply to the U.S. Department of Commerce by filling out their Form ITA-628. Most licenses are received within 15 to 30 days of request. A Destination Control Statement and the Import (or Export) Control Number shown on the license is placed on the bills of lading, invoices, and Export Declaration Form. The exporter records all items shipped on the back of the license, and returns it to the Department of Commerce.

Shipments cannot be diverted elsewhere or be in contradiction of U.S. law. Failure to use a license when required incurs fines of up to $10,000 and possibly up to five years imprisonment.

ANTITRUST LAWS AND TRADE ACTS

The antitrust laws consist of the Sherman Act, the Clayton Act, and the Federal Trade Commission Acts. Of these, the buyer needs to be wary of the Clayton Act and Robinson-Patman Act, which concern pricing and are seen as "restraint of trade" statutes.

Section 2 of The Clayton Act forbids price discrimination between different buyers where such actions serve "substantially to lessen competition or tend to create a monopoly in any line of commerce." It also forbids reciprocity-type arrangements, where the buyer, to get what he wants, must buy something unwanted.

The famous amendment known as the Robinson-Patman Act replaced and expanded the above Section 2 in 1936. It prohibits a buyer from knowingly inducing and buying at discriminatory lower prices than others pay. This act is designed to assure a seller's equality of treatment to all buyers. It also prohibits discounts, rebates, or allowances of commodities of like grade and quality that cause price discrimination.

Sellers can give lower prices that otherwise could be discriminatory if they have evidence that lower competitive prices exist. Domestically, buyers violate Robinson-Patman should they induce the seller to lower his price by giving false competitive price information. The buyer should never lie by saying, "I can buy that for $10 (or whatever) from your competitor." A good tactic is to say, "My target price is $10." Does any buyer know when his price is the lowest?

Reciprocal deals, such as, "If you buy my wine, I'll buy your flour," were at one time common in the United States. The practice became distasteful to buyers pushed to buy based on sales. It was replace by "Trade Relations." Domestic sales and buying arrangements cannot be legally tied together under U.S. law.

The Trade Act of 1982 allows U.S. companies to enter countertrade arrangements with offshore suppliers. Antitrust laws don't apply abroad. It is a common, acceptable type of international business arrangement. Such buying and selling are necessary to match foreign competition globally.

Some lawyers believe that the only risk would be harming a domestic competitor. A legal problem might result if a U.S. buyer trys to fulfill the terms of a countertrade arrangement by pressuring local suppliers to buy certain items. The buyer should avoid saying, "I won't buy from you unless you buy this so that we can compete abroad." This could generate antitrust actions. This is a specialized legal area, and specific counsel is needed on a case-by-case basis.

The United States uses varies tactics to stem the tide of imports. The Carter

Administration applied restrictions on shoes, color TV sets, and a "trigger price" mechanism for policing foreign steel sold below cost. There is, however, a political fear of imposing higher tariffs.

The Buy America Act of 1933 was passed to provide preference to U.S. suppliers when the federal government buys. Weakened by the Trade Agreement Act of 1979 and the Defense Acquisition Circular No. 76-25 in 1980, the Buy America Act can still apply where national security is at stake. For government procurement and purchasing by government contractors, it places significant restrictions on buying other than U.S.-produced items.

Many states have enacted legislation for some type of American preference policy. However, Buy America is not a factor in most commercial buying decisions.

UNITED NATIONS CONVENTION

"If it doesn't work, we'll sue 'em!" is sometimes the U.S. buyer's trained reaction. But internationally, that is not easy. Global buying was to have come under the "United Nations Convention on Contracts for the International Sale of Goods." Known simply as the 1980 Convention (CISG), it contains 101 articles, covering formation of contracts, as well as the rights, debts, and remedies.

About 60 nations have ratified CISG. Congressional concern over adoption of this little known code, coupled with lack of understanding by business lawyers delayed U.S. application of this universal "legal" business colde until 1988. It makes it easier for the seller to enforce verbal agreements or phone conversations.

If your contract is with a seller whose country also has approved, the new terms apply unless you specifically state *CISG does not apply*. Until the impact becomes clearer, buyers might better exclude them and call for the UCC.

GENERAL AGREEMENT ON TARIFFS AND TRADE (GATT)

International trade is conducted through bilateral and multilateral trade agreements, as well as under the General Agreement on Tariffs and Trade. "GATT" was created in 1948, when more than 60 governments signed the charter in Geneva, Switzerland. By 1986 membership had expanded to 92 nations.

During the depression in the 1930s, the Smoot Hawley Act put restrictions on exchange rates, and so on. Other nations responded with their own barriers to trade. The result was a stifling of world trade. Following World War II, the United States strongly advocated "Free Trade" to resurrect the devastated world's economies. A means to cut excessive tariffs was needed.

Most Favored Nation (MFN) policy calls for nondiscrimination in trade, extending to all nations the same customs and tariff treatment given to the "most favored nation." Since 1923, goods from countries dominated by communism, or denied MFN status, are excluded by U.S. law from this treatment.

When buying from a country with MFN status, a favorably low duty, usually about 4 percent, is levied. MFN tilts buying decisions away from nations without that status. Indicative of the importance of MFN status was its granting to Hungary and the resulting current growth in trade. Hungarian imports to America jumped 56 percent in 1989, and joint ventures have quadrupled.

MFN status changes with the times. Congress is debating taking MFN away from China, unless they change their human rights position. Now the USSR hopes to be granted MFN status.

GATT provides for periodic negotiations to reduce tariffs, settle disputes, and discuss ways to promote free trade. The agreement covers only the trading of goods. Negotiations are underway to expand GATT to cover services, but is difficult to negotiate. Through seven "rounds" of tariff reduction meetings, world leaders have met to resolve differences. Progress has been made in reducing U.S. industrial tariffs from 28 percent in 1960 to about a 4 percent average today.

The latest GATT negotiation, termed the Uruguay Round, appears headed for temporary defeat. The EEC refuses to drop farmer's export subsidies that the United States has tried to cut. Government subsidies can take the form of duty rebates, lower sales taxes, income tax concessions, transportation taxes, cash rebates, and lower interest rates on loans. Hopefully, a spate of retaliatory tariffs will be avoided.

"Antidumping" and "countervailing duties" are the internationally approved way under GATT to prevent unfairly priced products being sold at excessively low prices. Higher tariffs and surcharge taxes are permissible when there is a balance-of-payments problem.

Title VII of the Tariff Act of 1930, as amended by the Trade Act of 1974, provides for added duties when foreign goods are dumped in the U.S. market. Selling products at prices much lower abroad than at home is termed dumping.

Antidumping Duties

An antidumping duty may be assessed for imports sold to American buyers at prices less than their fair market value. As an example, a duty fine as high as 213 percent was put on imported bearings. Nine foreign bearing makers were selling at about one-third the price in their home countries. The offenders simply reduced their shipments from their home plants.

Shipments from Sweden dropped almost 20 percent in 1989, while shipments were increased as high as 543 percent from Austria, Spain, and Argentina.[1] Then, bearing shipments increased from plants in Spain, Poland, Mexico, Turkey, South Korea, and Hong Kong that don't make any bearings.

---

[1] 1990. Cat and mouse game. Forbes. May 28. p. 48.

The U.S. Department of Commerce (DOC) rules on dumping, making the price ruling based upon complaints presented. It is difficult to get the DOC to make a dumping ruling. To improve the chances for success of a filed complaint, critics want this authority transferred to the U.S. Trade representative.

Action against dumping is controversial, as seen by the recent try to impose a 35 percent penalty on Canadian housing shakes. A problem of using duties to protect American industry is that there is always a trade-off penalty paid by the American consumer.

A tariff was imposed that would have eliminated $350 million of Canadian lumber exports to the United States. Four thousand Canadian jobs would have been cut. While highly unpopular in Canada, it was considered by Americans as an acceptable way to react to severe hardship suffered by American labor. This action generated Canadian debate on punitive counter measures.

The final solution to the conflict was a 15 percent surtax that was imposed on Canadian lumber dealers by the Canadian government to prevent higher proposed U.S. tariffs. Though praised as a compromise, this action meant a 15 percent increase in cost to U.S. consumers.

Countervailing Duties

Foreign companies, as well as American, are often given government incentives and subsidies to export. Procedure calls for an investigation. The U.S. Trade Representative has a staff of 130 people who take up cases involving U.S. companies claiming they can't get into a foreign market.

Countervailing duties may be levied against any foreign government that permits or causes an unfair trade advantage within the United States. Many governments have been accused of violating U.S. trade laws by subsidizing their industries to gain an unfair advantage. For example, say the Greek government gives a 2-percent rebate to encourage export of a certain product. Spain does not. If Spain or the U.S. company complains, U.S. Customs might add a 2-percent countervailing duty to buys from Greece, to level the market.

A well-known complaint is the U.S. charge that government subsidies granted European farmers prevent U.S. agriculture produce sales. Many European companies are government-owned, so some people believe that the U.S. government should become a participant in their problems.

The Trade Act of 1974 also gave the President trade-easing authority. Provisions were made for economic help if American workers were hurt by imports. Two sections of this act are of interest:

Section 201 provides relief from injury caused, or threatened, by unfairly-priced imports. To date, only 12 of 60 cases have resulted in successful relief.[2]

---

[2] 1987. Trade. Congressional Research Service Review. February. p. 10.

Section 301, applied in 1985, empowers the President to "take all appropriate and feasible action...to enforce the rights of the United States under any trade agreement...to counter any foreign trade practice that is unjustifiable, unreasonable, or discriminatory and burdens or restricts U.S. commerce."

GLOBAL TRADE BARRIERS

Trade barrier issues are emotional subjects that have legal implications now, as many jobs are at stake. They include:

- Closed countries;
- Cartels and boycotts;
- Unfair pricing and protectionism;
- Counterfeiting and piracy of property; and
- Value added taxes.

Should these concern the offshore buyer? Yes, since surveys show that at least 11 percent of them have had a recent bad experience with counterfeiters.[3] Inferior products such as fasteners were made of boron, rather than carbon steel. Marked SAE Grade 8, these fasteners could become a hazard in high temperature applications.

Closed Countries

Closed countries shut off their import trade, and are a serious impediment to trade. Certain foreign governments play the protectionist game when they opt to selectively close their borders. Among those countries currently doing this, are Indonesia, Malaysia, Taiwan, Argentina, China, Brazil, Mexico, and Spain. This situation is constantly changing.

Some newer industrialized nations ban foreign firms from making investments or gaining control of native companies. India's market is partially closed. It's estimated that almost half of all trade is restricted in some way. As an example, a buyer can't import a product into Brazil if an equal is already made in-country. Yet this same government offers a variety of incentives to manufacture and export.

Most governments, including the United States, try to use their position to provide favorable conditions to win jobs and profits with exports. One way of gaining access to closed markets is to build a factory within that country. However, fortunately, most countries do not shut the door, even though they try to reduce imports.

---

[3] 1987. Counterfeiting remains tough nut... *Purchasing*. February 26. P. 20.

A cartel exists when companies that produce the same or similar products plan together to control their market pricing. A cartel will often agree to maintain or increase production, set prices, or decide the market share each participant will enjoy. By U.S. law, such action is illegal!

The Organization of Petroleum Exporting Countries, known as OPEC, is perhaps the most famous cartel. For several years it was successful in controlling the price of petroleum. The collapse of OPEC helped keep inflation down in the late 1980s. In the 1990s this cartel is beginning to regain power, and prices again have moved sharply higher. The Iraqi invasion of Kuwait and forced removal has introduced grave uncertainty as to the control of future pricing.

A boycott is the refusal to use, buy, or deal with others as a protest or means of coercion. Mainland China boycotts Taiwan, and India boycotts South Africa. The United States boycotts North Vietnam, Cuba, and now Iran. Boycotts are often punished by punitive taxes, if income is "boycott-tainted." Boycotts, while uncommon, are a rare problem for the buyer. For example, there have been Arab unsanctioned attempts to get U.S. buyers to boycott Israel's products. Some call for a boycott of South African goods. A buyer must not make any agreement involving a boycott, but must report such attempts to the government. Run to an attorney if faced with this issue.

Unfair Pricing and Protectionism

Organized labor is a major force trying to protect its jobs. Charges have been made of unfair trade practices in the shoe and textile industries, copper fabricators and miners, and others.

The Japanese are the target of U.S. anti-protectionist pressure. They have been known to use industry standards, regulations, commercial customs, product inspections, and so forth, to prevent imports. It's culturally difficult for them to accept foreign goods. There is pressure in Congress to block Japanese products in retaliation for our inability to break into some Japanese markets.

It's not solely the Japanese whose business practices raise legal issues. When companies can't resolve their complaints about unfair pricing, they have some relief under various trade acts.

Counterfeiting and Piracy of Property

Agreements that protect ownership are the Paris Convention for Patents, the Universal Copyright Convention, the Berne Convention for Copyrights, and the Madrid Agreement on Trademarks. Primary patent and copyright protection is under the World Intellectual Property Organization.

Gray market goods are authentic items brought into the country by unauthorized or unlicensed distributors. Customs doesn't appear attentive about the gray market. A problem with such gray market goods now is in electronics.

New technological developments speed around the world in months. Today, a company brings out a new product and it is copied in a matter of a few months or even weeks. Back a few years, a company had up to three years during which it could recover much of its research and development costs. Piracy of design speed today is discouraging some large research and development efforts.

Conservative estimates are that up to $25 billion of domestic trade is lost to illegitimate, counterfeit items sold in the United States annually.[4] The worst offenders have been Taiwan and South Korea. They've agreed to stop.

The United States won a victory in July 1986 in the settlement of the Section 301 case on protection from property theft against South Korea. Students in South Korea used textbooks illegally copied for about one-third the U.S. price. By stealing the designs or products, the R&D cost is cut, distorting true costs to bring a product to market.

It isn't enough to prove the pirating of patents. For example, Corning Glass Works proved use of its fiber optic products made by Japanese companies. The ITC ruled that Corning's patents were violated, but the law required proof of damage. The court ruled that Corning didn't prove damages.

An anti-counterfeiting code has been in existence to be reviewed by GATT since 1970. Some headway is being made, but getting a consensus remains difficult. The Gatt Round in Uruguay in 1986 took up the issue, but it is still under discussion in 1991.

The computer microchip industry claims that Japan and Taiwan not only dump their products, but also stole their copyrights and trademarks. Proposed 100-percent duties were proposed solely for products made by those companies who broke a trade agreement. Protection is needed for pharmaceutical and chemical products as well as computer software. The ITC decides proprietary rights and whether copyrights are violated. They decide injury to a U.S. company from foreign unfair trade practices. They do not determine *if* it occurs.

If the United States begins to make headway in solving some of these proprietary legal issues, it will help answer those who believe the rest of the world denies free trade. Moderates fear trade reprisals would undermine the world economy.

How can designs be protected if the American company is owned by foreign interests? Certain foreign governments feel that their citizens have a right to use whatever information is available. They go out of their way to protect that right.

Brazil's Congress passed the 1984 Informatica law. When in joint ventures with foreign firms, the Brazilians must own 70 percent of the stock and have "technological control" and "decision control." The means of enforcement are tax incentives and licensing of imports of foreign goods. The United States has threatened to retaliate with import restrictions if this continues. In India, a pharmaceutical company can't sell its own product, with the right given to a local pirate. The United

---

[4]Finn, Edwin A. Jr. 1986. That's the $60 billion question. *Forbes.* November 17. p. 40.

States is beginning to put pressure on those governments, finally backed by Japan and West Germany.

Appeals in U.S. patent-infringement suits go to the Court of Appeals for the Federal Circuit (CAFC). Of course, foreign companies have no monopoly on such disputes. Recent use of Polaroid's film by Kodak is an example. In 1990, the courts ruled that Kodak had to pay damages.

Value Added Taxes

Governments use taxes in various ways. Certainly as a way to raise money, they often influence trade by enhancing or discouraging it. Taxes are another tactic used for protectionism. Some 50 countries have a Value Added Tax (VAT). This VAT is widely used in Europe.

The United States has long complained about these discriminatory-type taxes. For example, the VAT is not imposed on goods that Europe ships into the United States, while American goods are subject to it when going into Europe. Thus, this tax discourages American exports.

Canada has a new business-transfer tax that is similar to a VAT, though it shouldn't affect their cost of products. The Goods and Services Tax (GST) is 7 percent of value that was imposed in 1991 to replace an older tax on manufactured goods.

The GST differs from a retail sales tax in that the tax is paid as value is added. For example an aluminum sheet is sold for $10 to a stamping plant that pays 70 cents of taxes at that time. The stamping plant sells to a fabricator and collects a 7-percent tax of $3.50. When the stamping company pays its tax, it gets to deduct the tax of 70 cents it has already paid to the aluminum mill. Each firm in turn does the same accounting until the consumer pays his 7 percent on the retail price. The Canadian government claims that consumers will pay no more, though the government collects its taxes faster. The level of taxation is of major importance in the business environment.

FOREIGN CORRUPT PRACTICES ACT

You can't move your shipment from a port. It seems that a gift might ease its release. When does a gift become a bribe? Is it any different if it's in an Italian or a Korean port?

"What will I do if he asks me for a bribe?" Examples have been told of Americans, upon completing a deal, being told what gift would be proper to celebrate the occasion. Bribery is not a crime in many developing countries. In fact it's often part of their heritage and isn't known as a bribe.

Most of the above are legal issues only for Americans because of a law called the 1977 Foreign Corrupt Practices Act. This act prevents U.S. businessmen from participating in the bribery of foreign government officials. It's a crime for American businessmen to pay for favors from foreign government officials or businessmen. An example of a potential buying problem is if a foreign official offers to arrange for purchases through his connections. Your challenge is to discern whether you are running into unnecessary government bureaucracy or whether their law mandates the administrative delay.

The law came upon the heels of Watergate. Large sums of money were paid to other nation's political parties and military officers that may have given approval for certain equipment purchases. About 400 corporations, including 117 of the top 500, were found to have paid out hundreds of millions of dollars for these nefarious services. The Security and Exchange Commission described this as a national crisis. Money was used to influence foreigners who had discretionary authority to assist the company to get or maintain business.

Trade arrangements often involve foreign government officials who must approve the deal, and will participate in and shape it. Dealing with governments has greater consequences than simpler negotiations with individual companies.

If a buyer has a shipment held in bureaucratic entangle, make sure that any service given is legitimate and not part of official duties. This is a sensitive area because people-to-people contacts are there, providing the potential for illegal payments.

This law doesn't prohibit a legitimate payment to clear a problem. In 1988 the Senate relaxed on this issue, stating that American businesspersons could pay, "if payments were legal in a foreign country if they were made to expedite routing government action." Corporations face fines up to $1 million and individuals $10,000 for violation of this law. Moreover, the employer cannot indemnify the individual. There is also a maximum jail term of five years. Because of this law, Americans while doing business abroad can break the U.S. law.

A buyer does not have to be a lawyer or legal expert to buy successfully offshore, but does need to know basic legal issues to avoid potential danger. Volumes could be written on legalities. However, the preceding review has covered most issues that buyers face when buying globally.

7

Constructing the International Purchase Order

The primary purpose of a purchase order is to get needed materials, supplies, and services. When making an offshore purchase, problems are minimal if buyers plan and draft a well-documented purchase order. The buyer has to think defensively when preparing his or her agreement and try to look forward to possible events that could go wrong. This is difficult to do, when everyone is enthusiastic to try the new offshore supplier.

Legal clauses usually state "Purchaser." Throughout this book, the author uses the word buyer for continuity. Either word is meant to include the company, importer, buyer, and so forth. Another legal word issue is contracts versus purchase orders. Contracts are usually more complex and detailed than purchase orders. Purchase orders are used to represent the contract instrument used in offshore buying.

DOCUMENTATION REQUIRED IN INTERNATIONAL TRADE

The primary documents required in international trade and those who will make use of them are shown in Figure 7-1. Most documents are obtained by the seller, but errors and delays are at your expense. The buyer must know what is needed and ask for some of them in the purchase order.

The Shipper's Export Declaration is commonly called the "Export Dec." It provides the local government with export statistical information, including the quantity, weight, value, identity of goods, exporter, consignee, manner of transport, port of export and carrier, port of unloading, and final destination.

The Import Declaration document is one of the copies of the Customs Entry form. It contains about the same information as the Shippers Declaration and must

PRIMARY DOCUMENTS REQUIRED IN INTERNATIONAL TRADE						
PRODUCT DESCRIPTION AND IDENTIFICATION ON ALL DOCUMENTS				USED BY: ✔ = YES		
DOCUMENT	PURPOSE	EXPORTER'S GOVERNMENT	EXPORTER	IMPORTER'S GOVERNMENT	IMPORTER	COMMON CARRIER
BILL OF LADING	RECEIPT FOR SHIPMENT BY SPECIFIED DATE, LINE OR SHIP		✔	✔	✔	✔
INSURANCE POLICY OR CERTIFICATE	COVER RISKS OF DAMAGE OR LOSS		✔		✔	✔
COMMERCIAL INVOICE	QUANTITY, PRICE, CURRENCY, PAYMENT DUE, CREDIT TERMS	✔	✔	TO DETERMINE APPLICABLE DUTY	✔	
SHIPPER'S EXPORT DECLARATION	SOURCE OF EXPORT STATISTICS IDENTITY OF EXPORTER, IMPORTER DESTINATION PORT, METHOD OF SHIPMENT, WEIGHT AND CLASSIFICATION	✔	✔			✔
EXPORT LICENSE	PERMISSION TO EXPORT	✔	✔			✔
IMPORT ENTRY	SOURCE OF IMPORT STATISTICS SAME AS SHIPPER'S DATA, BUT ADDS LOADING PORT AND COUNTRY OF ORIGIN			IMPORT STATISTICS	✔	
CERTIFICATES OF WEIGHT, CONDITION, MANUFACTURE, ETC.	PROOF PRODUCT MEETS SPECIFIED CHARACTERISTICS		✔	IF AFFECTS HEALTH OR SANITARY LAW	✔	
CERTIFICATE OF ORIGIN (FORM A)	ALLOWS IMPORT CONTROL, AND DETERMINES PROPER DUTY		✔	DETERMINE DUTY RATE & IMPORT CONTROL	✔	

POOLER & ASSOCIATES

ATS 9101108-2.0

FIGURE 7-1.   Primary documents required in international trade.

identify both port of loading and country of origin. It is used by the importing government for statistical import purposes.

Handshakes may still work for domestic purchases, but for international buys it is absolutely necessary to use written agreements and to back them up with proper written documentation. For major equipment buys, a formal legal document may be best. However, when buying production or maintenance-type items the buyer needs to control the paperflow. Use a purchase order, and spell out anything that is important.

An *implied* Contract doesn't have all terms reduced to writing nor discussed, yet the supplier knows what is wanted. Because of time taken to complete offshore buys, buyers may use a letter of intent. The letter of intent gets the seller to arrange early parts buys and plan his production schedule. It is binding and obligates the buyer to complete a purchase if it causes the seller to start action.

Buyers frequently ask, "What can I include in an international purchase order?" The reply is, "Put in anything you want." An international purchase order has many more details than does a domestic order. Sometimes it is five to ten times more lengthy.

A clear understanding of contract terms is vital in international buying. Written terms you choose don't have to mimic long-winded legalese or jargon. Spell specifics out in terms that are understandable to you and the supplier. Suppliers must know exactly what you expect of them. Working at distances of thousands of miles, there isn't always time for quick fixes that can temporarily ease problems on domestic buys.

WHAT THE IMPORTER/BUYER SHOULD SPECIFY

Because of language and business custom difference, give special attention to paperwork accuracy adapted to international buying. Spell out in separate provisions any transportation, insurance, marking, or packaging requirements. While not intended as 100-percent complete, here is a typical buyer's offshore checklist that might help:

1. Exact quantity.
2. Unit of purchase. (U.S. ton is 2,000 lbs or "short ton" versus the British 2,240 lbs "long ton." Buy in metric! The metric ton of 2,204.6 lbs, used for cargo freight, is normally figured at 40 cubic feet.)
3. Quality requirements must include an accurate and complete technical description.
4. Price, identified by currency (U.S. $ or yen, for example).
5. Invoice address: name and address.
6. Ship to information: name and address.
7. Type of packing and container.
8. INCOTERMS, or method of shipment and time required.
9. Method of payment (open credit, letter of credit, etc.).
10. Insurance details—extent of coverage and whether paid by buyer or seller.
11. Letter of credit cleared through your issuing bank.
12. Import license needed?
13. List of seller-executed documents required, such as:
    a. Packing list;
    b. Commercial invoice;
    c. Airway bill or bill of lading;
    d. Certificate of origin;
    e. Insurance certificate;
    f. Certificate of survey (manufacture, inspection, etc.);
    g. Other special documents required by FDA, FTC, Department of Fishery and Wildlife, and so on; and
    h. Special instructions.

KEY CLAUSES FOR OFFSHORE PURCHASES

A major cause of offshore sourcing difficulties comes mainly from improperly documented buying agreements. Consider the following instruction clauses for your purchase order in light of all provisions that appear in fine print on your company purchase order form.

#1. U.S. Court Jurisdiction Clause

No body of international law has been approved by all nations. However, by getting the seller to agree to U.S. legal norms, the buyer is in a stronger legal position. Write in the agreement to the effect:

> "This Purchase Order shall follow the body of law applicable to international contracts, including INCOTERMS. It is interpreted, governed, and enforced by the Laws of the State of (your State), the U.S. courts, and the Uniform Commercial Code and all laws applicable."

#2. Seller's Authority To Contract Clause

Some foreign salespeople haven't got authority to bind their employer. Avoid this problem by stating:

> "Seller represents and guarantees that this contract is signed by an officer of the company who has authority to commit the supplying company to performance of this contract."

#3. Entire Agreement Clause

This clause prevents a seller from later defending his mistake by saying to the effect, "Your letter or quality people told me to do it differently." The purpose is to strengthen written agreements.

> "This agreement shall solely control the term of Purchase and Sale of the products/services hereunder. Any contrary, different, or added terms in any purchase order, contract, sales acknowledgement, or other documentation of either party shall have no effect and this agreement shall override any such documentation. This agreement may not be changed or modified except by written notice signed by both parties."

When a seller makes a warranty orally and the confirming agreement between buyer and seller does not include this warranty, a problem may arise about whether the express warranty became part of the contract. Under the UCC, as part of the Law of Sales, the parole evidence rule states, "Oral or extrinsic evidence is not admissible to add to, alter, or vary the terms of a written contract."

#4. Assignment Agreement

You may want to prohibit assignment of the agreement or subcontracting to another party without your approval. To assure you know who is doing your work, use the clause:

> "This agreement may not be assigned to any other party, nor any interest transferred without the written consent of the other party. Furnishing of any products (other than

component and replacement parts) shall not be subcontracted by seller without the prior written consent of Purchaser."

#5. Quality and Reliability

In addition to description, specs, and sample of the item, reliability is of interest to you. State wording like this:

"Seller shall use effective quality and reliability control techniques in monitoring their processes and products. Seller shall provide and maintain a quality control system that will, as a minimum:
- List all critical and major characteristics.
- Specify details for quality audits, including characteristics to be inspected. Follow with agreed representative sample of all lots and frequency of inspection.
- Tender only supplies that have been inspected in accord with the quality control system and found to conform with the requirements of this agreement.
- Provide for qualification of new and revised products, and re-qualification in case of major product deficiencies.
- Provide for disposition of rejected samples.

"Surveillance may be by appointed representatives of Purchaser at Seller's plant. Buyer may choose to inspect products by Purchaser or its representative at any reasonable time during business hours. (Each company will specify details consistent with their purchases here.) Purchaser has the right either to reject or to require correction of nonconforming products. The purchaser shall accept or reject products as promptly as practical after delivery.
"Seller's compliance with this paragraph shall in no way relieve it of its responsibility and obligations otherwise assumed under the terms and conditions of this agreement."

Among items you may choose to check for quality are the processes being used, the techniques and controls employed, the finished product, plus other areas pertinent to the product, including test methods and test data that support the ratings.

You should clarify any allowances for deviations or substitutions. Any penalties for failure to meet quality standards should be specified.

#6. Payment Terms Clause

"Payment terms shall be Net 30 (or as negotiated), per the Letter of Credit (draft, or whatever) covering this purchase. Payment shall be in U.S. dollar funds (or whatever foreign currency). Documents to accompany shipment include items as spelled out herein below, or in the Letter of Credit."

#7 Price Adjustment Clause

All prices should be firm. However, you may have to call for a periodic review of prices on long-term contracts. If a blanket order price is subject to change, fix a ceiling to the amount of escalation by using the following pricing adjustment clause stating to the effect:

"Purchaser has the right to approve all price increases in advance. Any price increase is limited to:
- A (named) maximum percentage
- Shipments after (a set date)
- A (percentage) of the U.S. Producer Price Index for (site the specific items to be adjusted)
- A (maximum amount) increase allowable."

When you discuss the above escalation, also negotiate a discount for higher volume, and spell out those terms here. A special price adjustment clause designed to protect the buyer from large exchange rate fluctuations is covered in Chapter 11.

#8. Marking Instructions Clause

Based on the U.S. Custom's *Importing into the United States* guide recommendations, buyers should inform the supplier as follows:

"Mark and number each package legibly and conspicuously with the name of the country of origin and with such other wording as required by the marking laws of the United States. Observe closely the instructions detailed below (or that have been supplied to you)."

"Markings and labels must be in English, and may also be in the supplier's language. Marks and numbers are to be on the invoice and each package. Show our company name, address, and order number with two inch high stencil lettering in black waterproof ink. Use standardized international shipping and handling symbols adapted by the International Organization for Standardization."

#9. Communications Notice Clause

State place to which supplier is to send invoices and other data. Give the specific person that they are to contact for various reasons. Example:

"Any notice or demand required by any provision of this agreement shall be determined to have been given adequately if sent by registered or certified mail, return receipt requested, to the party at the following address: (name and address here)."
For shipment information, state:
"Seller shall furnish written documentation about shipping dates as requested by Purchaser. Seller shall furnish a monthly status report. Seller shall notify purchaser by telex within three (3) working days after each shipment of the vessel name, quantity shipped, and E.T.A. date."
For technical information, state:
"Communications about technical matters, of an engineering nature, quality questions, and so on, are to be by telex, FAX, or overnight electronic mail with confirmation by airmail."

After issuance of the purchase order, buyers should communicate by telex, FAX, or overnight electronic mail. Overnight electronic letter-quality mail now serves more than 117 European, Australian, and Asian cities. DHL offers World-wide Express to the major world trade cities. Using a machine is fast and, unlike a phone call, provides a written record. Time zones present no problems in contacting the other party.

Use airmail for confirming any verbal communication. A regular mail letter may take more than 30 days to reach its destination. Second class mail (sent by ocean carrier) often takes 3 or 4 months for delivery.

#10. Instructions to Offshore Supplier Clause

Based on Customs recommendations in its *Importing into the United States* guide that you inform the supplier, insert something such as the following:

> "Prepare your invoices carefully. Type them clearly...Mark and number each pack-age...and the goods legibly and conspicuously with the name of the country of ori-gin...and with such other marking as required by the marking laws of the United States. Observe closely the instructions...sent you (or detailed below) that have to be met when your goods arrive in the United States."

#11. Transmit Documents to Customs Broker

By having the supplier send data directly to the broker, time is saved to expedite customs clearance. The original documents, certificates, invoice, and bill of lading are usually put in a waterproof packet that is attached to the shipment container.

> "Send copies of all required documents as spelled out in this purchase order and our Letter of Credit Number (insert) directly to our customs broker, (yours inserted) Mr. Kevin Mark, Entry Customs, Inc., NY 10048."

#12. Certificates of Survey

Various types of certificates, such as a certificate of origin, and of insurance, are often needed. To receive exactly what you order, you should request various certificates. Depending on the purchased goods, you may want certificates of weight, manufacture, inspection, sanitary conditions, and so forth.

To assure you get them, include a certification clause both in your purchase order, and in any letter of credit, such as:

> "Seller must submit a Certificate of Origin Form A (or Insurance, etc.), stating the per-centage of Seller's product that is made or produced in his country. Submittal must be made on Form A."

Electrical and other codes are potential hazards to recognize in your purchase order. Codes are designed to protect consumers. Products and components must meet certain criteria to assure safety to the offshore buyer purchaser.

In addition to all the regulatory codes mentioned under legalities, examples of specialized U.S. technical codes to be met are Underwriters Laboratories (UL), ETL testing laboratories, ASHRE, ASME, AHAM, and so on, as required by U.S. markets. Approval of the above agencies takes place in advance, and usually requires a stringent test procedure. ETL will recognize UL approval, but UL will not recognize ETL approval. A buyer must assure that the foreign source can meet these approvals.

If the importer is to sell the purchased goods as received, the seller must sometimes deal directly with the technical code agencies for approval, before they can provide proper certification. In this case, use the following:

"Seller must submit proper certificate(s) that its products comply with OSHA, DOE, FTC, (AHAM, SAE, ASHRAE, ASME, or other) requirements and achieve Seller's published rated capacity and efficiency per submitted specifications."

When global sourcing for components used in buyer's products that are later sold in United States, Canada, and abroad, such components must meet the proper codes. Canadian Standards Association (CSA) approved products are required for items sold in Canada. CSA will only accept its own approval. Germany's TUV code requires certification by them of the manufacturer of steel from which products are made. Other worldwide markets sometimes require local code approvals, such as JIS in Japan and KIS in South Korea. This is a small sampling of stringent restrictions required.

If the buyer/assembler has to get approval for its complete product, use the following provision:

"Purchaser will also submit its products to get German TUV (or Canadian CAL, etc.) approval. Seller must submit proper certificate that its products comply with these requirements fully."

Inspection certificates are usually prepared by independent inspectors, who attest to condition, quality, or quantity of goods shipped. Buyers requiring foreign code certification may seek to hire well-qualified foreign inspectors. For example, SGS in Belgium is a special inspection agency that inspects for foreign buyers.

#13. Warranty Clause

The UCC states that express warranties are "any description of the goods, which is made part of the basis of the bargain." Without anything in writing, the UCC (Section Two, Part Three) provides minimum requirements in an implied warranty.

The buyer has a right to expect the goods to be merchantable, to "pass without objection in the trade under the contract description," and to "fit for ordinary purposes for which such goods are used." If the buyer refuses to disclose to the seller how the item is used, this can lead to a later dispute.

A warranty clause is mandatory for your protection, especially when dealing with third-party arrangements. *Warranties are negotiable!* A warranty is a promise by the seller to the buyer that the goods purchased are of a quality conforming to certain standards. An express (written) warranty defines the extent of coverage and is created in three ways:

1. By "affirmation of fact or promise made by the seller";
2. By description of the goods; and
3. By "sample or model."

In all three cases, the promise, description, or sample must become "part of the basis for the bargain." Spell out the obligations for warranties, repairs and so forth, in the contract.

> "Seller shall be responsible for warranties of merchantability and fitness for a particular purpose and assures the products are safe to use." (Purchaser should spell out any special features, etc.)
>
> "This warranty shall cover the first 12 months of use, or 18 months after purchase (or whatever). In the event of failure, the cost of replacement parts and labor will be reimbursed to the Purchaser by the Seller. Items that fail under warranty shall be returned to the factory at the Purchaser's expense. Seller may choose to replace defective item(s) with a new replacement. (Again, these issues are specific to the item.)"

A statement on a contract that the product is *As Is* or *With all Faults* negates the seller's warranty responsibility.

#14. Indemnification Clause

There are two areas to cover here. The first is personal or property damage, and the second is patent, copyright infraction, or trade secret theft. The later area looms even larger in offshore buying, where the exact origin of a product may be less clear than in domestic buying. Buyers want the supplier's assurance that they, the customer, are held harmless from suits for both areas.

Indemnification is controversial and often difficult to sell to suppliers because this clause is strongly for protection of the buyer. Include and use as much of the clause as possible to protect the buyer/importer if product or merchandise fails.

> "Seller covenants and agrees always to indemnify, hold harmless (including, but not limited to, the payment of all reasonable expenses and satisfaction of all judgments)

and defend Purchaser, its agents, and its respective directors, officers, employees, and successors and assigns against all claims for loss, damage or injury, and suits or actions brought against Purchaser or such other parties because of any third person, persons, or entities, because of any personal injuries received or sustained by such person or damage to tangible property, other than the product, caused by or growing out of any defects of the products supplied by Seller to Purchaser.

"Seller's obligations hereunder are conditioned upon Purchaser promptly notifying Seller of all such claims, demands, or legal proceedings. Seller shall have the right to control, manage, litigate, or compromise any such claim suit or demand; and Purchaser shall provide such information and aid in the defense as Seller may reasonable request. Purchaser agrees that it shall not compromise or settle any claim or case without the prior written approval of Seller.

"The indemnification shall not apply in event of misapplication of the product or improper installation, or Purchaser's negligence in handling or modification without Sellers's written consent, the cause of any injury to persons or damage to property. Except the foregoing, Seller will defend any suit and hold Purchaser and its vendees harmless against any claim, demand, cost, or loss arising from a suit or proceeding brought against Purchaser or its vendees, based on the claim that any product or part thereof furnished hereunder constitutes an infringement of any patent, copyright, or trade secret of the United States, if notified and given authority, information, and assistance for the settlement or defense of the same, other than for the assistance of Purchaser employees, shall be at Seller's expense; and Seller shall pay all damages and costs awarded therein against Purchaser."

Epidemic Failure Clause

Define epidemic failure as where failure occurs in "X" percent or more of total sales of the product to consumers within "Y" months of date of the supplier's manufacture of them. Negotiate the numbers. "X" at 3 percent and "Y" at 12 or 18 months is reasonable. Detail how the seller will repay you for such excessive defects by using this clause:

"An epidemic failure means a defect in materials or workmanship of a specific type that occurs or recurs in any part, component, accessory, or item of equipment of a product and that impairs the function, operation, or safety of such product: provided such failure occurs or recurs in three percent (3%) or more of the total sales of the products to consumers within eighteen (18) months from the date of manufacture.

"If such an 'epidemic failure, ' Seller shall remedy such excessive defects more than the three percent (3%) in one of the following ways to be selected by Seller at its option: 1. Repair such units, 2. Replace such units, 3. Credit Purchaser units at Purchaser's unit price set stated on the purchase order, or 4. Reimburse Purchaser for its reasonable expenses (including labor, materials, and the usual transport allowances in correcting the units)."

There is a chance the buyer can't get monies due from the foreign country because the native government may restrict or deny transfers of funds. In such cases, the buyer may choose to insist on an insurance policy in his favor, provided and paid for by the seller.

#15. Patent, or Proprietary Protection Clause

The warranty for patent infringement is one of the *warranties of title*. This clause can be included as the last paragraph of the indemnification clause as it's done in clause #14 above. However, it also stands alone.

Some lawyers have pointed out that Americans freely give or make available its information to the world. Many companies in effect give away their designs when buyers make price inquiries from offshore suppliers. In sending quote requests, the buyer has to be careful to send proprietary data fully protected. If the patent is not protected in the foreign country, it can be copied and made. Depending on the country in question, buyers may register new product designs (for example, with the Design Depository in the Hong Kong Design & Packaging Centre).

A distinction is drawn for proprietary protection of data of a technical or business nature that are classified as "trade secrets" or "confidential." These may be unpatentable, so by using the following clause, the buyer shows that data is submitted with restrictive provisions and establishes a proprietary or confidential relationship.

(Date)

To Christian Michael (person receiving disclosure);

The *Confidential Disclosure* of Pooler & Associates's (your company) computer related idea (...spell out the type of information disclosed) to me on this date, shall only be used for the purpose of quoting (or assembly, evaluating manufacture costs, etc.). The purpose for disclosure is to determine if this product has economic feasibility.

I agree to use this information mindful of Pooler & Associates (your company) patent pending application.

_____
Christian Michael (Signature of reviewer)

Simply providing your information without such a statement may put the data in the public domain.

The following addition to this clause helps protect the buyer if a patent is held by another party. Piracy of patents makes it possible that buyers might buy "stolen" goods. Certain foreign companies are known to allow use of others' inventions without permission. A genuine Rolex can cost $8,000. For less than $50, a look-a-like copy can be bought in South Korea. Sales of counterfeit trademark goods may be illegal in the United States.

The heavy liability for the buyer or importer reselling an item made by someone without a valid patent is great, with or without knowledge or intention on the part of the buyer. A precautionary protective clause should be part of the terms and conditions getting the seller to assume full responsibility.

> "Seller warrants that his product(s) are of his own design and manufacture, and any use of others patents or proprietary design has been cleared properly."

Before using these protective clauses, the buyer should refresh the legal chapter. Be aware that when the seller is making something conforming to the specifications of the your buying company, the liability could be solely yours.

#16. Taxes Clause

The offshore supplier knows the taxes imposed far better than the importer/buyer. Buyers don't like to be surprised by unexpected costs. Use this clause:

> "Supplier must bear the cost of present and future taxes for goods or transport imposed within his country."

#17. Cancellation Clauses

Spell out under what conditions either party can withdraw from the purchase.

Termination for Convenience
Most sellers balk at termination for convenience. It is difficult to get the seller's acceptance for this clause. However, it is done. An example of such a clause is as follows:

> "The Purchaser may terminate this order for convenience. In the event of such termination, Purchaser will reimburse Seller for all expenses incurred or committed up to the date of receipt of notice of termination."

Termination for Default Clause
An example is shown below:

> "If Seller fails to fulfill any of the terms of this order, or if Seller files a petition from bankruptcy, reorganization, assignment for benefit of creditors, or similar proceedings, Purchaser may by written notice to Seller, without prejudice to any other rights or remedies that Purchaser may have, terminate further performance by Seller. If termination takes place, Purchaser may complete performance of this purchase order by such means as Purchaser selects. Seller shall be responsible for any added costs incurred by Purchaser in doing so."

#18. Force Majeure Clause

Domestic disasters are known to the buyer quickly, unlike distant suppliers diffi-culties. This clause primarily protects the seller from liability from *Acts of God*, such as flood, fire, strikes, war. The clause can cover the buyer also. Make sure you state a deadline on when they have to inform you and your right to terminate without extra charge.

Buyer should stipulate this added paragraph:

> "Seller is responsible for notifying Purchaser within three (3) working days of occurrences that may prevent or delay seller performance. Notification shall be in writing and the Seller shall make every reasonable effort to resolve the Force Majeure occurrence as soon as pos-sible. Reportable occurrences would include (1) Acts of God, (2) civil uprising or war, (3) acts of the Government in either its sovereign or contractual capacity, (4) extreme weather conditions, fires, or floods, (5) epidemics or quarantine restrictions, (6) strikes, and (7) freight embargoes. Should the Seller be unable to fulfill the contract after a one-month pe-riod, the purchaser shall have the right to terminate the purchase order, with its only liabil-ity being to pay seller for products received by Purchaser."

Should such uncontrollable events deprive a company from receiving material, buyer is free to search elsewhere.

#19. Products, Service, and Replacement Parts Clause

Your interest here lies in any surprise changes in the design of items bought. Also, offshore suppliers may find it convenient to drop a product and not provide for replacement components later. Insert:

> "During the life of this agreement, Seller agrees to provide Purchaser a complete de-scription of any changes in form, fit, or function of component parts or accessories of products purchased. Seller agrees to furnish all component specifications and draw-ings for parts sold. Seller agrees to provide service and installation and/or data suffi-cient for service and installation.
> "Products shall include replacement parts or components of said products. Seller agrees to make available for replacement purposes for those products sold, functional fabricated or purchased parts (or acceptable substitutes) ten (10) years after date of last unit of production by seller. These parts are (name key parts here).
> "Seller must make available all nonfunctional parts for five (5) years after date of last production. (Spell out whatever was agreed.) Purchaser may buy replacement parts from others not a party to this agreement."

#20. Special Clauses for a Specific Country

You might include clauses suited to a particular offshore country. For example, these are useful when dealing with Hong Kong:

1. Late shipment penalty of 1 percent daily on unshipped balance due, with a cap of 25 percent of the order value.
2. Letter of credit amendment and discrepancy clause that holds supplier liable for any bank charges and commissions incurred by buyer and that result from supplier's failure to follow the L/C provisions.
3. Default compensation clause. Holds supplier liable for procurement costs incurred by buyer should supplier default his contract.

DISPUTE SETTLEMENT CLAUSES

The nature of the buying job is that buyers have to settle conflicts and disputes with suppliers and contractors. Buying is a friction-producing job, since the buyer must often question many aspects of a purchase. The buyer is in "conflict between two worlds"—that of the company he represents and that of the supplying interests. It takes a high degree of statesmanship to work in that environment.

Most commercial disputes that arise are settled amicably. The best inducement for settlements known is the understanding that the seller wants another sale, and the buyer likes and needs the materials. While a ship doesn't sink too often, pilferage or damage does occur, requiring buyer action. Despite the utmost care in preparing, the chance of an occasional sticky dispute is high in offshore buying.

The two clauses that follow are vital to the prevention of disputes and useful when one occurs. The challenge is to lessen the probability of having a dispute in the first place. A key to solving disputes is answering the questions, "Who has ownership of the goods," and "When do I take legal possession?" Are there guidelines that will help? Yes!

Commonly in use are the "Revised American Foreign Trade Definitions—1941." However, there are newer terms that made their debut in 1953 and later revisions, including those made in 1980. The International Chamber of Commerce has standardized and modernized 14 international commercial terms that are known as INCOTERMS. Buyers sometimes misuse such terms, because of confusion concerning their use and meaning.

The basic function of an INCOTERM is to call for the preferred method of shipment. They also spell out clearly the division of responsibilities and obligations between buyer and seller. The goods are legally delivered by seller to buyer at a point spelled out in the specific FOB within the IN-COTERM. Based on identifying the transfer point for possession of goods, an INCOTERM determines who will pay the costs and who assumes the risks.

#21. International Commercial Terms (INCOTERMS)

Insert:

> "This contract will be governed by the provisions of INCOTERMS. In case of dispute, the published reference by the ICC, specifying 'What the buyer and seller are responsible for' will apply."

In case of dispute, the buyer has a published reference, specifying "What the buyer and seller are responsible for."[1]

Lacking mention to the contrary, a purchase order is treated as a shipping point contract, with risk on the buyer when the seller has delivered the goods to the carrier. Usually at the point of ownership exchange, the buyer will take possession. He assumes the responsibility and risks for further transport and costs.

A distinction is made between who has possession and is controlling the shipment, and who bears the risk and responsibility to settle problems occurring during shipment. The buyer has to be wary. Under some terms, this risk has already passed to you, though the seller has paid for and is controlling the shipment.

The seller is responsible for invoice, packing list, certificate of manufacture or origin, export crating, and securing an export license, if needed. Maximum buyer responsibility is seen at the top left in Figure 7-2, a chart of buyer and seller

BUYER & SELLER RESPONSIBILITIES			LOADS INLAND VEHICLE	SHIPPING DOCUMENTS SELECT & LOAD SHIP	PAYS FREIGHT	OBTAINS INSURANCE	ASSUMES RISK DURING TRANSIT	PAYS DUTY
B = BUYER RESPONSIBILITY S = SELLER RESPONSIBILITY	INCOTERM	BASIC RESPONSIBILITIES						
MAXIMUM BUYER	EX WORKS	ORIGIN SPECIFIED AS TO PLANT SHIPPING DOCK.	B	B	B	B	B	B
	FOR/FOT	SELLER ARRANGES RAIL CARRIER. OBTAINS BILL OF LADING.	S	—	B	B	B	B
	FAS VESSEL FOREIGN PORT	SAME AS FOB EXCEPT BUYER PAYS FOR LIFTING.	S	B	B	B	B	B
	FOB VESSEL	SELLER ARRANGES INLAND SHIPPING TO SHIP DOCK.	S	S	B	B	B	B
RESPONSIBILITY	C & F	SELLER'S PRICE INCLUDES TRANSPORTATION.	S	S	S	B	B	B
	C I F	SAME AS C & F AND ALSO INCLUDES INSURANCE.	S	S	S	S	B	B
	EX SHIP	SELLER TO IMPORT SHIP LOADING.	S	S	S	S	S	B
	EX QUAY (DOCK)	SELLER PAYS TO IMPORT CUSTOMS.	S	S	S	S	S	S
MAXIMUM SELLER	FOB DELIVERED	SELLER PAYS ALL COST.	S	S	S	S	S	S

POOLER & ASSOCIATES

ATS 0101100-1.0

FIGURE 7-2. Buyer and Seller responsibilities.

---

[1] ICC's "INCOTERMS" booklet. ICC Publishing, 156 Fifth Avenue, Suite 820 New York, N.Y. 10010. (212) 206-1150.

responsibilities. The terms are shown in descending order toward maximum seller responsibility. A first buyer reaction frequently is to go for the highest degree of seller responsibility. However, there are many reasons why that won't be your best choice. (for example, you find the insurance premium is out of line and you can get it cheaper). Or you find that your traffic department wants tight control over shipment routing, tracing, and so on.

Seldom will buyers choose maximum responsibility using *Ex Works*. Firms using this term, such as banana plantations, have strong skills and want to control everything. Most buys will gravitate toward the middle, C&F, CIF, or Ex-Ship range. Let's review your options. The first four of these eight possession terms listed below are shipping point terms:

- Ex-Works
  Possession changes along with title at the seller's shipping dock, ready to ship but not yet loaded. The buyer is responsible for loading, transportation, insurance, duty, and customs clearance. This is a "native contract" with minimal risk to the foreign seller. Seldom used, this term is reserved to those buyers that have strong in-house transportation talent. For example, a large company when dealing with a small foreign supplier may expect to handle all the details to assure quality and reduce costs.
- FOR/FOT (Free on Rail or Truck) Refers to railway wagon
  This term is intended solely for goods transported by rail. Title passes to the buyer when the goods have been delivered to the rail carrier.
- FAS (Free Alongside Ship) To named port of shipment
  Seller provides transportation for the goods to the point of departure alongside the ship. The buyer has the responsibility to get ocean freight space, as well as marine and war risk insurance.
- FOB (Free On Board) Named point of shipment
  The price quoted applies only to an inland shipping point. The seller arranges for loading of goods on, or in, railway cars, trucks, barges, aircraft, and so on.

The following four are the "Destination Point" terms:

- C&F (Cost & Freight) Named port of destination
  This is a shipping point contract, though the seller pays the charges. Title and risk of loss passes to buyer when goods are delivered to carrier. Buyer must insure that he or she is protected.
- CIF (Cost, Insurance, and Freight) To named port of destination
  Same as C&F above, but seller also arranges and pays for insurance.
- Ex-Ship—Named port of destination
  This is an arrival contract. Title of goods changes when they pass over the ships rails at the U.S. entry port.

- EX-QUAY—Named port of import
  This is an arrival contract. Seller's price normally includes costs for goods plus all other costs to place goods on the quay (pronounced as key, it means a dock or wharf) at port of destination. If seller must pay the duty, clarify it by adding the words *Duty Paid* After the Ex-Quay.

The above eight, the most common INCOTERMS in use today, were adopted in 1953. The following two terms were added in 1967, as goods moved increasingly across national borders:

- Delivered at Frontier (DAF) Named place of entry at frontier
  Implies delivery to border of destination country of import, by either rail or truck. For the U.S. buyer, this applies only for shipments from Canada or Mexico.
- Delivered Duty Paid (DDP) Named place of destination in the country of importation
  This includes any mode of transport. Total landed costs to buyer's destination, including duty are paid by the seller.

With increased use of air transport, the following term was added in 1976:

- FOB Airport (DAP) Named airport of departure
  The buyer uses this term solely for air shipments. Seller pays all costs to departure airport, and buyer assumes possession at the import airport.

In 1980, the modernization of logistics brought about three more additions. As Customs adopts its new computerized systems, these terms are expected to gradually replace C&F and CIF, since they will get higher priority:

- Free Carrier (FRC) Named point
  This is for cases where the named point is a cargo terminal located either at a seaport or inland.
- Freight Carriage Paid (DCP) To named point of destination
  This is for land transport, but does include inland waterways. Seller pays freight to destination, but risks of loss are the buyers.
- Freight Carriage and Insurance (CIP) Paid to named point of destination
  Same as above DCP, but also includes insurance. It is similar to CIF.

These are the latest modern revisions, adaptable to multimodal forms of transportation. There are also other terms in use today. A buyer can make up combinations of terms for his or her FOB. As long as they are specific, they can work. The buyer should do this with caution, since the feature of predetermined responsibility is lost.

One buyer complained about bad mixups on several shipments. He was using a "shipping point" term. By designating his port of *entry* as a destination point, he bastardized the term. The seller interpreted the term to mean that the buyer paid for transportation and arranged the shipment, but the buyer expected the seller to handle it.

Referring to Figure 7-2, previously shown, buyers can quickly determine responsibility based on ownership. Assume that the buy was C&F and an insurance claim had to be filed. As the chart shows, it is a buyer responsibility. If there is a freight claim, it is up to the seller. If shipping documents are missing, that's a seller problem, and so on.

Of special concern is the trap in both the C&F, and the CI&F INCOTERMS! The buyer must get insurance when using C&F. While the exporter is responsible to get and pay for the insurance with CI&F, the buyer is still responsible for loss.

Warning! Stick with the proper terminology on the purchase order. Spell out easily misunderstood terms. These 14 up-to-date INCOTERMS are preventive aides for buyers, should disputes arise.

Alternate Dispute Resolution (ADR)

Disputes start with a conflict between two parties. The settlement steps arranged in increasing complexity are: 1. problem solving, 2. mediation, 3. arbitration, and 4. litigation. Perhaps buyer and seller, by using problem solving techniques, will reach a settlement.

If buyers focus objectively on the need of a resolution, and do not use a "We" versus "They" approach, most disputes can be settled amicably. If unable, the next higher level of settlement is pursued. There is a tendency in our litigious society to pursue a legal approach too quickly.

There are few substitutes for trust and a willingness to negotiate to clear a disputed commercial transaction. Is there a difference whether purchase is domestic or imported? Not in essence, but getting a foreign warranty honored can be more difficult. A purchasing manager told of a problem buying equipment from a U.S. company that sold Swiss machines. When the machine performed improperly and satisfaction was not received, the company sued. The American agent was judged not liable. Faced with recovering from the manufacturer by going through a foreign court action, where the buying company had no connections, the company conceded. This litigation action is much too uncertain, complex, and expensive and is least preferred of all the options available. They realized it was much cheaper to write it off as a lesson learned. Moral to the buyer? Get the obligations on warranties, repairs, and so forth, into your purchase order! This is especially important when dealing with three-party arrangements.

Settling consequential damages resulting from product failure indirectly is difficult. For example, a fuse blows and a factory shuts down for the day, sending

100 people home. A buyer might try to collect for the lost wages, but can't, as this is "consequential."

It's possible to contract for consequential damages by negotiation and stating that it is covered in your purchase order. Of course, there will be heavy costs charged into the pricing that will discourage most buyers trying for it.

What do you do when there is an unavoidable offshore dispute? Most embassies may offer some help. They have libraries with information on foreign trade, industry journals, and lists of overseas manufacturers and product catalogs.

While foreign service personnel may not act as legal representatives, they can provide support and make presentations for a U.S. firm in a trade dispute involving a settlement of more than $500. They need complete background to do this.

Visiting an American Chamber of Commerce abroad provides aid for overcoming local barriers, such as language, customs, laws and regulations. Commercial banks help by telling what they know about the reliability of local manufacturers.

In addition, there are specialists who can handle technical buyer/seller conflicts. Increasingly, resolutions have taken place through Alternative Dispute Resolution (ADR). ADR consists of mediation and/or arbitration.

Mediation

Mediation differs from arbitration, as the third party doesn't have the authority to settle, but merely aids in clarifying issues. Mediators have the right and responsibility to suggest compromises or solutions. The mediator is a neutral third party that acts as moderator between the disputants, trying to get the two parties to discuss and focus on the disagreement. The parties settle their own grievances.

Mediators are most desirable for small family businesses or an intra-company dispute, where the parties must keep working together. Lawsuits often leave parties unable or unwilling to do business again, as deep resentment continues.

Local agencies sponsored by local or state governments provide mediation service free of charge. They are not, however, equipped to handle offshore dispute settlements. Mediation is arranged by some foreign countries. An example is the Hong Kong Customs & Excise Department, which has an Overseas Trade Complaint Unit set up to help foreign (American) buyers in commercial dispute settlements.

Arbitration

The arbitrator acts as a type of judge. The United States has ratified the 1958 New York Convention on the Recognition and Enforcement of Foreign Arbitral Awards. The United Nations Commission on International Trade Law (UNCITRAL) issued a model Law on International Commercial Arbitrations. The UN established the World Arbitration Institute and the Federation of Commercial Arbitration Institutions to maintain and improve relationships between various agencies worldwide. There is close cooperation with this commission and the ICC.

It's possible to select neutral arbitrator specialists that live in neither country of the two parties in dispute. International buyers report that some foreign suppliers insist on moving arbitration into a neutral country, such as England or Switzerland. Otherwise, they may refuse to accept an arbitration clause.

Include a standard arbitration clause as shown below in the contract. Use of the clause gains advance agreement of the parties to arbitrate as part of their contractual understanding. Though the buyer fails to enter the clause on his purchase document, arbitration is still possible if both parties agree. It is, however, sensible to remove all doubt by acceptance. You may never need the clause, but, should need arise, it commits the two parties to a practical way to a neutral judgement.

The American Arbitration Association headquarters are at 140 West 51st St., New York, NY 10020 (212) 484-4000, and maintain offices in 30 cities. Founded in 1926, the AAA is a not-for-profit organization whose function is the "resolution of disputes of all kinds through the use of arbitration, mediation, democratic elections, and other voluntary methods." Lists of available arbitrators are made available to those using their services.

Claiming to have 60,000 experts in various fields or professions available to pass judgment, the AAA conducts workshops, seminars, and conferences to promote better understanding of the arbitration process.

#22. Arbitration Clauses

The American Arbitration Association suggests the following:

> "Any controversy or claim arising out of or relating to this contract, or the breach thereof, shall be settled by arbitration in accordance with the Rules of the American Arbitration Association, and judgement upon the award rendered by the Arbitrator(s) may be entered in any Court having jurisdiction thereof."

Frequently, AAA judgement is without pay as a public service in domestic squabbles. However, you must pay arbitrators on international cases, and you may pay an advance deposit. Administrative costs incurred are separate from the fees of any arbitrator(s).

AAA will provide a hearing room. The language used depends on the native languages of the parties. Listening to arguments from both sides, the arbitrator makes a decision that is not subject to legal action. Judgments are given in a short written form, but they are not published. An arbitrator can be challenged before a decision is reached and the AAA will determine whether to disqualify.

The other option is the International Chamber of Commerce's (ICC) Court of Arbitration. The ICC has an International Center for Technical Expertise that offers parties to furnish independent experts in dispute settlements. Its court works with the International Maritime Bureau (IMB), which combats maritime fraud. They provide help to overcome local barriers, such as language, customs, laws, and regulations. These wide contacts make them preferable for offshore squabbles.

If you wish to use the ICC, insert a clause as suggested by the ICC as follows:

"All disputes arising in connection with the present contract shall be finally settled under the Rules of Conciliation and Arbitration of the International Chamber of Commerce by one or more arbitrators appointed in accordance with the Rules."

To get further information write the ICC Publishing Corp. 156 Fifth Ave. Suite 820, NY, NY 10010 Tel: (212) 206-1150. Available are the following: "Guide to Arbitrations," ISBN number 92-842 1018-6, "Guide On Multi-Party Arbitration," "Arbitration Law in Europe," and "Rules for the ICC Court of Arbitration" (rules and conciliation costs).

Inclusion of the clause providing for use of either of these two organizations commits the two disputing parties to use this method to secure a neutral judgement. The procedures followed will be prescribed by the AAA or the ICC.

Remember, a legal court ruling can be challenged. However, when a buyer gives power to a third party to solve his dispute, an appeal from the award or decision is prohibited. It's to prevent recurring quarrels. In any case, ADR is less adversary and conducive to settlements in privacy, without large court costs. And the reputation of the parties is not at stake because of the confidentiality.

These "boilerplate" clauses won't all be used. They are only representative examples that you should adapt to the specifics of each negotiation and specifics of the purchases. Buyers must choose those to use in their purchase orders.

Ecological regulations affect procurement on issues such as PCB contamination and purity of water effluent, for example. Another factor is a social responsibility, as companies bear some accountability to societal needs. Minority suppliers and small business buying programs are domestic issues that are still part of any sourcing decision. These and other issues effect material supply and increase your coordination effort with others. They all lead to increased demands on suppliers that must be enforced through the buyer's purchase orders.

8

Meeting U.S. Customs Tariffs and Regulations

All goods imported into the United States are subject to duty or duty- free entry. All imported items are assigned a Harmonized Code number that sets the customs duty to be paid. The amount of duty depends on an items classification and the supplying country of origin.

Duty is a form of taxation used to protect a local market and to raise revenue. You must pay what is mandated, but, like taxes, why pay extra?

HARMONIZED TARIFF SCHEDULE OF THE UNITED STATES (HTSUS)

Tariffs change frequently. Get a copy of the loose-leaf edition of the "1991 Harmonized Tariff Schedule of the United States." The current HTSUS, put into place in 1989, provides description, classification code numbers, and duty rates. It classifies more than 5,000 article descriptions that are further subdivided into more than 25,000 commodities.

What goods are called determines how they are classified, which in turn sets the rate of the customs duty. Buyers need to interpret their buys and select the proper article description. Beside the item's name and code number in the HTSUS, you can quickly find that commodity's rate of duty.

Sometimes, by changing the description of the item purchased, another classification may have a lower rate of duty. For example, a regular watch is assessed a 20-percent rate of duty. A digital type with calculator qualifies as a "timing mechanism" at a 7.5-percent duty. Another example: At one time, if a "van" was shipped into the United States it incurred a 25-percent duty. However, if it was classified as a "truck" it only incurred 2-percent duty. This came to light in 1989 when Customs declared that vans were not trucks.

Still another example is the importation of cotton covers HTSUS 6302.21.10602, which has a duty of 23.8-percent. If the item could be properly termed cotton quilts, code 9404.90.9013, it would have a 14.5-percent duty. The amount of filler defines a quilt.

Even a simple change such as the location of a pocket may determine the classification. If located above the waist, it's a blouse. If the pocket is below, it's classified as a jacket.

A buyer could bring in an item as "aircraft part, or classify under a specific part, such as "hydraulic reservoir" or "landing strut." Classifications can be affected by width and thickness of belting material, or, if qualified, as power transmission belts. The point is that *changing the term that describes the item purchased may change the duty imposed.*

Use the Harmonized code as a guide and request a binding ruling from the Customs "Commodity Specialists," which rule on rates, markings, and value in advance. Ask for an "advisory ruling" about the exact duty, from your local Commodity Specialist. Or get a binding ruling from the National Import Specialist, located at #6 World Trade Center, NY, NY 10048.

A response is normal within 30 to 45 days. When you get a ruling, tell your local specialist, who may not know of its existence. This ruling is binding on all local commodity specialists within the United States.

ENTRY OF MERCHANDISE STEPS

The steps for customs clearance are entry, valuation, examination, appraisement, and liquidation. Entry can be made through almost 300 ports of entry into the United States. Imported goods are not legally entered until the entry process is completed.

Entry for consumption consists of filing documents to:

1. Determine whether merchandise may be released from Customs custody; and
2. Allow duty assessment and government statistics.

Delivery of the merchandise has to be authorized and estimated duties paid. Goods may be entered by the owner, buyer, or licensed customhouse broker. Customs does not require the importer to have a license or permit.

A bill of lading, airway bill, or carrier's certificate, stating the consignee, gives evidence of shipment and the right of the consignee to make entry. The "Carriers Certificate and Release Order" CF 7529 form is used on customs entries for air shipments in some ports. Sometimes, it may be used for ocean shipment.

Usually, a shipment is consigned to a specific company or individual, or "To order" (to the bank or to shipper). It depends on the method of payment. If consigned "To Order," the bill of lading properly endorsed shows the right to make entry.

You need an original bill of lading for the Steamship Company Release. If you don't have a B/L for an order consignment, get your bank to give you a "Bank Guarantee" (for a fee). Take it to the steamship line, telling them you want your shipment released. When you get the Bill of Lading, give it to the steamship company. Upon return of the guarantee, return it to your bank.

The importer arranges for examination and release of his or her goods. At present, for ocean shipments you can present import documents to customs five days before arrival and goods can be cleared in 24 hours or less, unless the shipment is subject to customs examination or a quota exists.

Entry for Consumption

Within five days after cargo has become available, an entry permit, Customs Form CF 7501 (Fig. 8-1)[1] must be filed with the inspector at the incoming pier or airline terminal, along with the estimated duty payment. A commercial invoice is also needed. It is a very important document, used to compute the amount of duty owed.

Customs wants *all* details on the invoice prepared according to Section 141.86 Customs Regulations and commercial practice. To instruct your supplier, spell out specifics in your purchase order. Any discounts, rebates, commissions, and royalties must be shown on the invoice. While the invoice may state quantities in weights and measures used in the United States, the Customs entry must state quantity in metrics.

Customs wants the Harmonized code number shown on the left hand side of the invoice, close to the name of the item being imported. This is usually done by the person preparing the customs entry form.

Errors or questions concerning the invoice result in Customs sending you CF 28 Request for Information. Perhaps they have questions about commissions or assists. You may be told to furnish copies of your PO, breakdown of costs of components, and so forth. CF 29 is the Notice of Action form used to advise you of rate or classification changes. It is checked to show proposed action, or action that has been taken. The importer/buyer must respond to these inquiry forms promptly. You will certify that your answers are true and correct.

Immediate Delivery Entry

Suppose you have reason to get your goods at once—fresh fruit from Canada or Mexico, an article for urgent display at a trade show, or perhaps delicate equipment susceptible to damage? An alternate entry allows for immediate release of a shipment by using special permit Entry/Immediate Delivery Customs CF 3461,

---

[1] All Customs forms are obtainable from the U.S. Government Printing Office. Commercial printers also sell the CFs in quantity.

DEPARTMENT OF THE TREASURY
UNITED STATES CUSTOMS SERVICE

ENTRY SUMMARY

Form Approved OMB No. 1515-0065

(1) Entry No.	(2) Entry Type Code	3. Entry Summary Date	
4. Entry Date	(5) Port Code		
6. Bond No.	7. Bond Type Code	8. Broker/Importer File No.	
9. Ultimate Consignee Name and Address	10. Consignee No.	(11) Importer of Record Name and Address	(12) Importer No.
		(13) Exporting Country	14. Export Date
		(15) Country of Origin	16. Missing Documents
State		(17) I.T. No.	(18) I.T. Date
(19) B/L or AWB No.	20. Mode of Transportation	21. Manufacturer I.D.	22. Reference No.
(23) Importing Carrier	24. Foreign Port of Lading	25. Location of Goods/G.O. No.	
26. U.S. Port of Unlading	(27) Import Date		

(28) Line No.	30. (A) T.S.U.S.A. No. B. ADA/CVD Case No.	(29) Description of Merchandise 31. (A) Gross Weight B. Manifest Qty.	(32) Net Quantity in T.S.U.S.A. Units	33. (A) Entered Value B. CHGS C. Relationship	34. (A) T.S.U.S.A. Rate B. ADA/CVD Rate (C) I.R.C. Rate D. Visa No.	(35) Duty and I.R. Tax Dollars	Cents

(36) Declaration of Importer of Record (Owner or Purchaser) or Authorized Agent

I declare that I am the

☐ importer of record and that the actual owner, purchaser, or consignee for customs purposes is as shown above. OR ☐ owner or purchaser or agent thereof.

I further declare that the merchandise

☐ was obtained pursuant to a purchase or agreement to purchase and that the prices set forth in the invoice are true. OR ☐ was not obtained pursuant to a purchase or agreement to purchase and the statements in the invoice as to value or price are true to the best of my knowledge and belief.

I also declare that the statements in the documents herein filed fully disclose to the best of my knowledge and belief the true prices, values, quantities, rebates, drawbacks, fees, commissions, and royalties and are true and correct, and that all goods or services provided to the seller of the merchandise either free or at reduced cost are fully disclosed. I will immediately furnish to the appropriate customs officer any information showing a different state of facts.

Notice required by Paperwork Reduction Act of 1980. This information is needed to ensure that importers/exporters are complying with U.S. customs laws, to allow us to compute and collect the right amount of money, to enforce other agency requirements, and to collect accurate statistical information on imports. Your response is mandatory.

↓ U.S. CUSTOMS USE ↓		TOTALS	
A. Liq. Code	B. Ascertained Duty	(37) Duty	
	C. Ascertained Tax	(38) Tax	
	D. Ascertained Other	(39) Other	
	E. Ascertained Total	(40) Total	

(41) Signature of Declarant, Title, and Date

PART 1 — RECORD COPY

Customs Form 7501 (030984)

88

☆ U.S. GOVERNMENT PRINTING OFFICE: 1990—262-008-26711

FIGURE 8-1. Entry summary CF 7501.

shown in Figure 8-2. I. D. Entry should be submitted in advance of arrival to the district Customs director. This form certifies that a bond is current and that requirements for entry have been met. Upon approval, delivery is authorized and you are free to take over the shipment. Within ten days of arrival, the importer must still file an Entry Summary CF 7501.

"Demurrage" is the payment to be made to the stevedores for holding goods beyond the allowed time. Goods not cleared within the prescribed period are considered unclaimed. Customs sends unclaimed merchandise "into General Order."

A General Order warehouse is the storage location, and if a container is consigned to it, the cost to reclaim your merchandise can be as high as $2,000 in the port of New York for a one-month stay (exclusive of duty). General Order charges from the warehouse include the cost to remove goods from the dock and take them to the warehouse for storage. If not claimed within one year, goods may be sold by auction.

Mail Entry

For small shipments of parcels valued under $1,250, mail entry has its advantages. The post office delivers to the consignee, collects the duty at that time, and makes the entry. The packages must have a customs declaration attached that is available at post offices worldwide. A commercial shipment must contain an invoice or statement of value and the package is marked "Invoice enclosed."

Bonded Warehouse Entry

If it is desirable to postpone the release of your goods, use this type of entry to store goods until exported or entered later. A warehouse receipt usually negotiable, is issued for the stored goods. On any portion of goods shipped out of the country from the warehouse, no duty is due. An example of use would be where a quota existed preventing entry at the arrival time. Or, should you believe a rate of duty will drop shortly (as happened recently when Hungary was granted Most Favored Nation status), a shipment can be temporarily stored for later release.

While in the warehouse, your goods can be cleaned, sorted, repackaged, but not manufactured. Goods can be held for up to five years. "Duty Paid Warehouse Withdrawal For Consumption" CF 7505 is used by the withdrawer when removing goods at any time. Any duty or taxes are not due until the goods are withdrawn from the warehouse and entered officially into the United States. The rate of duty is the one in effect at the time of removal.

A bonded warehouse is an approved facility that is either separate or a segregated part of a storage building. Or the warehouse can be part of an importer's premises that is in conformance with Customs direction. The warehouse is secured by

TABS:

DEPARTMENT OF THE TREASURY
UNITED STATES CUSTOMS SERVICE

Form Approved
OMB No. 1515-0069

ENTRY/IMMEDIATE DELIVERY

19 CFR 142.3, 142.16, 142.22, 142.24

1. ARRIVAL DATE	2. ELECTED ENTRY DATE	3. ENTRY TYPE CODE/NAME	4. ENTRY NUMBER
5. PORT	6. SINGLE TRANS. BOND	7. BROKER/IMPORTER FILE NUMBER	
	8. CONSIGNEE NUMBER		9. IMPORTER NUMBER

10. ULTIMATE CONSIGNEE NAME	11. IMPORTER OF RECORD NAME

12. CARRIER CODE	13. VOYAGE/FLIGHT/TRIP	14. LOCATION OF GOODS—CODE(S)/NAME(S)
15. VESSEL CODE/NAME		
16. U.S. PORT OF UNLADING	17. MANIFEST NUMBER	18. G.O. NUMBER	19. TOTAL VALUE

20. DESCRIPTION OF MERCHANDISE

21. IT/BL/AWB CODE	22. IT/BL/AWB NO.	23. MANIFEST QUANTITY	24. TSUSA NUMBER	25. COUNTRY OF ORIGIN	26. MANUFACTURER NO.

27. CERTIFICATION	**28. CUSTOMS USE ONLY**
I hereby make application for entry/immediate delivery. I certify that the above information is accurate, the bond is sufficient, valid, and current, and that all requirements of 19 CFR Part 142 have been met.	☐ OTHER AGENCY ACTION REQUIRED, NAMELY:
SIGNATURE OF APPLICANT	
X	☐ CUSTOMS EXAMINATION REQUIRED.
PHONE NO. DATE	
29. BROKER OR OTHER GOVT. AGENCY USE	☐ ENTRY REJECTED, BECAUSE:
	DELIVERY AUTHORIZED: SIGNATURE DATE

Paperwork Reduction Act Notice: This information is needed to determine the admissibility of imports into the United States and to provide the necessary information for the examination of the cargo and to establish the liability for payment of duties and taxes. Your response is necessary.

Customs Form 3461 (112085)

FIGURE 8-2. CF 3461 immediate delivery entry.

Customs. Since 1982, Customs does not oversee the entry or withdrawal of goods. However, the warehouse manager must have records available for Customs inspection at any time.

Customs Bond

A customs bond is a signed contract that insures performance imposed by law. The bond may be in negotiable or nonnegotiable form. There are usually three parties to a Customs bond: 1. the principal (your company), 2. surety, and 3. the beneficiary (the U.S. Customs Service). Surety is a third party who agrees to pay if the conditions of bond are not met, meaning that the principal can't or won't pay.

Customs Bond form CF 301 (Fig. 8-3) is filed with the Regional Commissioner of Customs. The principals must sign the form that spells out their limits of liability. The bond covers either a single transaction, or, if continuous, the bond remains in force for one year and is renewed each period unless terminated.

Types of Transportation Entries

Customs routinely advises carriers that goods are subject to inspection by "Transportation Entry and Manifest of Goods Subject to Customs Inspection and Permit" CF 7512. A short serial numbered card, Transportation Entry and Manifest of Goods CF 7512-C, is checked to show the type of entries listed below:

- Immediate Transportation Entry
- Transportation and Exportation
- Warehouse Withdrawal for Transportation
- Immediate Exportation

It also is a permit to proceed. Goods moving to a duty-free zone could use Immediate Transportation Entry. To clear Customs at a different port than arrival, the merchandise may be transferred "In Bond" to that other customs area. An example would be to unload goods in the Port of New York and deliver part of the shipment by bonded carrier to Canada.

Goods entering the United States solely to be reshipped to a third country can come in without duty payment. An Immediate Exportation or I. E. Entry is prepared when merchandise is exported immediately from the same port of entry. These special-type entries should be reviewed with Customs. They are indicative of the arrangements that can be worked out.

Use of Quota Entry

Historically, world trade is encouraged, but in the 1970s, protectionism began creeping back. Two million American textile and apparel workers, one million auto

DEPARTMENT OF THE TREASURY UNITED STATES CUSTOMS SERVICE **CUSTOMS BOND** 19 CFR Part 113	CUSTOMS USE ONLY	Approved through 01/31/91 OMB No. 1515-0144 BOND NUMBER¹ (Assigned by Customs) FILE REFERENCE	Execution Date

In order to secure payment of any duty, tax or charge and compliance with law or regulation as a result of activity covered by any condition referenced below, we, the below named principal(s) and surety(ies), bind ourselves to the United States in the amount or amounts, as set forth below.

SECTION I—Select Single Transaction OR Continuous Bond (not both) and fill in the applicable blank spaces.

	Identification of transaction secured by this bond (e.g., entry no., seizure no., etc.)	Date of transaction	Transaction district & port code
SINGLE TRANSACTION BOND			

	Effective date	This bond remains in force for one year beginning with the effective date and for each succeeding annual period, or until terminated. This bond constitutes a separate bond for each period in the amounts listed below for liabilities that accrue in each period. The intention to terminate this bond must be conveyed within the time period and manner prescribed in the Customs Regulations.
CONTINUOUS BOND		

SECTION II— This bond includes the following agreements.² (Check one box only, except that, 1a may be checked independently or with 1, and 3a may be checked independently or with 3. Line out all other parts of this section that are not used.)

Activity Code	Activity Name and Customs Regulations in which conditions codified	Limit of Liability	Activity Code	Activity Name and Customs Regulations in which conditions codified	Limit of Liability
☐ 1	Importer or broker..............113.62		☐ 5	Public Gauger.......................113.67	
☐ 1a	Drawback Payment Refunds............ 113.65		☐ 6	Wool & Fur Products Labeling Acts Importation (Single Entry Only)..........113.68	
☐ 2	Custodian of bonded merchandise.......113.63 (Includes bonded carriers, freight forwarders, cartmen and lightermen, all classes of warehouses, container station operators)		☐ 7	Bill of Lading (Single Entry Only)........113.69	
			☐ 8	Detention of Copyrighted Material (Single Entry Only)..............113.70	
☐ 3	International Carrier..............113.64		☐ 9	Neutrality (Single Entry Only)............113.71	
☐ 3a	Instruments of International Traffic.113.66		☐ 10	Court Costs for Condemned Goods (Single Entry Only)...............113.72	
☐ 4	Foreign Trade Zone Operator.............113.73				

SECTION III— List below all tradenames or unincorporated divisions that will be permitted to obligate this bond in the principal's name including their Customs Identification Number(s).³ (If more space is needed, use Section III(Continuation) on back of form.)

Importer Number	Importer Name	Importer Number	Importer Name
		Total number of importer names listed in Section III:	

Principal and surety agree that any charge against the bond under any of the listed names is as though it was made by the principal(s). Principal and surety agree that they are bound to the same extent as if they executed a separate bond covering each set of conditions incorporated by reference into the Customs Regulations into this bond.

If the surety fails to appoint an agent under Title 6, United States Code, Section 7, surety consents to service on the Clerk of any United States District Court or the U.S. Court of International Trade, where suit is brought on this bond. That clerk is to send notice of the service to the surety at:

Mailing Address Requested by the Surety

	Name and Address	Importer No.³		
PRINCIPAL⁴		SIGNATURE⁵		SEAL
PRINCIPAL⁴	Name and Address	Importer No.³ SIGNATURE⁵		SEAL
SURETY⁴·⁶	Name and Address⁶	Surety No.⁷ SIGNATURE⁸		SEAL
SURETY⁴·⁶	Name and Address⁶	Surety No.⁷ SIGNATURE⁸		SEAL
SURETY AGENTS	Name⁹	Identification No.⁹	Name⁹	Identification No.⁹

PART 1—U.S. CUSTOMS

Customs Form 301 (092189)

86

FIGURE 8-3. Customs bond CF 301.

workers, 500,000 steel workers, and 20,000 copper workers were idled, and about 150,000 fabrication workers were out of jobs. The United States set quotas on steel, sugar, petroleum, and meat.

An import quota is a quantity control on certain items for a time period as provided in the HTSUS. The argument for quotas is that they protect U.S. industry and jobs. The threat of quotas also provides incentives for foreign manufacturing here at home.

Buying goods abroad because of lower prices, better quality, or unavailability here increases American consumers' buying power. So a higher standard of living results. While imports provide capital and jobs for foreigners, they also cause domestic price discipline and incentive for innovation.

Arguments against quotas are that they protect high cost and inefficient producers, and cost the U.S. consumer dearly. For the long term, American products must be competitive in the world marketplace. Also, it makes it more difficult to buy quota items. Opponents say that, rather than keeping goods out, quotas actually keep our domestic prices high and guarantee the foreign seller his U.S. market share.

Quotas are used by many governments. Quotas set limits for autos in Italy, France, and Britain. Quotas can be placed into four distinct groupings:

1. Agricultural-type products, under Section 22 of the Agricultural Adjustment Act.
2. National security, under direction of the Department of the Interior.
3. International commodity control agreements, such as for cotton and coffee.
4. Specific industry quotas. Examples are to protect the dairy industry, watches, and steel.

Watches and movements are under control of the Departments of Interior and Commerce. Certain dairy products come under the Department of Agriculture during the quota period.

There are two types of quotas: 1. absolute and 2. tariff-rate. The first, absolute, is the most common and direct, and is known as "first come, first served." It limits by specified number how many can be imported. When the entire quota is filled, no more goods can come in during the quota period. Meantime, warehouse entries may be made pending the reopening.

How does Customs prevent one importer from grabbing all the available quantity at the absolute quota opening? Customs explains it this way, "When the total quantity for which entries filed at the opening of the quota period exceeds the quota, the merchandise is released on a pro rata being the ratio between the quota quantity and the total quantity offered for entry. This assures an equitable distribution of the quota."[2]

---

[2] 1990. Importing into the United States, *U.S. Customs Service Booklet.* March. p. 59.

Some absolute quotas are global, while others apply to certain countries. The following absolute quotas apply to the European Community countries only: candies, apple and pear juice, ale and bear, and white wine.

Some typical absolute quotas are for certain textiles from certain countries and is the most common of quotas. Textile articles such as shirts require a visa (a permission from the foreign government to export). The invoice should be visaed (stamped) by the foreign government.

Others are for sugar, syrups, and molasses, 1701 and 1702 HTSUS. The 1987 Farm Act requires the United States to prop up the sugar industry through a quota instead of subsidies. We use sugar beets, which are more expensive to raise than sugar cane. Costs to consumers are about double in the United States over what the rest of the world pays. An estimate is that this quota costs the consumer $76,000 for each American job in the sugar industry.

The second type of quota is based on tariff-rate. This type provides for imports of a specified quantity of a product at a reduced rate of duty. Any quantity can be imported at any time, but all quantities over the quota ceiling are charged a higher duty. These quotas may be by trade agreement or may be strictly voluntary between countries.

When a quota exists, clearance documents can't be presented until the shipment arrives. When the tariff-rate quota is filled, further entries are at a higher rate. An example of a tariff-rate type quota is tuna fish, item 1604.14.20 of the HTSUS. The Department of Fishery and Wildlife SF 370 and SF 371 forms are used for clearance of tuna fish. Tuna fish is admitted in the early part of the year and quotas are quickly filled.

The Bureau of Customs controls the listing of all commodities subject to quotas and enforces regulations of other government agencies that apply. The list of quota items often changes. For current information, check the Quota Desk at Customs, 1301 Constitution Avenue NW, Washington, D.C. 20229 (202) 566-8592.

Voluntary Restraint

There are voluntary restraint agreements on about one-third of the U.S. market. Their main intent is to make it unlikely that America would impose absolute quotas or take measures to counter. The U.S. Congress is now under intense pressure to stop the erosion of American trade and loss of jobs. A series of trade bills have been resisted by the Administration. Under Japan's voluntary export restraint program, they limit cars and machine tools shipped annually to the United States.

Customs Duty Valuation

A tariff is a "list of duties," a schedule or system of fees. Duties are determined by Customs. They are usually at an "ad valorem" (according to value) rate and are a percentage of the dutiable transaction value. Transaction value is defined as "the price the buyer actually pays the seller." It includes packaging costs and the value of any "Assists" that are not included in the price itself. Customs wants to capture the value of any value added offshore.

Some articles are dutiable at a specific rate of duty, such as so much per pound or barrel. Still others are a combination of both ad valorem and specific rates. An example of compound rate would be a duty of $1 for each item imported plus 10 percent of the item's dutiable value.

Definition of Assists

The buyer is responsible to declare any assist as described below, *if supplied by the buyer* for the supplier's use to produce the goods imported. The reasoning is that such furnished items reduce the supplier's transaction value for the imported items. For Customs to collect the proper duty, assists have to be declared.

Assists include any materials or items that are part of the finished imported item, as well as any supplied tools, equipment, dies, or molds that were used in production. Products consumed in the production of the merchandise are included, as well as design drawings and development work, if done outside the United States, by anyone other than the buyer's fellow company employees.

All assists must be declared on the invoice and other papers used for entry. If separate payments for such assist items were made, they must be summarized on the invoice used for custom purposes. Should this information not be available at the time of entry, assists and the duty due on them should be made known to Customs as soon as possible after entry.

Examination

Before the goods are released, the Customs district or port director may choose to examine the merchandise. Examination may be made on the docks for bulk shipments, at container stations, cargo terminal, or your premises. Examination determines:

- The value of the goods and their dutiable status;
- Whether goods are those that are invoiced;
- Whether the goods were marked with the country of origin or require special marking or labelling and if done properly;
- If any articles are prohibited; and
- Whether the goods are properly invoiced or are more or less than ordered.

Perhaps 5 percent of goods are physically inspected. Certain goods may be weighed or measured. Shortages noted by Customs can reduce the amount of duty levied. If the buyer detects the shortages after entry but before liquidation, an allowance can be made.

What happens if your shipment arrives in a damaged condition? If salvageable, customs clearance based on reduced value is pursued. However, reduction of duty for any articles made of iron or steel being discolored or rusted is not allowed.

Country of Origin Marking Requirements

Section 304 of the Tariff Act states that each imported article is to be marked in "a conspicuous place as legibly, indelibly, and permanently as the nature of the article permits, with the English name of the country of origin, to indicate to the ultimate consumer in the United States the country in which the article was manufactured or produced."

If the article is used in a process or for manufacturing, the manufacturer is the ultimate consumer. This marking must be permanent, and it must be large and legible enough to "be read easily by a person of normal vision." The supplier must use the words, "Made in..." or "Product of...". Adhesive labels aren't recommended, but are okay if approved.

Exempted from individual marking of country of origin are articles that: 1. can't be marked, 2. would be damaged, 3. would be excessively expensive to mark, or 4. entered into warehouse for immediate export. Examples of industrial type exceptions to unit identification are ball bearings, bolts and nuts, chemicals, glass, lumber, paper, watch springs, and wire. Regardless, the outermost containers must be marked.

Failure to mark the items properly can mean a marking duty at time of import. The marking penalty is equal to 10 percent of the customs value of the article. An item marked to induce the public to believe that it was manufactured in a foreign country other than in which it was manufactured is not permitted. Such an article is subject to seizure and forfeiture under Section 42 of the Trade-Mark Act. If you believe your imports can't be marked, get advice from Customs rather than presume it's not needed.

Certificate of Origin

An UNCTAD Certificate of Origin Form A, as seen in Figure 8-4, is often needed for goods more than $1,000 in value. A certificate permits buyers to gain duty-free or reduced rate under the GSP provision or other trade arrangement. To secure reduced tariffs, a minimum of 35 percent of local content is usually required.

At its discretion, Customs may ask for your certificate. The certificate provides you, your company, and the U.S. Customs assurance of the specific country in which the products or goods were manufactured. When required, it is proof of the origin of any materials and labor used to produce the goods. It also helps deter the seller from subcontracting or farming out work without the buyer's knowledge.

Usually, the Certificate of Origin is issued or approved by the chamber of commerce from the shipping country. They are sometimes signed by consulates and trade associations officials. Exporters get the form from their governments.

Revenue Canada   Revenu Canada
Customs and Excise   Douanes et Accise

CANADA — U.S.
FREE TRADE AGREEMENT

EXPORTER'S CERTIFICATE OF ORIGIN

ACCORD DE LIBRE-ÉCHANGE ENTRE
LE CANADA ET LES ÉTATS-UNIS

CERTIFICAT D'ORIGINE DE L'EXPORTATEUR

1 Goods consigned from (Exporter's business name, address, country, tax identification number)
Marchandises en provenance de (nom ou raison sociale, adresse et pays de l'exportateur et son numéro d'identification aux fins de l'impôt)

2 If Blanket Certification : S'il s'agit d'un certificat général, en indiquer la

Effective Date
Date d'entrée en vigueur _____

Expiration Date
Date d'expiration _____

3 Goods consigned to (consignee's name, address, country)
Marchandises expédiées à (nom, adresse et pays du destinataire)

4 Producer's name, address, country, tax identification number (if different from exporter)
(nom, adresse et pays du producteur et son numéro d'identification aux fins de l'impôt (s'ils diffèrent de ceux de l'exportateur)

5 Origin Criteria for goods covered by this Certificate

A. Wholly produced or obtained in Canada or the United States; or

B The goods have been transformed in the United States or Canada so as to be subject

1) to a change in tariff classification as described in the Rules of Annex 301.2 or

2) to a change in tariff classification as described in the Rules of Annex 301.2 and the value of originating materials plus the direct cost of processing in Canada or the United States is not less than 50 percent or as required by Section VI Rule 15 of Annex 301.2 70 per cent of the value of exported goods; or

3) to Rule 5 Section XII of Annex 301.2 or

C No change in tariff classification because goods and parts are provided for in the same tariff subheading or goods were imported in unassembled or disassembled form and were classified pursuant to General Rule of Interpretation 2a) of the Harmonized System; and the value of originating materials plus the direct cost of assembly in Canada or the United States is not less than 50 per cent of the value of exported goods

Critères d'origine pour les marchandises visées par le certificat

A Les marchandises ont été entièrement produites ou obtenues au Canada ou aux États-Unis, ou

B Les marchandises ont subi aux États-Unis ou au Canada une transformation qui

1) entraîne un changement de leur classement tarifaire, prévues dans les règles de l'annexe 301.2, ou

2) entraîne un changement de leur classement tarifaire conforme aux règles de l'annexe 301.2 et ou fait en sorte que la valeur des matières originaires du Canada ou des États-Unis ajoutée au coût direct de leur traitement n'est pas inférieure à 50 p. 100 de leur valeur à l'exportation ou, comme le prévoit la règle 15 de la section VI de l'annexe 301.2 à 70 p. 100 de cette valeur, ou

3) répond aux exigences de la règle 5 de la section XII de l'annexe 301.2 ou

C Aucune modification au classement tarifaire n'est requise parce que les marchandises et leurs parties sont classées dans la même sous-position tarifaire ou qu'elles ont été importées sous forme non montée ou démontée et classées conformément à la règle générale d'interprétation 2a) du Système harmonisé et que la valeur des matières originaires ajoutée au coût direct de leur montage au Canada ou aux États-Unis n'est pas inférieure à 50 p. 100 de leur valeur à l'exportation

6 Special Declaration for textile products, subject to tariff rate quota

A Apparel goods cut and sewn in Canada or the United States from fabric produced or obtained in a third country

B Non-wool fabric and non-wool made-up textile articles, woven or knitted in Canada from yarn produced or obtained in a third country

Déclaration spéciale pour les articles textiles assujettis à des contingents tarifaires

A Vêtements taillés et cousus au Canada ou aux États-Unis dans des tissus produits ou obtenus dans un pays tiers

B Tissus et articles textiles autres qu'en laine tissés ou façonnés au Canada à partir de filés produits ou obtenus dans un pays tiers

Origin Criterion (see fields 5 or 6) Critère d'origine (voir les zones 5 et 6)	8 Description of Goods Désignation des marchandises	Tariff Classification (to six digits) Classement tarifaire (6 premiers chiffres)	9 Gross weight or other quantity Poids brut ou autre quantité	10 Invoice Number(s) and Date(s) Numéro et date de la ou des facture(s)

11 Certification of Origin

I certify that the information and statements herein are correct, and that all the goods were produced in Canada or the United States that they comply with the origin requirements specified for those goods in the Canada - United States Free Trade Agreement; and that further processing or assembly in a third country has not occurred subsequent to processing or assembly in Canada or the United States

I agree to maintain and to present upon request the documentation to support this certification and, if this is a blanket certification, to inform the importer or other appropriate party of any change that would affect the validity of this certification

Certificat d'origine

J'atteste que les renseignements et énoncés fournis dans les présentes sont exacts, que toutes les marchandises ont été produites au Canada ou aux États-Unis, ou elles répondent aux exigences relatives à l'origine prévues dans l'Accord de libre-échange Canada - États-Unis et que tout complément de traitement ou de montage dans un pays tiers n'a pas eu lieu après leur traitement ou montage au Canada ou aux États-Unis

Je conviens de conserver et de produire sur demande les documents à l'appui du présent certificat et, dans le cas d'un certificat général, d'informer l'importateur ou toute autre partie intéressée de tout changement qui influerait sur la validité du certificat en question

This certificate consists of _____ page(s)
Ce certificat comprend _____ page(s)

Place and Date / Lieu et date   Authorized Signature / Signature autorisée   Title / Titre

FIGURE 8-4.   Certificate of origin.

Anyone can buy it from the Director, Technical Assistant Project/GSP, UNCTAD, 1211 Geneva 10, Switzerland.

Appraisement

After entry is made, but before liquidation, the Customs Service finalizes its appraisal decision. To compute the value of shipment for Customs declaration purposes, any foreign currency denoted must be converted to a U.S. dollar amount by using Customs conversion rates. Conversion is per provision 31 U.S.C. 5151. The *date of exportation* is used to certify a rate, regardless of time of payment for the goods themselves. These rates are set by Customs and must be used. For estimation purposes, they are close to the published exchange rates in the New York Times, and so on.

For customs purposes, U.S. Custom exchange rates are certified by the Federal Reserve Bank of New York on the first day of each calendar quarter. If the exchange rates vary more than 5 percent, Customs uses that day's rate.

Liquidation

Duties are not official until "liquidated" (completed) after several weeks or months. Customs has one year from date of entry to liquidate or to tell the importer that the entry is to remain open. Any under- or overpayment is rectified.

Penalties for Improper Declaration for Customs
Periodic inspections and reviews by commodity specialists can uncover errors. What if you make a mistake? Sometimes penalties are imposed to assure proper collections, depending on whether the error was: 1. intentional, 2. gross negligence, or 3. just plain negligence. Whether the importer informs Customs or Customs makes the discovery on its own affects the amount of the penalties. Penalties as high as eight times the normal duty have been reported. Also, the merchandise may be seized to assure payment of the penalty.

However, don't blindly accept penalty charges! They can be reduced. Customs may have incorrect information. Check it out and discuss before paying. In case of fraud, sanctions provides a maximum of two years imprisonment, or a $5,000 fine, or both.

Protests
Importers have the right to disagree with a Customs finding. Should there be disagreement, a protest application Form 19 must be filed within 90 days from the date of liquidation. All customs forms and records used must be retained for at least three years after final liquidation.

In the rare case where the protest fails and the importer still disagrees, the last resort is to file a summons in the U.S. Court of International Trade. Litigation action requires filing within 180 days after denial of your protest.

Customs Fees Charged

Since 1987, a Customs merchandise processing fee (MPF) has been imposed on the value on all imports. Also, fees for travelers from overseas amount to $10 for each arrival except those in transit. This revenue is to help pay for customs and immigration checks.

Much opposition has been raised about the current (1990) 0.17 percent MPF charged. Critics claim that it is unfair to U.S. business, contrary to GATT, and unnecessary, since "In fiscal year 1989, Customs collected $18.6 billion, a return of just over $18 for every dollar appropriated for the Service."[3]

The Customs and Trade Act of 1990 reaffirmed the fee for goods more than $12,300, though it did create a minimum charge of $21 with a cap of $400 that will save large importers money. Goods under $1200 have a tier fee structure: $2 for an automated, non-Customs-prepared entry and $8 for any Customs-prepared.

HOW CUSTOMS BROKERS HELP
IMPORTING BUYERS

For most overseas purchases, the manufacturer or a foreign freight forwarder will arrange to get the product out of the foreign country.

Buyers may handle their own import clearance paperwork, insurance, and follow up. If a buyer has at his or her disposal a staff, he or she may not want outside help. Left alone, however, the buyer may need this aid as he or she begins to deal overseas. You can get rid of all details of the importing transaction. Give the job to a customs broker.

A customs broker making the entry must be licensed by the Treasury Department. The Customs Broker Act of 1984 specifies new licensing provisions that became effective in 1986. Every brokerage house must have at least one individual licensed broker in each of their offices. While not mandated by law, most brokers will require a Power of Attorney CF 5291 from your company. This should be done well in advance of arrival of the first shipment. The customs broker is supposed to provide you with his or her experience. Knowing as much about customs regulations as possible is most helpful to the buyer. However, brokers can't know your business or products as you do.

Upon arrival of goods into the United States, customs brokers arrange to clear

---

[3]1990. Leo, Robert J., AAEI V.P. & Counsel. 10 Reasons to Repeal Customs User Fee. *Global Trade.* October p. 30.

your shipment through U.S. Customs and have the goods delivered to the next carrier. They will see that all documents are executed as required. A customs broker will act as a clearing agent, moving goods through customs.

The practicing broker has experience with transportation, marine insurance, banking requirements, and credit procedures, as well as the rules of Customs. Naturally, he or she has contacts with many others located globally that may be called on as required.

They will help with:

1. Advice about classification and appraisement of merchandise, import tariff law, and regulations. (Most brokers are not well informed about your technical products.)
2. Receive shipping documents, and prepare proper customs release papers.
3. Expedite cargo with steamship and airlines to get fast progress through ports of import.
4. Handle import documentation to clear Customs.
5. Arrange delivery to inland plant or warehouse storage.
6. Arrange necessary bonds required.
7. Provide advice when asked.

Some forwarders and brokers may carry errors and omissions insurance. Therefore, the buyer should try to get restitution if an error causes losses.

How To Pick a Customs Broker

Most buyers will recommend a broker whom he or she uses. Most custom brokers themselves say that most of their new business comes from referrals. However, some competitive importers don't want to suggest a broker to others who import their type merchandise. Failing in any referral search, brokers can be located easily in the local Yellow Pages. They are also listed with the National Customs Brokers and Forwarders Association at 5 World Trade Center, New York, NY 10048.

After locating brokers, and before hiring one, find out if they handle your kind of commodities. Most brokers do not specialize, but they may be unaccustomed to certain terms, such as electronic or technical. If a broker specializes in air shipments at a major airport, he or she may be a poor bet to do a job where the problems are at the Mexican border. In short, a broker should preferably be where the action takes place. Many brokers are diversified and handle all modes of shipment. You want a broker you can locate and talk to when needed. Make sure he or she can be reached quickly.

Fees charged vary from port to port. They are based on volume and type of work done, and are subject to the buyer's negotiation skills. It is a competitive business, and enough volume should make the fee negotiable. Brokers typically charge fees of $75 to $125 per transaction. Sometimes, small air shipments can be handled for as low as $40. While brokers and forwarders should be competitive, it's smart to get several fee prices from time to time, to compare cost.

A warning—don't give money to brokers for them to pay your customs duties or freight charges! Should payment not be made for any reason, you alone are responsible. Customs will bill you along with a penalty for failure to pay. Buyers should either pay the duty directly or give a check to your broker payable to the U.S. Customs Services.

ELECTRONIC DATA INTERCHANGE (EDI)

An array of new computerized systems are being used, from the experimental stage to a variety of operating applications, including transferring bills of lading. The Port of New Orleans was one of the first to inaugurate a computerized customs system, called CRESCENT. Their system is said to track ships and container, check the movement of any hazardous cargo, send the export declaration, and notify the broker of the ship's arrival. Data to brokers lets them speed up the customs process.

ORION is the Port of Charleston's EDI system, which interfaces with U.S. Customs' Automated Manifest System (AMS) Many other ports also have their own systems underway.

Users with the Automated Broker Interface (ABI) can get "paperless" entry using the entry module. Automated Commercial System (ACS) allows entry without CF 3461, as the paperless term only applies to picking up the merchandise. The Entry Summary CF 7501 is still given to Customs afterwards.

A paperwork glut exists as Customs paperwork has more than doubled this decade. An estimate is that about 8 million customs entries are filed annually. U.S. Customs is pushing to automate, and EDI for Administration Commerce and Transportation (EDIFACT) is striving for standardization of trade terms on invoices. Use of EDI should allow shipments to pass through customs in hours, rather than the current days. The experience at the NY/NJ Harbor during the first year of startup was about a 3-day delay to clear paperwork, 48 hours more than the old manual method. As the bugs were worked out, time is now being saved.

Today, about 22 percent of all goods are cleared using EDI. This is projected to be about 30 percent by next year. Automation will allow perhaps 80 percent of the goods to be precleared before arriving in the port. Customs would like a paperless system eventually. This depends on the Automatic Invoice Interface (AII), which ties in with the FCC, FDA, and Fish and Wildlife, which are not now automated. U.S. Customs has decided that electronically documented shipments will be cleared through customs first. This is the incentive for companies to gear up and use modern documentation.

9

U.S. Programs Benefiting the Importing Buyer

Trade policies affect rates of duty charged. Penalties imposed on exporting nations take the form of higher duties that hurt the buyer. In similar fashion, benefits may be given to other nations that give buyers reduced costs. The result is that buying decisions enforce the intended aim to encourage or discourage imports.

The buyer should assure that available benefits to importers are known and used. Among benefits under Customs regulations are Temporary Free Entry, Duty-free Reentry of Goods Sent for Repairs or Replacement, Carnet Entry, and Section 807 Entry.

SPECIAL IMPORTATIONS

Temporary Importation Under Bond (TIB entry) is useful if merchandise is not for domestic sale. Usually, the bond posted will be for double the estimated duty. The item will be exported within the terms of the bond to avoid liquidation damages in the amount of the bond.

When would you use TIB entry? Use it if you want to test an item for supplier qualification. Or an offshore supplier has a special testing device for repairing your purchased parts. Afterwards, you can't sell these items in the United States, but must export or destroy under Customs supervision.

Customs will advise how to destroy the goods. Emphasizing the strict control for disposing items, one customs broker told where they had to use a hammer to break thousands of useless hand mirrors. CF 3495 is sent to customs asking them, "Do you want to examine before we destroy?" This allows Customs to tell you what they want done in advance. Failure to reexport or destroy under Customs supervision incurs a penalty of twice the normal duty.

Duty-free Reentry of Goods Sent for Repairs or Replacement

When exporting materials to be repaired, altered, or replaced, the equipment can be sent under "Registration" to avoid paying duty again upon the items' return to the United States.

A "Certificate of Registration" CF 4455 may be used for materials to be repaired, altered, or replaced. It states, "Duty-free entry is claimed for the described articles as having been exported without benefit of drawback and are returned unchanged except as noted."

Carnet Entry

A small benefit, but one nonetheless, is use of an ATA carnet, which is an international customs document. The ATA carnet's name stands for the French and English "Admission Temporaire—Temporary Admission," and grants temporary entry to many countries without paying duty.

A buyer might use a carnet to take samples abroad to show the quality of product desired, without the need to pay any foreign duties or post bonds. It allows the holder to take merchandise samples or professional equipment temporarily into many foreign countries without making customs entries.

Carnets are issued for a fee by local carnet branches of the ICC, and are honored in 40 countries. U.S. Customs has authorized the ICC's New York office, 1212 Avenue of the Americas, New York, NY 10036 as "the United States issuing and guaranteeing organization." Carnets are valid for up to one year.

Partial Duty Exemption, Section 807

This type of entry takes advantage of low-cost offshore labor and permits a reduction of duty. Assume you make children's dresses, but your domestic costs make you noncompetitive. You precut your cloth to size, and send it to Haiti for finished sewing. Upon return of the dresses, you pay duty only on value added plus freight and insurance to ship there. It works the same if you are sending partially assembled or knocked down parts out of the country to finish. You enter the goods under section 807, Section 9802.00.80 of the HTSUS.

Items are imported the same way as other imported goods. However, the buyer must furnish Customs with details about the assembly operation that is performed abroad. A "Foreign Assemblers' Declaration" is endorsed by the importer.

Add to your purchase order:

"I (name) declare that, to the best of my knowledge and belief, the (your items) were assembled in whole or in part from fabricated components (list and describe) below, which are products of the United States."

In computing the duty, the *full value* of the goods is used. An allowance is made for those items that are U.S. products. Labor and fabrication costs are part of the total costs, along with general and administrative expenses. Any materials and components supplied free to the assembler are computed at their cost plus transportation and insurance to deliver to the offshore assembly plant.

Products may be marked, "Assembled in (country) from U.S. components (or materials)." Country of origin must appear on the documents. There are no restrictions against the assembly using a mixture of foreign components in the assembly. However, only the U.S. supplied component(s) qualify for the duty reduction.

No operation other than assembly is permitted (for example, sewing the cut cloth, soldering, gluing). The normal requirements for labelling, quota, and hazards still apply.

GENERALIZED SYSTEM OF PREFERENCES (GSP)

The GSP is a program for free rates of duties for merchandise from beneficiary developing independent countries to help their economic growth. The United Nations Conference on Trade and Development (UNCTAD) formally approved GSP in 1968. Start up required a waiver in 1971 of Most Favored Nation clause of GATT that forbade discriminatory international trade. Today, 27 countries grant GSP benefits to help developing nations improve their economic status through more exports.

The U.S. GSP began in 1976 and has been extended to July 4, 1993. Items are identified by an "A" in the tariff schedule, which denotes duty-free entry. An "*" placed after the A denotes that merchandise from some nations may be excluded from the exemption.

Under the Generalized System of Preferences, duty-free entry is allowed for more than 3,800 tariff schedule subheadings, from over 130 "Beneficiary Developing Countries" (BDCs). Industrialized countries are encouraged to import from the emerging nations by benefiting from their duty-free treatment.

Among "developing nation" countries benefiting are Argentina, Brazil, Egypt, Haiti, India, Israel, Mexico, Poland, Yugoslavia, and about 110 other countries and 30 territories, many of which are small islands.

The Trade Act of 1974, Tariff Schedule T-146, states, "Whenever an eligible article is imported into customs territory of the U.S. directly from a developing country, it shall receive duty-free treatment...provided that the direct costs of processing operations performed is at least 35% of the approved value of such article at time of its entry into the customs territory of the U.S." Proof of country where manufactured is needed for duty-free entry under GSP.

The economies of the Four Tigers—Hong Kong, South Korea, Taiwan, and

Singapore—grew so fast that they no longer warranted inclusion. Taiwan has no national debt and ran a $13 billion trade surplus with the United States. U.S. imports under GSP rose from $3 billion in 1976 to $18 billion in 1988, dropping to $10 billion in 1989.

The list of items and countries eligible changes often. Buyers should learn if their commodities can be brought into the U.S. duty-free or with special lower tariffs. On the job, the buyer finds out the benefits that may apply under all such agreements by review of the HTSUS.

Items for military contracts are entered duty-free. For other items, unless the item is also duty-free, there are three rates of duty for an item. The HTSUSA (Fig. 9-1) shows differing duties for classes of goods from various countries. Take time to study this figure carefully. On the job, you have to interpret such pages. Let's review the keys to possible lower duties. For example, look at code 8418.61.00 heat pumps. The rate for most favored nations (MFN) also appears in Column 1, under the General heading.

Goods entitled to duty-free treatment or entered at a reduced rate of duty are listed under the Special heading in Column 1. This includes programs such as GSP, Israel Agreement, and so on. A certificate of origin may be required when entering merchandise under the Special heading.

The rate for Communist-bloc countries appears in Column 2. For example, the same item bought under the U.S.-Israeli Agreement would have zero duty, compared to 35 percent if bought from Bulgaria.

BILATERAL AND MULTILATERAL TRADE AGREEMENTS

The most famous of the multinational treaties is the Geneva Accord on Trade and Tariff, which extended the same customs and tariff treatment given to the most favored nation. There are several special agreements of benefit to the American importer. Usually, agreements are geographically grouped. A recent example of a bilateral trade treaty is the 1990 trade agreement between the United States and Chile. A Council on Trade and Investment will meet to reduce tariffs further and increase trade. The United States sells capital goods and agricultural chemicals while Chile ships copper, fruits and vegetables, and wine.

Other examples of multinational treaties are the free trade associations that foster unrestricted trade among its members. Among well-known associations are those countries in the Pacific Rim that formed the Association of South East Asian Nations (ASEAN). Members include Indonesia, Malaysia, the Philippines, Thailand, and Singapore, which are also listed as beneficiaries under GSP. The European Free Trade Association (EFTA) includes Austria, Denmark, Norway, Sweden, Portugal, Switzerland, and the United Kingdom. The Latin American Free Trade Association (LAFTA) includes Argentina, Bolivia, Brazil, Chile, Columbia, Ecu-

HARMONIZED TARIFF SCHEDULE of the United States (1991)

Annotated for Statistical Reporting Purposes

XVI
84-17

Heading/ Subheading	Stat. Suf. & cd	Article Description	Units of Quantity	Rates of Duty — 1 — General	Rates of Duty — 1 — Special	2
8418 (con.)		Refrigerators, freezers and other refrigerating or freezing equipment, electric or other; heat pumps, other than the air conditioning machines of heading 8415; parts thereof (con.):				
8418.30.00	00 3	Freezers of the chest type, not exceeding 800 liters capacity......................	No......	2.9%	Free (A,C,E,IL) 2% (CA)	35%
8418.40.00	00 1	Freezers of the upright type, not exceeding 900 liters capacity......................	No......	2.9%	Free (A,C,E,IL) 2% (CA)	35%
8418.50.00		Other refrigerating or freezing chests, cabinets, display counters, showcases and similar refrigerating or freezing furniture...	....	2.9%	Free (A,E,IL) 2% (CA)	35%
	40 0	Freezing................................	No.			
	80 1	Other..................................	No.			
8418.61.00		Other refrigerating or freezing equipment; heat pumps: Compression type units whose condensers are heat exchangers..........	....	2.9%	Free (A,B,C,E,IL) 2% (CA) 1/	35%
	40 7	Finned coil type....................	No.			
	80 8	Other..............................	No.			
8418.69.00		Other.................................	....	2.9%	Free (A,B,C,E,IL) 2% (CA) 1/	35%
	10 5	Icemaking machines: Self-contained, cube and flake with a capacity not exceeding 227 kg...............	No.			
	15 0	Other.......................	No.			
	20 3	Drinking water coolers, self-contained..........................	No.			
	25 8	Soda fountain and beer dispensing equipment.........................	No.			
	45 4	Centrifugal liquid chilling refrigerating units: Open-type.......................	No.			
	50 6	Hermetic-type...................	No.			
	55 1	Absorption liquid chilling units....	No.			
	60 4	Reciprocating liquid chilling refrigerating units...............	No.			
	90 8	Other refrigerating or freezing equipment: Household.....................	No.			
	95 3	Other........................	No.			
8418.91.00	00 9	Parts: Furniture designed to receive refrigerating or freezing equipment......	X.......	2.9%	Free (A,B,E,IL) 2% (CA)	35%
8418.99.00		Other.................................	....	2.9%	Free (A,B,E,IL) 2% (CA)	35%
	05 6	Refrigeration condensing units: Not exceeding 746 W...........	No.			
	10 9	Exceeding 746 W but not exceeding 2.2 kW..............	No.			
	15 4	Exceeding 2.2 kW but not exceeding 7.5 kW..............	No.			
	20 7	Exceeding 7.5 kW but not exceeding 22.3 kW.............	No.			
	25 2	Exceeding 22.3 kW.............	No.			
	50 0	Other: Parts of combined refrigerator-freezers fitted with separate external doors and parts of household type refrigerators..................	X			
	60 8	Other..........................	X			

1/ Duty suspended on certain articles originating in the territory of Canada. See subheading 9905.84.10.

FIGURE 9-1. Harmonized tariff schedule of the United States.

ador, Mexico, Paraguay, Peru, Uruguay, and Venezuela. The Caribbean Free Trade Association (CARIFTA) members are the United Kingdom's Cook Islands and includes Guyana from South America.

Common Markets

A common market seeks to use a common economic system, taxes, and foster trade enhancement among its members. The European Economic Community (EEC) covers Belgium, France, Germany, Italy, Luxembourg, Netherlands, the United Kingdom, Denmark, Ireland, and Greece.

1992 has been set to further remove many of their trade barriers, customs clearance, and border crossing delays. They have established the European Community Unit (ECU), which is a mix of their member currencies. One of the current stumbling blocks to implementing these changes is the United Kingdom's wanting to keep its pound sterling. Also, Germany's having financial difficulties absorbing East Germany into the fold, and having stayed somewhat aloof of the Gulf War allies could cause delays with full implementation.

Another common market is The Central American Common Market (CACM), which includes Costa Rica, El Salvador, Guatemala, Honduras, and Nicaragua. The Caribbean Common Market (CARICOM) includes Antigua, Bahamas, Barbados, Belize, Dominica, Grenada, Guyana, Jamaica, St. Lucia, St. Vincent, Trinidad and Tobago, and the territory of Montserrat.

Listed below are other important bilateral agreements of use to buyers and importers:

- U.S.-Canada Free Trade Agreement
- Caribbean Basin Initiative Act
- Israel Free Trade Area Agreement

U.S.-Canada Free Trade Agreement

The world's number one trading partnership is between the United States and Canada. While the United States buys slightly more from Japan, Canada reciprocates more making for an excellent mutual exchange. The U.S.-Canada Free Trade Agreement calls for a free trade area and all tariffs to be dropped by January 1, 1999.

The FTA is intended to strengthen and benefit U.S. and Canadian producers and promote productivity, full employment, and friendship. Further, it should contribute to expansion of world trade. Some Canadians and Americans have concerns about the agreement. To allay these, Prime Minister Mulroney often refers to enhanced trade or freer trade, while President Bush talks of fairer, competitive trade or free trade.

Events have changed since the 1911 Canadian Manufacturers Association slogan, "No truck or trade with the Yankees." Removal of some restrictions on U.S. imports that Canada proposed in 1985 was believed by proponents to be helpful to Canadian industry in preserving businesses and jobs. Canada wants the benefits of open trade, but also wants to keep its cherished independence. One common force for accommodation is the knowledge that the EEC has unified trade barriers facing the outside world. Proponents feel that North America needs a united approach.

The weakness of the Canadian dollar makes up for the relative inefficiency of many Canadian companies versus their U.S. competition. Canada shuns equity of the two dollars, for their manufacturing could be at a disadvantage.

Total Canadian world trade for 1990 was $190 billion. Exports were about $100 billion and imports $90 billion. 16 percent of Canadian jobs are said to be U.S. export–dependant. Exports solely to America are $66 billion, almost 70 percent of all Canada's exports.

The cross-border movement of goods has increased as expected. During 1989 exports from the United States to Canada increased by 3 percent, while imports from Canada remained about even. In 1990, greater progress is expected. Some items bought by U.S. buyers are: automobiles (which are one-third of all U.S. trade), newsprint, lumber, wood pulp, minerals, fish, and beverages. Canada buys from the United States the following: coal, iron and steel, some cars and parts, fruits, cotton, textiles, and petroleum and chemical products.

To claim benefits under this FTA, simply add the letters "CA" as a suffix to the HTSUS number on the CF 7501 entry form. CA stands for Canadian Agreement; C is the Agreement on Trade for Civil Aircraft and B is the Auto Production Act.

General Rules of Origin define those items that qualify for FTA benefits. The Exporter's Certificate of Origin, Customs Form 353, used by Americans, and a similar bilingual form for Canadians is important. While it does not have to be used for entry, it must be produced upon Customs request.

One of the Rules of Origin requires that 50 percent of the value of the goods must be either U.S. or Canadian in origin to get duty-free or special duty under this agreement. These are elaborate rules detailing phased tariff reductions of specific items. The buyer will want to get a copy of this agreement, published by Customs.

The United States is now negotiating a similar trade agreement with Mexico. The goal is to bring together American capital and technology with Mexican labor. Mexico can be an attractive alternative to the Pacific Rim. Their low labor rates and dropped import licenses, as well as a gradual reduction of corporate taxes to 35 percent by 1991, all help. Also, customs duties are substantially reduced. Mexico now allows 100 percent foreign-owned investment for businesses of $100 million or less in assets.

The President's Enterprise for the Americas initiative seeks to expand the U.S.-Canadian type agreement throughout North, Central, and South America. Since Canada wants to be included in Mexican trade, plans have begun on a North American FTA.

The Caribbean Basin Initiative (CBI)

The Caribbean Basin Economic Recovery Act, known as CBI, was designed to help 22 smaller nations, by eliminating duties on U.S. buys. The CBI was enacted during 1984 and expires September 30, 1999, unless extended. "E" is the symbol in the Special column of the HTSUS, denoting when it applies. Most products from the area are eligible, but must meet a 35 percent of appraised value requirement. An asterisk after the E denotes that the item may be excluded from free-duty status from some of the countries.

This act may not have given a big boost to Caribbean imports because many of the countries were already entering free under GSP. However, other similar agreements with Columbia, Ecuador and Bolivia, and Venezuela that are not in the CBI are in the negotiation stage.

Israel Free Trade Area Agreement

The Israel agreement is another similar deal signed in 1985 that calls for elimination of most tariffs within 10 years. The letter(s) "I" or "IL" appearing in the HTSUS Special column denotes that, if the item is imported from Israel, it's duty-free or has a reduced rate of duty. The "I" is added as a prefix to the HTSUS on CF 7501 entry document.

An item is a "Product of Israel" if it meets the 35 percent rule. Like other FTAs, the formal Certificate of Origin, Form A is not required, but must be produced if requested by Customs.

Transfer Pricing An Issue

As with any agreement, fairness will keep it productive for both parties. Neither party wants something bought from an offshore country to be treated as a native product. Now, transfer pricing (how prices are set crossing countries borders) are a rising concern. Some foreign companies reportedly declare little profit in the United States.

The U.S. Internal Revenue Service worries that high prices for the transfer of goods may allow little U.S. tax revenue. The IRS estimated that of $450 billion of products sold by foreign-based suppliers in 1990, they reported losses of $1.5 billion.[1]

Here is how an offshore supplier's transfer pricing to evade taxes might work. A German company makes an item for $10 and sells it for $10 to its subsidiary in Ireland. Selling at no profit avoids Germany's 48-percent tax. The Irish subsidiary sells the item for $20 to another U.S. subsidiary and pays 4-percent tax on $10

---

[1]Martz, Larry, and Rich Thomas. 1991. The corporate shell game. *Newsweek*. April 15. p. 48.

profit, or 40 cents. In turn, the U.S. subsidiary sells the item for $20, its fair market value. No U.S. profit, so no 34-percent taxes due. All the money is made by the Irish, who "lend" money to the United States for future growth!

Conversely, if transfer prices are too low, they might damage U.S. ability to compete. The World Trade Institute, One World Trade Center, New York, NY. has a special program on this pricing issue. The aim is to lessen future fair market pricing disputes.

FOREIGN TRADE ZONES AND SUBZONES

Duty-free entry into the United States is used where goods are moving on to a free trade zone (FTZ). When the entry is made, you or your broker files Application for Foreign Trade Zone Admission and/or Status Designation, CF 214 (Fig. 9-2). This form is signed by the District Director of Customs and the zone proprietor, authorizing transfer and under what conditions.

Technically, an FTZ is a secured site legally considered outside a nation's customs territory. Goods can be brought into the zone without duty. Goods within an FTZ, for business purposes, remains within the International Zone of Commerce. There is no time limit about how long you may keep goods in a zone.

The *prime aim is to create American jobs*. The Foreign Trade Zones Act of 1934 allowed buyers to make use of a much neglected buying tool. Many buyers fail to make use of zones because they don't know how they work. Should the merchandise be reexported, duty is not levied. Another advantage is the cash savings as funds are freed. Duty drawback, while a profitable activity, is not necessary, when an FTZ is used.

Zones are used by both importers and exporters. They allow a U.S. manufacturer to produce some portion of their products outside the United States, import them duty-free into the trade zone, and finish them using domestic labor and parts. The products are then reexported without paying any duty. With customs approval, it is possible for foreign machinery to be temporarily removed from a zone without formal entry for the performance of certain limited operations. Afterwards, the machinery is returned into the same zone with the same status as when removed.

FTZs are sizable. There are about 175 FTZs (Appendix B) now in use within the United States, with perhaps another 50 applications being processed. 14,000 people are employed in these zones. About $15 billion flows through them. 40 percent of goods are said to be exported from the zones, with the balance of 60 percent ultimately being imported into the United States.

The U.S. Foreign Trade Zones Board is overseen by three members. The chair is the U.S. Secretary of Commerce. The other two members are the Secretary of the Treasury and the Secretary of the Army (because most deep water ports were built and maintained by the U.S. Army Corps of Engineers). Alternate delegates are appointed, by the above three, to the board.

FORM APPROVED. OMB NO. 1515-0086

CENSUS USE ONLY	DEPARTMENT OF THE TREASURY UNITED STATES CUSTOMS SERVICE APPLICATION FOR FOREIGN TRADE ZONE ADMISSION AND/OR STATUS DESIGNATION 146.12-15, 146.21-22, 146.25, Customs Regulations 400.800, Foreign Trade Zone Board Regulations	1. ZONE NO. AND LOCATION (Address)	
		2. DISTRICT/PORT CODE	

3. IMPORTING VESSEL (& FLAG)/OTHER CARRIER		4. EXPORT DATE	5. IMPORT DATE	6. ZONE LOT NO.	
7. U.S. PORT OF UNLADING		8. FOREIGN PORT OF LADING		9. BILL OF LADING/AWB NO.	10. INWARD M'FEST NO.
11. INBOND CARRIER		12. I.T. NO. AND DATE		13. I.T. FROM (Port)	

14. STATISTICAL INFORMATION FURNISHED DIRECTLY TO BUREAU OF CENSUS BY APPLICANT?　☐ YES　☐ NO

15. NO. OF PACKAGES	16. MARKS, NOS. AND COUNTRY OF ORIGIN	17. DESCRIPTION OF MERCHANDISE	18. TSUSA NO.	19. QUANTITY (TSUSA)	20. GROSS WEIGHT	21. SEPARATE PEXT VALUE & AGGR CHGS.

22. I hereby apply for admission of the above merchandise into the Foreign Trade Zone. I declare to the best of my knowledge and belief that the above merchandise is not prohibited entry into the Foreign Trade Zone within the meaning of section 3 of the Foreign Trade Zones Act of 1934, as amended, sections and 141.11, Customs Regulations, and section 400.801, Foreign Trade Zones Board Regulations.

23. I hereby apply for the status designation indicated:

☐ NONPRIVILEGED FOREIGN　☐ PRIVILEGED DOMESTIC　☐ NONPRIVILEGED DOMESTIC　☐ ZONE RESTRICTED

☐ PRIVILEGED FOREIGN: There is filed herewith a Zone Customs entry in triplicate in connection with this application for privileged foreign status.

24. APPLICANT FIRM NAME	25. BY (Signature)	26. TITLE	27. DATE
F.T.Z. AGREES TO RECEIVE MERCHANDISE INTO THE ZONE	28. FOR THE F.T.Z. (Signature)	29. TITLE	30. DATE

PERMIT	Permission is hereby granted to transfer the above merchandise into the Zone.	31. DISTRICT DIRECTOR OF CUSTOMS: BY (Signature)	32. TITLE	33. DATE
PERMIT	The above merchandise has been granted the requested status.	34. DISTRICT DIRECTOR OF CUSTOMS: BY (Signature)	35. TITLE	36. DATE

PERMIT TO TRANSFER	37. The goods described herein are authorized to be transferred:　☐ without exception　☐ except as noted below			
	38. CUSTOMS OFFICER AT STATION (Signature)	39. TITLE	40. STATION	41. DATE
	42. RECEIVED FOR TRANSFER TO ZONE (Driver's Signature)	43. CARTMAN	44. CHL NO.	45. DATE

CUSTOMS REPORT OF MERCHANDISE RECEIVED AT ZONE	46. To the District Director of Customs: The above merchandise was received at the Zone on the date shown except as noted below:		
	47. CUSTOMS OFFICER AT STATION (Signature)	48. TITLE	49. DATE

Paperwork Reduction Act Notice on Reverse)

GPO 946-691

Customs Form 214 (10-09-81)

FIGURE 9-2.　Application for foreign trade zone admission CF 214.

Specialists located at customs offices or ports of entry can provide on-the-spot information about a trade zone in their area of interest. Questions should be directed to your district Director of Customs.

A listing of current foreign trade zones in Appendix B shows location of each U.S. zone. You may want to delve further into one located nearby for your use. For a copy of the latest listing, get "Annual Report of Foreign Trade Zones." It lists the merchandise imported into them and operators names, addresses and phone numbers. Write to: Foreign Trade Zones Board, Department of Commerce, Washington, D.C. 20230.

Look at all the events that can be done to your buys within these zones. Goods may be stored, exhibited, assembled, processed, sorted, manufactured, repaired or altered, and repackaged—all without paying duties or taxes, until the goods are moved into a country's customs territory. Any duty then due is only on the import value.

Another example of use might be to save transport costs by shipping unassembled furniture or machinery into the FTZ. After assembly, they're shipped to nearby users or consumers. For example, your company wants to import components but control the final assembly process. By bringing in components of special ovens that may carry a higher duty than finished ovens, and assembling in the zone before importing into the country, the *lower duty is selected*. An example is assembled watches from Taiwan that are uncased for reassembly after import into U.S. territory.

An important feature of an FTZ is to have goods available for immediate delivery. Say you ship foreign-made goods out of a warehouse over time. By bringing the goods into the zone and paying duty as the goods are withdrawn, the payment is stretched out. Of course, the cost of zone storage is usually higher versus storage in the company's own plant. This has to be weighed.

Suppose a fragile item has considerable losses in transit or storage by liquid evaporation or rapid deterioration. By culling, sorting, and so forth, you'd pay duty only on what you accept.

If your company buys several electronic components and simply assembles into your control box, why pay duty and then claim drawback upon exportation? Any domestic items taken into a zone to be incorporated into your product is reentered to "customs territory" free of duty or tax.

Every port of entry may have a zone within which any state inventory taxes are waived. Typical is the Greater Syracuse Foreign Trade Zone, Ltd., the Syracuse Chamber of Commerce started in 1981. A 64,000-foot warehouse is managed by a warehouse operator.

Subzones are smaller locations that may be owned by a city or a specific company to create jobs. Subzones of Zone 90, Onondaga County (Greater Syracuse) FTZ, were created in 1985 at two area companies—Chrysler/GM joint-venture New Process Gear Division and Smith Corona Corp. This activity allowed

and their overseas trade and be more competitive when competing with
~ ......s.

Foreign Countries Use FTZs

The Japanese-owned U.S. plants are making use of these zones too. Automotive plants in California, Ohio, and Tennessee, where Toyota, Honda, and Nissan are located, got these concessions to locate there.

FTZs are not restricted to the United States. Perhaps four hundred exist globally. Other countries used them before we did. Germany, France, and many others use them extensively. Developing countries use them to encourage foreign trade within their borders. For example, the Turkish free trade zones advertise that they provide "access to the most dynamic, liberal and stable economy in the Eastern Mediterranean." Their FTZs are located at Turkish ports Mersin and Antalya, on the northern shore of the Mediterranean Sea.

Buyers can use trade zones to improve their companies' cash flow and reduce costs, too. For example, say you buy polished brass lamp castings from India. Your company modifies and reships to Europe. The changes are to drill two 1-inch diameter holes to allow wires to pass through after attaching the socket. Different designs dictate where the holes are drilled. The lamps are noncompetitive in Europe if made in the United States. By shipping the brass into an FTZ in Turkey, and sending someone in to drill the holes, the cost is greatly reduced. Repacked into proper containers with correct language labels, the finished lamps can be shipped throughout Europe without any U.S. or Turkish duty due. Of course, the lamp may still be dutiable to the customer at its final destination.

DUTY DRAWBACK SAVINGS

Another benefit that results only *after duty has been previously paid* is termed "drawback". Drawback is an old concept going back to the U.S. Tariff Act of 1789, which was enacted by the First Congress. It's still in effect. Its purpose has always been to encourage American commerce or manufacturing. It enables a manufacturer to compete in foreign markets without having the duty as part of his product costs.

Drawback is covered under Customs Law, 19 U.S.C. Section 1313. This may be studied by anyone about to begin a new program of drawback. What is drawback? It's a refund on U.S. Customs duties paid upon importing materials or goods that are at later date sold abroad. Under drawback, 99 percent of the amount of duty paid can be recovered. The 1 percent is retained by Customs to defray their costs.

How much profit is your company giving up because of failure to use duty drawback? "Department of Commerce estimated that only $300 million was paid out last year (1989), while reexports should have generated $3 billion."[2] It's estimated that only 10 percent of U.S. companies take advantage of the program to get credit for such duties paid that can be refunded.

Few today are the U.S.-produced items that lack certain foreign produced components or items. Larger companies reclaim, but from the author's seminar experiences, few people in smaller and medium-sized companies have been exposed to the act. Some American buyers also forget that Canada is a "foreign country" when applying drawback.

Just who is eligible to collect those dollars in drawback? Any buyer or importer who: 1. exports items bought offshore, or 2. manufactures using items from offshore and then sells his or her product abroad. Also, a manufacturer or exporter who: 1. buys duty-paid items from an importer, 2. exports finished articles that contain imported portions. or 3. buys domestic items that are produced from some or all imported materials.

The buyer normally has up to three years to file a claim. The product might have been stored in a warehouse up to three years before leaving the United States. Five years is the maximum time that can pass between the original buy and reexporting the final product. This time limit is not extended.

Because a drawback system costs money to operate, it pays to first do an economic feasibility study. Data input is required from purchasing, sales, export operations, finance, and production. To obtain drawback, a proposal is filed with the Regional Commissioner of Customs, and the Drawback and Bonds Branch of Customs, 1301 Constitution Avenue, N.W., Washington D.C. 20229. Your proposal and the Customs approval letter are termed a drawback contract. For some items, steel, and component parts, submission of a formal proposal is not required.

To start the collection process, proof of importation, receipt, or use is required. *CF 7501* Entry form is used as a certificate of delivery of imported goods and is one of the acceptable proofs. Proof of receipt must show quantities, date received, and payment of duty.

Another "Proof of Use" used is the buyer's company monthly inventory reports or dated production schedule. Other documentation usually required includes:

1. Notice of Exportation of Articles with benefit of Drawback CF 7511-B (filed by freight forwarder with Customs at the Port where the export took place);
2. Certificate of Manufacture and Delivery CF 7577, A or B;
3. Drawback Entry for Exported Articles, CF 7573 (used where #3 above is used); and
4. Drawback Entry and Certificate of Manufacture for Exported Articles CF

---

[2]1990. Milosh, Eugene J. AAEI-Customs alliance signals smoother sailing for business. *Global Trade*. October p. 20.

7575 A or B (used where combined entry and an abstract from manufacturing record is enough).

Manufacturing Drawback

Duty drawback under Direct Identification can result when the exported product is made from specific imported material. Drawback is payable to the exporter of record, who has the right to claim, unless the manufacturer reserves the right to claim drawback himself. Drawback is designed to assist a manufacturer to be competitive. To do so, the manufacturer must know, prior to his contract, that the drawback is obtainable. For manufacturing drawback entry use CF 331 (Fig. 9-3). The reverse side (not shown) is for declarations and signatures.

Let's consider an example. Say that a Pennsylvania stamping plant imports hot-rolled steel for its stampings. It then ships to a Virginia plant that manufactures and in turn exports its finished product overseas. The Virginia plant is entitled to recover the duties paid originally by the Pennsylvania plant, unless the stamping plant gets concurrence that they can collect the drawback. Usually, since the importer has the data to proof import duties paid and the exporter has the data to prove export, the two parties team up to gain the drawback.

In 1958, drawback was expanded when the law allowed an exporting U.S. firm to substitute "in like kind" an American-made product of the same kind and quality as the import. This is called functional equivalence or substitution drawback. It doesn't matter whether the actual imported merchandise or the domestic is used for export. This makes it possible to obtain drawback advantage without maintaining separate inventories.

Same Condition Drawback

Goods brought in that do not conform to specifications are eligible for drawback when returned. This is Same Condition Drawback and does not have to be applied for in advance. A drawback entry is made on Customs Form 7539 "J" (reverse side of "C") shown in Figure 9-4. The form can be checked as either "Exported in the same condition as when imported," or "Destroyed under Customs Supervision."

This form certifies that duty has been paid and that the merchandise is the same in quantity, quality, value, package, pieces, and so forth, and no refund has been made by drawback or otherwise. The customs official will execute and sign this form, initiating your Net Drawback to be refunded.

Approved through 10/31/88 OMB No. 1515-0148.

DEPARTMENT OF THE TREASURY
UNITED STATES CUSTOMS SERVICE

**MANUFACTURING DRAWBACK
ENTRY ᴬᴺᴰ/ᴼᴿ CERTIFICATE**

19 CFR 191

Section I		
Type of Document	A. ☐ DRAWBACK ENTRY FOR EXPORTED ARTICLES (ENTRY)	1. NUMBER
	B. ☐ CERTIFICATE OF MANUFACTURE AND DELIVERY (CM)	1. NUMBER
	C. ☐ CERTIFICATE OF DELIVERY OF IMPORTED MDSE. (CD)	1. NUMBER
		2. DATE DOCUMENT FILED (MMDDYY)

II. ENTRY (Claim) RECORD

3. ENTRY TYPE CODE	4. PORT CODE	5. CLAIMANT (Importer) ID No.	6. REFERENCE No.	7. FILED BY

8. ☐	APPLYING FOR ACCELERATED PAYMENT (Complete Items 10-14.)	9. ☐	AUTHORIZED FOR EXPORTER'S SUMMARY PROCEDURE (Complete Items 10 and 11.)

10. BOND NO.	11. BOND TYPE CODE	12. DUTY REFUND $	13. I.R. TAX REFUND $	14. CLAIMED TOTAL REFUND

III. AUTHORIZATION | FILED IN COMPLIANCE WITH 19 CFR 191 | 15. PURSUANT TO 19 U.S.C. 1313 (Indicated Below) OR 19 U.S.C. 1309(b) (Indicated Below) ☐a ☐b ☐d ☐e ☐f ☐g ☐h | 16. T.D. No./APPROVAL

IV. IMPORTED DUTY-PAID MERCHANDISE OR DRAWBACK PRODUCTS

17. DESCRIPTION (Quantity, Kind, and Quality)

18. IMPORT ENTRY NUMBER(S)	19. DATE:		20. PORT WHERE FILED	21. QUANTITY DESIGNATED	22. IMPORTED BY	23. IF 1313(b), DATE:		24. CM/CD NUMBER
	19a. OF IMPORT	19b. OF LIQUIDATION				23a. REC'D AT FACTORY	23b. USED IN MFR.	

25. VALUE AT FACTORY	26. QUANTITY OF WASTE, IF ANY	27. FACTORY VALUE OF WASTE

28. QUANTITY/DESCRIPTION OF MERCHANDISE USED

29. QUANTITY/DESCRIPTION OF ARTICLE(S) PRODUCED	30. DATE PRODUCED	PLEASE CONTINUE ON BACK OF FORM.

CUSTOMS USE ONLY

USE ITEMS 31-35 TO DESIGNATE A CM OR CD.

31. BEGINNING QUANTITY	32. CHARGED QUANTITY	33. BALANCE	34. DRAWBACK ENTRY NO., CM, or CD NO. TO WHICH CHARGED	35. GROSS PER UNIT DRAWBACK

SELECTIVITY	ACCELERATED		LIQUIDATED	
	I.R. TAX AMOUNT: $		I.R. TAX AMOUNT: $	
LIQUIDATOR CODE (INITIALS)	DUTY AMOUNT: $		DUTY AMOUNT: $	
	TOTAL AMOUNT: $		TOTAL AMT: $	

SEE BACK OF FORM FOR PAPERWORK REDUCTION ACT NOTICE.   Customs Form 331 (052285)

FIGURE 9-3. Manufacturing drawback entry and/or certificate CF 331.

DEPARTMENT OF THE TREASURY
UNITED STATES CUSTOMS SERVICE

**DRAWBACK ENTRY COVERING
SAME CONDITION MERCHANDISE**

19 CFR 191.2, 181.4, 191.141, 191.156, 191.165

OMB NO 1515-0020

1. Drawback Entry No.

2. Drawback Entry Date

3. Location of Merchandise (Pier, etc.)	4. Exporting Carrier		5. Port of Exportation (Code)	6. Ultimate Port of Destination
7. Name of Person or Business Paying Duty	8. Importer of Record Name		9. Imp. of Rec. ID No.	10. Processing District/Port (Code)
11. Importing Carrier		12. Port of Importation	13. Date of Importation	14. Date Released by Customs

★	15. MARKS AND NUMBERS OF PACKAGES	16. QUANTITY	17. DESCRIPTION OF MERCHANDISE	18. VALUE	19. DUTY PAID
IMP.					
EXP.					

20. In Compliance with 19 USC 1313 (J) I declare that the merchandise was not used and that it was or will be: ☐ Exported in the same condition as when imported OR ☐ Destroyed under Customs supervision

declare that the indicated duty was paid on the merchandise described in this entry, that it is to be or was exported to the country indicated, and that it is not to be consumed or retained within the limits of the United States or its possessions; I further declare that: to the best of my knowledge and belief the said merchandise is the same in quantity, quality, value package pieces etc. except as noted or Affidavit as specified in this document; that no allowance or reduction of duties has been made, and that no part of the duties paid has been refunded by way of drawback or otherwise

21. Signature of Declarant	22. Date	23. Name and Address of Declarant

24. Name of Firm/Address

25. Check any that apply: ☐ Accelerated Payment Requested ☐ Filed Under Exporter's Summary Procedure ☐ Proof of Exportation Attached

We hereby authorize the below named person to make entry and collect drawback on the goods described above

26. Name of Person Authorized to Collect Drawback (if other than exporter)	27. Address
28. Signature of Exporter	29. Date	30. Name and Address of Exporter

31. AFFIDAVIT

The undersigned hereby certifies that the merchandise herein described is the same and in the same condition as that merchandise imported under Consumption

Entry No. _____ at _____ on _____, and the undersigned further certifies that this

merchandise was not subjected to any process of manufacture or other operation except the following allowable incidental operations: _____

The subject merchandise will be destroyed under Customs supervision or exported at _____ on or about _____
The undersigned consents and agrees to keep open its factory and/or place of business and to keep records relative to this transaction available for examination at all reasonable hours by authorized Government officers, for a period of 3 years from the date of payment of the drawback claim. The undersigned is fully aware of the sanctions provided in 18 U.S.C. 1001 and 18 U.S.C. 550.

32. Date	33. Signature/Title/Company Name

ENTRY RECORD

34. Claimant ID No.	35. Reference No.	36. Duty Drawback (Acc.)	37. I.R. Drawback (Acc.)	38. TYPE CODES Entry 42 Bond	39. Bond No.	40. Port Code
41. Import Entry No.(s)		Date(s)			42. Import Entry Liq. Date(s). If Known	

CUSTOMS USE ONLY

STATEMENT OF EXAMINING OFFICER

43. ☐ Prior notice of intent to export is hereby waived.	44. ☐ Customs has decided not to examine the merchandise and it may now be exported	45. ☐ CF 3499 attached

46. ☐ Customs examination is required:

47. Location of Examination

48. Date of Examination

49. Location of Goods if to be destroyed

50. ☐ I have examined the merchandise and found it to be the same merchandise described above, in the same condition as imported, or changed in condition as allowed by law

52. Title of Examining Officer

51. ☐ Same condition drawback cannot be authorized for the following reason(s):

53. Signature of Examining Officer and Date

LADING REPORT

54. Date Laden	55. Port Code	56. Carrier
57. Destination	58. Exceptions	

I certify that the packages described above were laden for export.

59. Signature of Lading Officer	60. Date

LIQUIDATION DATA

	61. Duty Paid $		62. I.R. Tax Paid $	63. Liq. Date
		ACCELERATED	NOT ACCELERATED	
64. Gross Drawback	$		$	68. ☐ REFUND
65. Less 1%	$		$	69. ☐ INCREASE
66. Less Acc Drawback Refund	$			70. ☐ NO CHANGE
67. Net Drawback	$		$	71. Liq. Code/Initials

★Attach Additional Sheets, if Necessary

"J" Side

Customs Form 7539 (032384)

FIGURE 9-4.   Same condition drawback entry "J" CF 7539.

Rejected Merchandise Drawback

To recover duty already paid for rejected goods that do not conform to specifications and are to be returned to the seller, use side "C" (reverse side of "J") of Customs Form 7539 (Fig. 9-5). This return must be within 90 days of receival, with an extension for good cause, that must be in writing.

BENEFITS FROM FOREIGN GOVERNMENTS

Recall that benefits given to offshore suppliers by their governments to encourage exports often result in benefits to American buyers. Ask if your supplier has access to subsidies or reduced taxes. Or does their country offer insurance covering exchange rate risks? Alert buyers will find enticements to buy offshore. A few examples follow:

"Import Financing" are provisions for preferential finance that exists for importation of manufactured goods from Brazil's government under FINEX. Mexico's Fomex programs also encourage import of their goods, and Mexico's Maquiladora program is an unqualified success.

A Maquiladora is a Mexican-located company that, under Mexican law, may be 100 percent foreign owned. The Mexican border town is no longer exclusively an American venture. Japan's dozen plants are far below the 750 U.S. border plants that import U.S. components duty-free and then reexport assembled products that are taxed on value added only. Mexico's weak economy allows labor rates that are far lower versus Asia's today. Sony operates a TV plant in Tijuana, and Sanyo Electric is doubling its 7-year-old plant, making small refrigerators and electric fans for the United States.

Over 1,400 Maquiladora plants exist that are owned by companies from the United States, Japan, Sweden, France, Canada, Taiwan, Hong Kong, and Korea. Sometimes they're joint ventures. They can be set up anywhere except Mexico City.

Mexican workers, mostly women, now earn just under $1/hr. The Mexican "maquiladora" approach fits into the supply system of many American companies. Components and subassemblies that are made in the United States by sophisticated technology can be shipped into Mexico duty-free for final assembly. Upon completion, the products are returned to the United States for sale. Any duty charged will only apply to the "value added" value of the labor. Such companies can import under bond, free of Mexican duties, all the machinery and tools they use to make anything for export from Mexico.

An added advantage is that the U.S. company now has duty-free access to the Mexican market for part of the output. However, if items are sold in Mexico, a special permit is needed, as there are restrictions as to where these items may be sold there.

DEPARTMENT OF THE TREASURY
UNITED STATES CUSTOMS SERVICE

DRAWBACK ENTRY COVERING REJECTED MERCHANDISE

OMB NO 1515-0020

1 Drawback Entry No.

2 Drawback Entry Date

19 CFR 191.2 191.4 191.142 191.165

3 Location of Merchandise (Pier, etc.)	4 Exporting Carrier		5 Port of Exportation (Code)	6 Ultimate Port of Destination
7 Name of Person or Business Paying Duty	8 Importer of Record Name		9 Imp of Rec ID No	10 Processing District/Port (Code)
11 Importing Carrier		12 Port of Importation	13 Date of Importation	14 Date Released by Customs

★	15. MARKS AND NUMBERS OF PACKAGES	16. QUANTITY	17. DESCRIPTION OF MERCHANDISE	18. VALUE	19. DUTY PAID
IMPORTED					
EXPORTED					

20. ☐ The merchandise does not conform to sample or specifications in the following particulars (Submit samples or specifications if available).

21. ☐ The merchandise was shipped without consent of the consignee.

I declare that duty (as specified above) was paid on the merchandise described in this entry and that the merchandise is to be exported to the country indicated, and is not to be consumed or relanded within the limits of the United States or its possessions. I further declare that, to the best of my knowledge and belief, the said merchandise is the same in quantity, quality, value and package, as specified in this entry, that no allowance nor reduction of duties has been made, and that no part of the duties paid has been refunded by way of drawback or otherwise.

22 Signature of Declarant	23 Date	24 Name and Address of Declarant

25 Name of Firm/Address	26 Import Entry Liq Date, If Known

We hereby authorize the below-named person to make entry and collect drawback on the goods described above

27 Name of Person Authorized to Collect Drawback (if other than exporter)	28 Address

29 Signature of Exporter	30 Date	31 Name and Address of Exporter

Entry Record	32 Claimant's Name	33 Claimant's ID No.	34 Ref No. (If Applicable)	35 Import Entry No.	36 Entry Date	37. Codes		
						Entry 43	Bond	Port

CUSTOMS USE ONLY

EXAMINATION

PACKAGES DESCRIBED ABOVE RECEIVED IN CUSTOMS CUSTODY.

38 Date received in Customs	39 District and Port	40 Exceptions

41. I found that the merchandise ☐ does ☐ does not bear evidence of deterioration, and ☐ does ☐ does not bear evidence of having been in use since release from Customs custody. I have examined the merchandise and found it to be identical to the merchandise described above, except as follows: (Item 40) →

42. The merchandise ☐ does ☐ does not conform to sample or specifications for which the order was placed. (This item to be completed only when claim is made of failure to conform to sample or specifications).

43 Date	44 Signature of Examining Officer/Title

LADING REPORT

45 Date Laden	46 Port Code	47 Port of Destination	48 Exceptions

49 Carrier

I certify that the packages described above were laden for export.

50 Signature of Lading Officer	51 Date

LIQUIDATION

Liquidation Data   Net Drawback

52 Liq Date	53 Gross Drawback $	54 If Manual, Issued To
55 Reliq Date	56 Less 1% $	Paperwork Reduction Act of 1980—Notice. We request the information on this form to enforce the laws of the United States, to fulfill the Customs Regulations, to ensure that the claimant is entitled to drawback, and to have the necessary information which permits Customs to calculate and refund (or increase) the correct amount of duty and/or tax. Your response is mandatory and to your benefit.
57 Liq Code/Initials	58 Net Drawback $	59 ☐ Refund ☐ No Change

RETURN THIS FORM TO THE DISTRICT NAMED ABOVE.

★ Attach Additional Sheets, If Necessary

"C" Side

★ U.S. GPO: 1989-262-001/02764

Customs Form 7539 (032384)

FIGURE 9-5. Rejected merchandise drawback entry "C" CF 7539.

10

Methods of Payment

"You know we always pay our bills after we get an invoice," a perplexed buyer exclaimed to another. "But this offshore supplier says it will collect by writing their own check. Hey, what gives?"

This offshore supplier, like many others in Far East countries, wants an alternative payment method called "Letter of Credit" (L/C). Most European and some South American suppliers don't wait for buyers to pay by invoice. Rather, they present a draft to a bank that triggers payment, against the buyer's funds.

A draft is simply a check-like form drawn on a bank. This is called "payment by collection," a method that is less expensive than a formal letter of credit. Under both of these payment terms, the supplier will save money and gain certain advantages. Before you automatically accept any credit terms, remember that payment terms of any kind are negotiable. Before you negotiate anything, pause to consider possible payment options available and their benefits to you.

The offshore supplier prefers payment before shipping (preferably cash). Most buyers would prefer to pay after they use or sell the goods. This is known as consignment. When you pay an invoice after you receive the goods, it's known as open account.

Creditworthiness becomes a dominant issue in offshore buys. Several credit payment methods built on the concept of "constructive delivery" are used to break that standoff between buyer and seller. Banks play the role of giving their assurance of payment, provided the supplier presents certain documents as stipulated in the buyer's conditions.

PROVISIONS AND DEFINITIONS

Documentary credits and letters of credit, often termed simply "credits," means any arrangement by which the payment stalemate is broken. Banks in more than 160 countries subscribe to agreed rules for documentary credit banking procedures, as last amended in 1983. The International Chamber of Commerce spells out the details in its UCP 400, or "The Uniform Customs and Practices for Documentary Credits."

The ICC consults bankers and the United Nations Commission on International Trade Law. UNCITRAL provides a forum that allows consultation of various parties on defining and simplifying international banking. The importing buyer should be somewhat familiar with these UCP 400 rules.

Liabilities and Responsibilities

Banks must examine all documents with care to see that they appear on their face to meet the terms and conditions of the credit. The issuing bank is bound to provide payment funds as long as the documents meet the terms of the credit.

If a bank feels that the documents are not correct and refuses them, it must give notice to that effect. Banks assume no responsibility for accuracy or falsification of any documents, such as guarantees of description, quantity, weight, quality, condition, packing, delivery, value, or even existence of the goods.

The supplier will state a requested method of payment in his or her quotation. Remember that you, the buyer, are responsible to stipulate clearly the documents and conditions of payment. As the UCP 400 banking regulations state, "Banks assume no liability for errors in translation or interpretation of technical terms and reserve the right to transmit credit terms without translating them."

To understand the procedures, the buyer should devote some thought to how the supplier gets his or her payment. The terminology that has grown up around payments confuses some stateside buyers.

METHODS OF PAYMENT

The methods of payment in international trade are shown in this Buyer's Payment Risk Assessment Chart (Fig. 10-1). The highest risk results if the buyer is paying cash in advance as shown at the top left. Chances are that most buyers would shy away from that arrangement. The lowest risk is shown at the bottom as payment after delivery, either on consignment or for an extended term. Of course, if a buyer can pay for materials after receipt, it's easier to withhold payment and secure prompt restitution.

"Open account" follows the same routine as domestic purchases. The supplier ships the goods and sends an invoice. The buyer pays the bill after he or she is satisfied that the goods are as ordered.

Open Account

The "open account" method of payment, normally used in U.S. domestic trade, means that the goods are sold on credit. Payment is made without any documents

BUYER'S PAYMENT RISK ASSESSMENT CHART

PAYMENT METHOD	TIME OF PAYMENT	GOODS AVAILABLE TO BUYER	BUYER'S RISK
CASH IN ADVANCE	BEFORE SHIPMENT	AFTER PAYMENT	RELIES ON EXPORTER TO SHIP AS ORDERED
LETTER OF CREDIT CONFIRMED	AFTER SHIPMENT & DOCUMENT PRESENTED	AFTER PAYMENT	ASSURES SHIPMENT MADE, BUT RELIES ON EXPORTER
DOCUMENTARY COLLECTION:			
SIGHT DRAFT WITH DOCUMENT AGAINST PAYMENT (D/P)	ON PRESENTING OF DRAFT TO BUYER	AFTER PAYMENT TO IMPORTER'S BANK	AS ABOVE, UNLESS GOODS CAN BE INSPECTED BEFORE PAYING
TIME DRAFT WITH DOCUMENT AGAINST ACCEPTANCE (D/A)	ON MATURITY OF DRAFT	BEFORE PAYMENT, AFTER ACCEPTANCE	AS ABOVE
OPEN ACCOUNT	AS AGREED, BY INVOICE	BEFORE PAYMENT	NONE
EXTENDED TERMS, OR CONSIGNMENT	AS NEGOTIATED	AFTER DELIVERY OF PROMISSORY NOTES	NONE

POOLER & ASSOCIATES

ATS 9101108-4.0

FIGURE 10-1. Buyer's payment risk assessment chart.

other than an invoice. The invoice is the document that triggers payment. This method can sometimes be negotiated between long-time offshore partners, as for a domestic buy. Time for the supplier to collect is affected by distance and processing time by banks, exchange availability, local regulations, and sometimes political actions. Items from nearby countries may be paid in two weeks. However, others may take several months.

Delays in processing payments across borders ties up suppliers' capital. For this reason, open account usually isn't allowed by most offshore sources and is prohibited by law in many countries. For example, because of banking restrictions, Brazil prohibits payment of funds leaving the country within one year. Payment for equipment may be spread out up to five years.

Other than a consignment, open account is the most favorable term possible for the buyer. Offshore suppliers sell this way only to buyers they know well. It is the most economical method of payment, as the buyer can pay an invoice as for a domestic buy. Between these payment extremes are several alternate methods.

All credits must clearly state whether they are available by sight payment, by deferred payment, by acceptance, or by negotiation. For most offshore buys, we can place payment methods into three major groups used by businessmen for international trade: 1. collections, 2. letters of credit, and 3. Bankers Acceptances. Let us address each of these payment methods in turn.

Collections

A collection consists of payment upon tendering to banks of the proper documents associated with a purchase. The financial document is the sight or time draft. This collection method is easier than the formal letter of credit procedure and costs less.

Traditionally, Europeans don't generally send an invoice for payment. In this method, a draft is presented by the supplier that triggers payment. The draft method is either:

1. A clean collection (meaning no other documents are required beyond the draft).
2. Part of the documentary collection, explained above, consists of the financial document, plus specified commercial documents such as a bill of lading, invoices, and certificates of origin. Sometimes, other certificates such as inspection and insurance are needed.

The draft cannot be cancelled without agreement between the parties. It resembles a bank check. Two types are used. The first is called "documents against payment" (D/P), where the documents are released to the buyer upon payment of the draft. The other is called "documents against acceptance" (D/A), where payment is made when the goods are accepted by the buyer.

The draft will be either: 1. sight draft or 2. time draft. A sight draft is commonly used. It means that payment will be made upon presenting, or on "sight," of the draft.

A "time draft" is a payment to be made within a stipulated time after being presented. TENOR is a term applying to the time delay in payment, normally 30 or 60 days. An "arrival draft" is a special type of sight draft that is payable only after goods arrive at a named port.

A draft may be used to collect for goods shipped before on open account. Arrangements can be made for direct mail collection (DMC), with the documents and instructions sent by the supplier directly to the presenting bank. Forms are supplied by the supplier's bank.

"Swift" message payment is the term used to describe the process where banks can transfer funds for payment the same day by telex. This costs an extra $10 to $15, which is charged to the beneficiary of this fast service.

About 35 percent of all world trade use some form of documentary draft collection as the means of payment. The collection method is more prevalent when there is a trusting relationship. The letter of credit is more binding and preferred by some suppliers.

The collection method offers some buyer benefits, such as:

1. Convenience—You avoid time and cost of opening a letter of credit.
2. Savings—Supplier may pass on savings to you, or you can negotiate for a lower price based on his or her savings.
3. Payment flexibility—It is easier to get finance incentives that banks and certain foreign governments, such as Brazil and Mexico, provide. Payments

may be stretched out with interest charges, especially for large capital equipment purchases.

4. Delayed payment—Collection method favors negotiation for a payment time delay.

The buyer should work with the banker directly or through his company's finance department. Fees amount to between $50 and $100 per transaction for bank services that are normally paid by the importing buyer. The buyer may be tempted to name a local as the issuing bank, but should refrain from doing so. Unless the local bank has the staff and connections to negotiate the letter, the buyer will incur extra fees when the local bank engages an international out-of-town bank to process.

Letter of Credit

A letter of credit is primarily for the protection of suppliers. Sometimes, buyers can negotiate to have the supplier waive the credit. However, certain governments require an L/C by law, and the parties have no choice but to comply. Buyers should know how to make the L/C work for them.

At the request of the applicant, the buyer's issuing bank arranges to make payment to a third-party beneficiary. The supplier's "advising bank" actually makes the payment to them after receipt of the funds from the buyers' "issuing bank." The supplier will be paid if contract conditions are met. It protects the supplier as the bank assumes the obligation to pay against presentation of required documents. There are many variations of such credit arrangements that are separate transactions from the sale of goods.

Credits may be either 1. revocable or 2. irrevocable. A "Revokable L/C" can be cancelled at anytime without consent of the supplier. Most credits are issued as an "Irrevocable L/C," which means they cannot be cancelled with consent of the supplier. This feature protects both the bank and the supplier. Otherwise, the bank is at risk because it tendered its credit guarantee. The word "Irrevocable" must appear on the document; otherwise, it is considered revocable.

Letters of credit must be arranged by the importing buyer. At the buyer's request, an L/C is executed by the "issuing bank," which guarantees payment. This bank commitment is usually required by many foreign suppliers before they will make or ship. This protects their payment risk and transfers it to the bank. About one-third of offshore payments use this method. We must understand the mechanics of the various forms of letters of credit.

The buyer may keep application blank copies of his or her issuing bank's L/C request form at his or her desk. The data should be filled in and forwarded to the bank for execution. The terms "opener of credit," "buyer," and "importer" are the same. Your bank's application form is requested and filled out. A favored customer may receive a series of numbers in advance, or may call the banker to complete the form based on the data given over the phone.

Figure 10-2 diagrams the letter of credit sequence of events required as explained below:

- Supplier and buyer agree on the purchase.
- Buyer applies to his "issuing bank" for an L/C.
- Issuing bank prepares the letter and forwards it to supplier through supplier's foreign "advising bank."
- The advising bank forwards the letter to the supplier.
- Supplier prepares shipment and presents goods to carrier.
- Supplier then sends the draft for payment to their advising bank.
- Supplier forwards document copies to buyer or buyer's broker to clear customs in advance.
- Advising bank forwards draft and documents to issuing bank.
- Issuing bank reviews documents and honors supplier's draft by making payment.
- Issuing bank gives shipping document packet to the buyer, who is free to take goods (if not already cleared).

Figure 10-3 shows how a letter of credit appears when issued. The cost to the buyer is small. One-tenth of 1 percent of the invoice price is typical, with a $65 minimum charge. Most banks have set "advisory" fees. An example would be $85

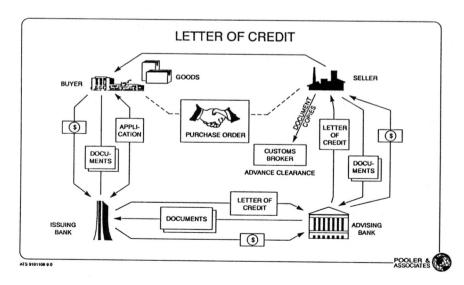

FIGURE 10-2.   Diagram of L/C sequence of events.

FE 421 (7-66)

CHEMICAL BANK NEW YORK TRUST COMPANY
P.O. BOX 1585, CHURCH STREET STATION   NEW YORK, N. Y. 10008
INTERNATIONAL DIVISION

IRREVOCABLE COMMERCIAL
LETTER OF CREDIT

JULY 5, 19..

CUSTOMER'S NO.

TO

Jose Doe & Cia.
Manizales
Colombia

OUR CREDIT: LC
(to be mentioned on all drafts and communications relative thereto)
ADVISED BY CABLE AND AIRMAIL THRU:
BANCO DE BANCO
MANIZALES, COLOMBIA

000-234567

BY ORDER OF

JOHN SMITH & CO.
1234 Wall Street
New York, N. Y. 10005

FOR ACCOUNT OF (SAME IF LEFT BLANK)

GENTLEMEN:
            WE HEREBY ESTABLISH OUR IRREVOCABLE CREDIT IN YOUR FAVOR, FOR THE ACCOUNT INDICATED ABOVE,
FOR A SUM OR SUMS NOT EXCEEDING IN ALL ·
THIRTY SIX THOUSAND SIX HUNDRED TWENTY FIVE DOLLARS UNITED STATES CURRENCY
($36,625.00 USC)

AVAILABLE BY
YOUR DRAFT(S)   AT   SIGHT ON US

FOR   FULL   INVOICE VALUE OF MERCHANDISE TO BE DESCRIBED IN INVOICE AS:

            500 BAGS COFFEE F.O.B. MANIZALES.

DRAFT(S) MUST BE ACCOMPANIED BY:
1. COMMERCIAL INVOICE IN TRIPLICATE.
2. CUSTOMS INVOICE IN DUPLICATE.
3. FULL SET CLEAN ON BOARD OCEAN BILLS OF LADING ISSUED TO ORDER OF CHEMICAL BANK NEW
     YORK TRUST COMPANY, MARKED NOTIFY JOHN SMITH & CO., 1234 WALL STREET, NEW YORK,
     N. Y. 10005, DATED NOT LATER THAN SEPTEMBER 19, 19..

EVIDENCING SHIPMENT FROM COLOMBIAN PORT TO U.S.A. PORT.
PARTIAL SHIPMENTS ARE PERMITTED.
TRANSSHIPMENT NOT PERMITTED.

MARINE AND WAR RISK INSURANCE TO BE EFFECTED BY BUYERS UNDER BLANKET POLICY NUMBER 12345
ISSUED BY YORK INSURANCE CO.

THE AMOUNT AND DATE OF NEGOTIATION OF EACH DRAFT MUST BE ENDORSED ON THE REVERSE
HEREOF BY THE NEGOTIATING BANK OR BANKERS.
WE HEREBY AGREE WITH THE DRAWERS, ENDORSERS AND BONA FIDE HOLDERS OF DRAFTS DRAWN UNDER
AND IN COMPLIANCE WITH THE TERMS OF THIS CREDIT, THAT THE SAME SHALL BE HONORED UPON
PRESENTATION AND DELIVERY OF DOCUMENTS AS SPECIFIED ABOVE TO THE DRAWEE IF DRAWN AND
NEGOTIATED ON OR BEFORE SEPTEMBER 30, 19..

VERY TRULY YOURS,

PROVISIONS APPLICABLE TO THE WITHIN MENTIONED CREDIT
This credit is subject to the Uniform Customs and Practice for Documentary Credits
(1962 Revision), International Chamber of Commerce Brochure No. 222.

XXXX

AUTHORIZED SIGNATURE

FIGURE 10-3.   Sample letter of credit.

to "advise" for a L/C. There is usually a minimum fee for administrative costs. For a major repeat customer, a bank may provide the service free. For a new, higher risk account, the fee may be 2 percent. When the bank has little confidence in the customer, it prefers to refuse the business rather than increase their fees.

Variations of Letters of Credit

The L/C can be either "Straight" or "Negotiable." A straight letter means that payment will be to the sole beneficiary who can hold and endorse the draft. Negotiable means that payment will be expanded to honor drafts from any negotiator or party.

Two classes of L/Cs are cash and confirmed types. A cash L/C requires the buyer to pay in advance before receiving the shipment. This is normally used when dealing with Eastern Bloc countries. Within the free world, buyers of most reputable companies seldom have to use this method. The buyer pays cash in advance only if there is no other choice.

"Confirming" occurs when either the issuing bank, or a second U.S. bank, confirms the L/C, guaranteeing payment. Confirmation means that the payment risk is minimal to the supplier. The major banks, such as Lloyds of London, do not require such action. Banks sometimes have possession of goods that they don't want because of a bad risk. So fees are imposed to cover this risk. The minimum fee charge is between $100 and $200 for a confirming guarantee.

A standby letter of credit, with its deferred payment credit, is, from a banker's point of view, an unsecured loan. When used, it is accepted by the issuing bank. Standbys differ in that neither party expects to draw against the credit. They expect that the account party will honor its payment.

The standby L/C means that the bank will pay, but will take title until the merchandise is paid for. An actual example will serve to illustrate the point. A U.S. firm needed a major purchase from Japan to be shipped to its Brazilian plant. However, the Japanese refused to accept a Brazilian P.O., mindful of a then poor credit rating for Brazil, where the government dictated a delay of payments. The solution was the standby L/C. If, for any reason, the Brazilian division did not make a payment on time per its contract, the U.S. parent guaranteed payment within 24 hours by wire to the Bank of Tokyo. This broke the impasse and allowed the buy to proceed.

The standby irrevocably binds the bank, so it is more expensive than a one-time transaction. The cost is about one-half of 1 percent and could be higher, depending on the buyer's credit risk.

Another alternate is a "revolving L/C," which permits flexibility for payment of any shipment up to a certain value, say $5000. As payment is made, the amount of credit returns to the original amount. Revolving L/Cs can be either "cumulative" or "non-cumulative." Cumulative allows the volume of what wasn't used in January to be used in February.

"Amendment" is a change to an original L/C to be used only in event of need, such as a performance bond.

Banks are automating their L/C procedures. Some provide a floppy disk to enable the buyer to get a credit issued using a personal computer. Also, many banks allow questions and responses through your PC (connected by modem to the bank mainframe), with no manual intervention.

Bankers Acceptance

Assume an importer has arranged an L/C that requires him to pay upon sight. Expecting to sell the goods shortly, the importer/buyer doesn't yet have enough funds to pay. Bankers acceptance allows release of goods upon the bank's payment of the draft. By drawing on the bank, independent of the letter, the buyer gets funds to take possession of his goods. When the sale has been made, the importer will then pay the acceptance at its maturity or due date. This is a marketable IOU.

Bankers acceptance provides financing by the bank's promise to pay the face amount of the draft to any holder who presents it at maturity. Acceptance is created from either an L/C or time draft drawn independently. Acceptance shows a willingness to pay a time draft or bill of exchange. The bank has the importer/buyer simply write the word "accepted" on the time draft or bill and sign it.

"Eligible acceptance" means it is eligible for a more favorable rate. This is proof a banker's acceptance complies with Federal Reserve regulations. As a negotiable instrument, the Federal Reserve Bank can discount it.

DOCUMENTS NEEDED FOR CREDITS

There is a 21-day grace period to fix or clarify a discrepancy without penalty. Bankers say that about 90 percent of all L/Cs are completed without delay, though about half of all L/Cs are classified as "unclean," meaning there were some discrepancies encountered. If documents are not executed within the 21 days allowable time limit, the documents are considered "stale" and a discrepancy exists. There is a "discrepancy charge" invoked whenever a bank runs into a delay that it didn't cause preventing performance.

Transport Documents

The bill of lading can be an ocean bill or airway bill, depending on the carrier. Unless a credit specifically calls for an on board transport document, banks will accept one that says goods have been taken in charge, or are received for shipment. On board or shipment can be shown by wording stating the loading of a named vessel, or stating, "received for shipment." Often, a stamp "on board" is used on the bill with the date loaded.

If credit calls for prepaid freight, the bank will see that payment is indicated. Any notation stating that goods are in defective condition will cause refusal of documents. "Consignment" of the bills of lading allows the item to be physically transferred to the buyer or appointed party, with title belonging to supplier. When the item is resold, payment is made.

The bank may want to be the consignee to protect itself since it guarantees payment. This means that the buyer cannot take possession of goods without paying the bank. An L/C can be transferred to another party, but in doing so, all credit rights are given up.

If, for any reasons, transport documents are missing, what can a buyer do? Get a "Steamship Guarantee" or "Airway Release," which is an indemnity letter issued by a bank to the carrier requesting release of merchandise without the original bills of lading. By waiving the L/C, the draft is paid, so the buyer can take possession of his or her goods. The buyer gives up any rights and protection he or she may have under the L/C, but it allows him or her to get the goods promptly.

Insurance Documents

Buyer's instructions to suppliers must be in the purchase order. However, banks that release your payment are not bound by anything other than their credit terms. So the insurance document should be an essential part of any credit document.

You should put on your letter of credit application that *either a policy or a certificate of insurance* is to be part of the documentation. This assures insurance is in force, or relieves the buyer from responsibility to pay.

Insurance may be taken by anyone with an insurable interest—that is, anyone who would suffer loses if the cargo is damaged or destroyed. The insurance amount is to be value of goods plus 10 percent to protect the interests of the supplier/exporter, buyer/importer, and the bank issuing the letter of credit. Whether a party has an insurable interest is determined by your purchase order terms.

When the supplier has insured the goods while enroute, the certificate can be made payable directly to your company, "To Buyer" or "To Whom It May Concern." The latter is common, as goods may be resold or rerouted while in transit. The type of insurance should be stipulated, such as where a credit covers "insurance against all risks."

If the buyer is responsible for insurance, he or she must be sure to buy a policy for at least the risks mentioned in the letter of credit, and be in negotiable form. The insurance document must be signed by the insurance company underwriters or their agents. Ask for the original and two copies.

The policy must be effective not later than the "on board date" on the bills of lading. Payment is to be in the currency specified in the contract.

Commercial Invoice

An invoice is an essential part of a credit, and should be made out to whomever applied for credit. Invoices for more than the credit may be refused. The description of goods must coincide with that on the credit.

When applying for an L/C, since an invoice is not yet issued, the bank needs a "Pro-forma Invoice" (simply the supplier's quotation on the same form as his invoice). However, you can use "preliminary advice." This is usually a teletransmission giving brief information of the credit, with details to follow. This starts the L/C paper process.

The buyer must see that the supplier/exporter has furnished a complete and accurate commercial invoice. The exporter must sign the invoice, certifying that it is true and correct. This supplier's invoice states the amount of money and the currency they expect for payment, as well as country of origin. It should reflect all the details of the transaction, in English!

Poorly issued foreign invoices cause most problems encountered. The broker can work with copies in most instances. Fax is okay to make the customs entry. A "Pro Forma" invoice made out by you as importer is acceptable. It's simply the importer's statement of value, or price paid in an an invoice-like form. The formal invoice must be produced within 50 days from entry only upon Customs request.

Other Documents

A certificate of origin and other certificates of survey for inspection, and so on, may be needed. If credit calls for check for weight, banks will accept a weight stamp or declaration of weight superimposed on the transport bill, unless credit specifically calls for a certificate.

MISCELLANEOUS CREDIT PROVISIONS

Several provisions should be reviewed. They include quantity and amount, partial shipments, expiry date and presentation, loading on board (Shipment), date terms, and transfer and assignment.

Quantity and Amount

The letter doesn't assure the buyer of getting exactly what was ordered. That is why buyers insist on the right of inspection before shipment. It does, however, insure that the documentation and procedures will be in proper order. The bank will pay the supplier only when the purchase conditions, as spelled out in the letter, are met.

The dollar value stated on the L/C cannot be exceeded. Quantity in the shipment may vary by more than or less than 5 percent. However, if the L/C stipulates an exact quantity of containers or packing units, changes are not acceptable.

Partial Shipments

Partial shipments are allowed unless the credit document says otherwise. If shipments are to be by installments within periods stated in the credit, and shipments are not made, the credit ceases to be available.

Expiry Date And Presentation

The buyer should always specify an expiry date for presentation of documents for payment or acceptance. Banks will refuse documents presented to them later than 21 days (unless otherwise specified) after the date of issuance of the transport document(s). This allows the buyer to cancel the order for the supplier's failure to deliver on time. If a buyer wants to extend the expiration date, he or she may. Using the expiration date can be a forceful expediting tool. Threatening to let the lapse cut off payment often brings results.

Loading on Board (Shipment)

The term "shipment" is understood to include the expressions "loading on board," "dispatch," and "taking in charge." "On or about" means that a shipment is to be made from five days before to five days after the specified date.

"First half" of a month is construed as from the 1st through the 15th. "Second half" is from the 16th to the last day of each month. The terms "beginning," "middle," or "end" of a month are taken as from the 1st through the 10th, 11th through the 20th, and 21st through the last day.

Date Terms

"Extended terms" allows delay in payment (for example 60, 90, 180 days). 360 days is usually the maximum used. "Long-term financing" means that payments may be stretched out, especially for capital equipment purchases.

Transfer and Assignment

A transferable credit allows the beneficiary to request the bank to pay to or accept from one or more other parties (second beneficiaries). A credit can be transferred only once. Buyers might specify transferability if their purchase might be diverted to a third party. A beneficiary has the right to assign any proceeds to which entitled, regardless of whether the credit is transferable.

For several reasons, the trend to more overseas sourcing in the 1980s has been unprecedented. Before issuing the purchase order and paying, the buyer must decide what currency to use.

Ideally, bankers say, two to four banks are involved in a credit process. Though, in some transactions, as many as nine banks may become a party. An international bank vice president stated that 93 percent of all world trade transactions are settled in U.S. dollars. Also, the American dollar is also the basis for currency exchange. For example, a purchase by an Italian company from one in Germany is usually made in dollars. So many dollars are deposited abroad for European trade that the funds are termed Eurodollars. Naturally, there is interest in the value of the U.S. dollar.

When requesting quotes, get the prices in both U.S. dollars and the foreign currency. Then, you should consult with finance before making major buys. You should be up-to-date on currency fluctuations if you are to protect your buy from foreign currency exposure. This is the subject of the next chapter.

11

Protecting Your Buy from Foreign Currency Exposure

Buyer Michael insists, "I'll buy only with good-old U. S. bucks, so there is no confusion about *what* we'll pay." Michael negotiates with England's Chris & Mandy, Ltd. for 10,000 woolen blankets at $40 each. The deal is set for delivery in six months. Michael is among those buyers who don't want to worry about exchange rates, or get in currency translation problems.

During a later staff meeting, his supervisor remarks, "The pound is down sharply versus the dollar. We must have made out on this blanket buy deal. How much extra profit did we make now that the dollar is so strong, Michael?"

What was Michael's major mistake? He paid with an appreciating dollar that gave the supplier extra profit. His major failing was that he did not communicate. Moreover, in the above simple scenario, several important issues are evident:

- Currency translations can affect your offshore buy.
- You must decide in which currency to negotiate and make payment.
- You should always proceed in accordance with your management's objectives.
- You must communicate with both finance and management.
- The impact of exchange rates and translation losses on profit should be understood.

Importing buyers' objectives include protection of product costs by making sure their costs don't rise because of currency fluctuation. Management needs to know the exact dollar value to be paid if profit objectives are to be met. Depending on how exchange rates swing, they can make a buy look good, or reflect a poor judgment call by the buyer.

Exchange rates are affected by complex forces. These include 1. the differences of inflation and interest rates between the supplying country and the United States,

2. government policies affecting the growth of the money supply, and 3. currency speculation.

FOREIGN EXCHANGE MARKET
TERMINOLOGY

Transactions such as lending, borrowing, swapping, and repaying make up the international financial trading system. "Foreign exchange" is conversion of funds of one country's currency into usable funds from another. We buy another currency, paying the bank as a supplier. When currency "A" buys less at a future date of currency "B," then "A" is said to be trading at a discount to "B." The opposite is true when "A" buys more. In that case it is trading at a premium to "B." "Hard" currency is the term applied to those likely to maintain or increase in value versus the U.S. dollar. "Soft" currency refers to those likely to decrease in the future.

The rate that the exchange takes place varies frequently. Daily rates are published in most major newspapers. There can be a slight difference in rates, depending on whether you are selling or buying a currency. A "bid" is the price that a pricemaker is willing to pay for a foreign currency. An "offer" is the price that a pricemaker is willing to sell a foreign currency.

A "spot" quote may be used for either the purchase or sale of a foreign currency. It is for immediate acceptance, and the currency must be received or delivered within two days to consummate the transaction. The "dealing date" is the date that the deal was made. The "value date" is the day that the deal is to be settled by either delivery or receipt of funds.

Funds Do Not Flow Between Countries

There's a misconception that money flows between countries. If a U.S. bank loans money to Brazil, it is called a "capital outflow" because it accepted Brazil's IOU. The dollars don't leave the U.S. bank, but are on deposit as a liability from Brazil—a "capital inflow."

As an example, our U.S. dollars are said to be going into Japan because of the huge trade deficit. The dollars that purchase Japanese cars do not go to Japan, they remain here. However, they do revert to Japanese ownership. There is simply a shift in assets controlled. The dollars stay in America. The exception to this is when a traveler takes dollars and spends them outside the United States.

It will help to understand this concept by explaining the use of "Eurodollars." These are U.S. dollar accounts held by Europeans on bank books outside the United States. Because these accounts exist in Europe, natives can make financial deals easily to trade with the United States. Eurodollars are listed on futures markets as a separate currency unit.

If the Japanese pile up so many excess dollars here (the dollar trade gap is about

$50 billion), what can they do with them? They can spend them, or invest them in physical assets, such as buying U.S. Treasuries, building manufacturing plants here, or even raising cattle to send home, which is what they are doing. So is it a surprise that Japanese are increasingly owning homes, factories, and so forth, in the United States?

Corporations are affected by currency exchange even if they do not export their products or have foreign operations. Unless they face no competition in their domestic market, they are still affected. Operating exposure involves noncontractual matters, revenue, cost, and profit. Companies selling within the same marketplace, but getting materials or using labor from different countries, are affected differently.

The magnitude for gain or loss is seen from reports of currency translation loses, recently as high as $763 million for a prominent computer company and $553 million for a U.S. oil company.[1]

The buyer faces uncertainty when a currency exchange takes place. If a U.S. company sells wheat to India, it is not paid in rupees, but by dollars in the United States. The Indians obtain those dollars by either buying them or by selling something else to Americans. Another alternative is for India to sell something to a third country, which pays them with assets convertible into dollars. India can use these dollar denominated assets to pay for the U.S. wheat.

Blocked Funds

Sometimes a company wants to get its funds out of a country, but it can't. A company may be prevented from transferring its fund assets because of foreign government policy. This action helps keep the currency from being depleted, and helps support the value of the local currency. Possibly, no one will buy the assets, or will pay little because of a lack of confidence in that currency.

Developing country currencies are sometimes difficult to swap. If not a major currency, we may have to deal in third countries. For example, buying from Turkey, whose currency (the lira) is not freely exchangeable, the supplier might favor the deutsche mark for payment. Nobody wants to hold fast-depreciating currency. Borrowing local currencies helps alleviate the need to have dollars to do business overseas.

Where the fund exchange process is difficult, blocked funds present companies with four options:

1. Wait it out.
2. Sell at a loss.
3. Swap funds (credits) with other companies.
4. Write-off as a total loss.

---

[1]*Fortune* magazine. November 26, 1984. p. 119.

Companies maintain informal networks to effect these transactions that are made to break logjammed funds. Such transactions are unpublished off-the-book accounting and are not included in any statistical data. When American executives travel, the cost is often paid by the host country's division as one way to use blocked funds.

The extent of these blocked funds is unknown, but probably amount to several hundreds of billions of dollars. The third world debt crisis has caused corporations to become ingenious at devising means to effect transfers. One way of getting some relief is to maintain banking ties within the host country that help get local government support. Most governments' policies make it easy for a company to spend within its borders. For this reason, some companies choose to retain and grow the funds in that country.

Currency value has both a "level" and a "volatility" factor to be considered. Level is the number of pounds or marks required to buy one dollar. Volatility measures the rapidity of those currency fluctuations or level changes.

Some buyers believe that if they leave funds in that currency's national account, currency value is unaffected. That's true. For a transaction denominated in dollars, the company that expects to pay a certain number of dollars will pay precisely that amount. This company will have sold its product using components at foreseen costs. As a result, the company's profit was as planned. However, consider the possibility that they purchased the components in another currency that dropped versus the dollar.

The company would have gained from reduced cost when they converted their dollars to make the payment. Conversely, if the currency had increased in value versus the dollar, the company would have lost some of its profit due to the increased cost.

To decide in which currency to buy, buyers should study:

* Inflationary or deflationary trends of the two currencies;
* Relative value of the U.S. dollar to other currencies; and
* Current exchange rates.

Inflation, the key to price forecasting, is a rapid rise in prices over a short time. The result is a sharp erosion in buying power of the currency used to buy. As an aerial navigator, the author learned that, if you watched your compass heading and knew the wind direction and velocity, you always knew where you were. Inflation is like economic windage. If you know or can project the expected inflation for what is to be bought, you can forecast prices accurately. However, as one economist said, "Forecasting is difficult, especially when it's in the future."

Global competition changes with the amount of inflation and affects your negotiations. High inflation encourages inventory growth. Low inflation induces cash discounts.

Economists distinguish between two types of inflation:

1. "Demand-pull," when more people want what you want; and
2. "Cost-push," when costs incurred are pushed up by costs incurred as reflected in the prices charged.

While U.S. inflation was almost 14 percent in 1980, it dropped to 2 percent in 1987. It currently is around 5 to 6 percent. The collapse of OPEC kept oil prices and inflation down in the mid 1980s. Inflation hasn't eased worldwide. Quite to the contrary, it has intensified. From a global perspective, the world's prices are increasing about 15 percent annually. Much worse are developing nation prices, which are growing at an annual rate of almost +57 percent, with Latin America's rate at 185 percent. Examples of super high inflation as of January 1990 are: Argentina 4000 percent, Brazil 1500 percent, and Peru 2775 percent.

Why worry about inflation? Inflation determines future price trends. Also, relative inflation of a supplier's currency versus the U.S. dollar is the basis for exchange rate differentials. Inflation is an old phenomenon. A chart exists showing more than 700 years of inflation. The Bible tells of inflation of the denarius at the time of Jesus. History teaches us what happens when inflation has gotten out of hand.

Governments often try to freeze prices by fiat, but this doesn't work for long. Prices finally break out and may go "through the roof" before they readjust. In Germany in July, 1923, 3.5 percent of the country's tradespeople were unemployed. By September the unemployment rate rose to 9.9 percent and by December it jumped to over 28 percent. The high unemployment rate was a result of failure to maintain a stable economy and stable prices for goods and services. Inflation was so rampant in Germany that, during the peak of the inflationary period, it cost millions of marks to mail a letter.

Many Europeans still recall the devastating U.S. inflationary binges of the 1970s that hurt Europe. These experiences, added to their post World War I and World War II experience, helps explain the German paranoia about inflation, causing many of today's economic disagreements with the United States, Japan, and others.

Can the buyer do much about inflation? Yes. Some techniques would be:

- Refusing to pay increased prices;
- Ignoring an inflated price and issuing the purchase order with the old price; and
- Awarding the business to someone else, but only after warning that business could be lost.

Perhaps you can think of other techniques?

VALUE OF THE U.S. DOLLAR

An overvalued dollar hurts U.S. export volume, but encourages importing. A currency is said to be overvalued if it can buy more from abroad than at home, or undervalued if the opposite is true.

The dollar peaked in the winter of 1984, at a high of 54 percent above its average price in 1980. Since 1984, the dollar has dropped to the point where it is currently down about 40 percent against the Japanese yen, the German mark, and other major currencies. In early 1991, the dollar bought 136 Japanese yen, 1.56 German marks, and $1.20 Canadian dollars. The dollar's loss since 1984 against the Taiwanese, South Korean, Hong Kong, Venezuelan, and Australian currencies has been about 5 percent. The dollar has held steady versus several other currencies, including Mexico and most European countries.

Governmental Influence on Exchange Rates

Psychology has an important influence on short-term price levels. Currency speculators fuel the currency exchange markets at the IMM, with their efforts to take advantage of short-term movements in spot and futures prices in volatile currencies. Industrial hedgers deal in these same markets.

Currency values change rapidly for a variety of reasons that may prompt intervention by various governments seeking to protect their self-interests. By tightening or relaxing the money supply growth, central banks can cause interest rates to rise or fall.

During the first quarter of 1985, ten central banks sold 10 billion dollars to help trigger the dollar's fall. By September of that year, Japan, the United Kingdom, Germany, and France had coordinated monetary policy with the United States. This "Gang of 5" sold another 10 billion U.S. dollars, pushing the dollar down even more. This group has since expanded to seven, with the addition of Canada and Italy.

Government intervention affects psychology over the short term, but for the long term, a consistent monetary policy is helpful. Acting as a deterrent to governmental use of this leverage is the need to meet other major goals of fiscal policy. These goals often include control of inflation, reduction of unemployment, judicious use of deficit spending, and tax reform. All these monetary and fiscal policies affect exchange rates and are, in addition, nationalistic and political issues.

If you decided to convert dollars into another currency, consider the following examples. Brazil's inflation has been 1500 percent per annum and their "parallel" (black) market allows you to make more than a 40 percent premium over the official rate by selling your dollars to individuals. The parallel market is so common in Brazil that this exchange rate is published daily in the newspapers.

The Brazilian government, wanting to make this rate official, has created a new "dolar turismo," available only to foreign tourists at hotels, banks, and government-approved exchange stations. These approved stations will exchange your dollars into cruzeiros at a rate of 70 percent more than the "official" rate. This tourist rate is only 10 percent lower than the black market parallel rate. Only the naive will exchange money at the official rate under such conditions.

In Ecuador, the black market buys and sells dollars at twice the official rate. In Chile, the black market rate premium is about 20 percent. Peru's black market offers only a slight advantage. In these countries, exchangers wave a pocket calculator in the air signalling they're available.

In some Eastern European countries (Czechoslovakia and the Soviet Union come readily to mind), you can get more than twice the official dollar rate on the black market. Poland's "premium" exchange rate is 6,000 zlotys per dollar. That is 5,000 zlotys above the bank rate, and only 200 zlotys below the black market rate.

Black market trading is done openly with taxi drivers and dealers who move through hotel lobbies. They constantly approach travelers. Beware though—undercover sting operations have been reported. Don't deal with strangers, especially in an alley! Visitors have to be careful that they're not robbed during these exchange deals.

In all countries, count your money carefully as shortchange artists abound. Buy on weekdays when banks are open. When banks are closed, rates are often less favorable elsewhere. Deal in your currency of choice. French francs are preferred in Africa, while the mark is wanted in some Eastern European countries.

Overcoming the Exchange Rate Roadblock

To gain experience in overcoming the exchange rate roadblock identified earlier in this book, fill in the conversion blanks for Table 11-1. Use the exchange rates from Table 11-2 that reflects rates at which foreign currency is exchanged on a specific date (March 10, 1991 in our example). The U.S. $ equivalent in column #1 is the rate for selling foreign currency; column #2 is the rate for buying that foreign currency. To convert into currency/U.S. $, use the rates from column #2 and multiply by $1000. Then answer the questions asked.

Conversion of foreign currency values for U.S. Customs purposes is covered in provision 31 U.S.C. 5151 based on the rates certified by the Federal Reserve Bank of New York.

This chapter seeks to apply some of the new knowledge gained from earlier chapters. At the end of this chapter, questions are answered and computations worked out for you in Table 11-9. Throughout this chapter, please do not read further until you've answered any questions asked and computed values. Buyers must work with this financial data, not simply be told the answers. An old proverb says "To do is to understand." Learning to apply principles on-the-job is how we

TABLE 11-1.   Foreign exchange rate exercise

1. Assume you have $1,000. Using rates shown in Table 11-2,
   Column #2, convert it into the following currencies:

   a. British pound   = _____ x $1000 = _____
   b. Canadian $ = _____   _____
   c. French franc   = _____   _____
   d. Mexican peso   = _____   _____

2. When you exchange money abroad, where do you usually get the highest value?
   a. at hotel
   b. bank
   c. store
   d. individuals

   Take a trip to Brazil to buy an aquamarine stone for $1000.
3. Where do you get the best exchange value here?
4. Should you try to buy with dollars?
5. If paying in cruzeiro, when should the purchase be made?
   a) Immediately upon arrival.
   b) Just as you leave?
   c) It doesn't matter.

TABLE 11-2.   Foreign currency exchange chart

March 10, 1991 Country	Currency	Column #1 U.S. $ Equiv.	Column #2 Currency/U.S. $
Australia	Dollar	.7689	1.306
Brazil	Cruzeiro	.00466	220.00
Britain	Pound	1.8680	.5383
Canada	Dollar	.8622	1.1598
China	Renmimbi	.191494	5.221
France	Franc	.1888	5.2420
Germany	Mark	.6387	1.5657
Hong Kong	Dollar	.1283	7.7938
Israel	Shekel	.4992	2.0033
Italy	Lira	.000860	1162.40
Japan	Yen	.007325	136.52
Mexico	Peso	.000336	2973.00
South Korea	Won	.001381	724.00
Sweden	Krona	.1738	5.7545
Switzerland	Franc	.7324	1.3653
Taiwan	NT Dollar	.0374	26.76
USSR	Rouble	.6153[a]	1.6250

As published in *Wall Street Journal*, *New York Times*, and so on, daily.
[a]Not freely traded. Official rate shown, but actually trades at about 6.2 roubles/U.S. $ = 16 cents.

become professional buyers. Remember, we can learn to fish from a book, but we can only catch fish when actually fishing.

MINICASE: MAKING A THIRD COUNTRY BUY

Using a minicase is as close as we can simulate the real world of global buying. We'll explore how customs duties affect buying decisions and how to protect against currency fluctuations. Buyer Michael can buy water heaters from three offshore sources. Quality is equal, so it is not an issue. Michael is about to place his purchase order with one of these sources for 4,000 instantaneous gas water heaters. 2, 000 are to be shipped direct to an Italian affiliate who will pay in lira. The other half is to be shipped to the company's California plant.

Of the 2,000 heaters to be shipped stateside, 500 will be reshipped to Tijuana at a border maquiladora operation for assembly and sale to the South American market. Five hundred will go to Canada. The remaining 1,000 will be used in the United States.

Michael prepares a price quote summary for heaters that is shown in Table 11-3. Fill in the missing data by using the conversion rates table used earlier. Don't read further until you've completed this chart. Answers are in Table 11-10.

TABLE 11-3.   Fill-in quote summary for heater buy

	Quote price	$Equiv.	Unit Price
Germany	65 marks	—	—
Bulgaria	35.00 $ U.S.	—	35.00
Israel	95 shekels	—	—

If this buy were similar to a domestic buy, where a customs duty doesn't exist, the best buy would be from Bulgaria. However, Michael cannot ignore the duties.

How Customs Duties Affect Buying Decisions

The purchase order terms control prices for all shipments. Looking up his Harmonized Code reference, Michael excerpts the HTSUS data shown in Table 11-4 that covers this type equipment. Michael knows that a buy from Germany attracts an MFN duty of 4 percent in Category 1 under the General heading. The IL denotes that Israel is duty-free under the Israeli Agreement. Bulgarian items attract a 45 percent rate, as shown in category 2.

Compute the customs duty to be paid by Michael for the 2,000 heater shipment to be shipped to the United States on March 10, 1991. Use this analysis outline in Table 11-5 to compute and study the impact of duties on the buying decision.

TABLE 11-4.   Referencing the harmonized code

Code	Description	Units	Rates of Duty		
				1	2
		Qty.	General	Special	
8419	Machinery, for treatment of materials by a process involving a change of temperature, etc.				
8419.11.00 00 5	Instantaneous gas water heaters		4%	Free (A*, E, IL) 3.6% CA	45%

Keys: General is MFN; A is BDCs and * indicates exceptions; E is Caribbean Initiate, and IL is the Israeli Agreement; CA is the Canadian FTA.

TABLE 11-5. Computing duty for the buy

	Ad Valorem[a]	% Duty	Customs $ Pd.	Total P.O. Costs w/o Freight
A. If shipped from German source?				
B. Shipped from Bulgarian source?				
C. Shipped from Israeli source?				

[a]Denote the value of 2,000 heaters in U.S. dollars for Customs

Michael knows that customs duty is based on the published exchange rates for the date of shipment. See answers in Table 11-11 later.

Now, ignoring freight costs but including duty, which country presents the best buy? Continue reading only after you've checked out the total costs.

Michael decides that the best buy is from Germany. While an American buyer only converts his dollars, a global buyer dealing with buyers in different countries will be called upon to convert other currencies. How much in lira will the Italians pay to the Germans?

The U.S. dollar is the common denominator known. Try the formula in Table 11-6 which makes it easier to visualize the conversion. The same result would be gained by using an alternate: lira/$ divided by mark/$.

TABLE 11-6.   Exchange formula to convert marks to lira

$$\frac{\text{Italian lira}}{\text{U.S. \$}} \times \frac{\text{U.S. \$}}{\text{German mark}} \times \frac{\text{marks}}{\text{unit}} \times 2{,}000 \text{ heaters} = \text{lira}$$

This minicase further expands outlook and knowledge by pondering and answering the following questions:

- Does Michael have to pay full U.S. duty?
- Can the buyer use a free trade zone or drawback?
- Will the U.S.-Canada Trade Agreement allow these heaters to be shipped through Canada and brought duty-free to the United States?

The answers to the lira conversion and these questions are at the end of this chapter in Table 11-12.

Buy in U.S. Dollars or Foreign Currency?

The question now is, "Should Michael buy in U.S. dollars or the foreign source currency?" Let's assume that, by the time shipment is made, the foreign currency rises 10 percent relative to the dollar. Michael would have been better off if he had negotiated and paid in dollars. The supplier would receive 10 percent less value to accept dollars that must be converted. However, if the foreign currency dropped 10 percent (dollar rises), then Michael would have paid 10 percent extra if he had paid in dollars.

Of course, if the supplier leaves his dollars on deposit in the United States, to pay for something bought here, there is no exchange effect. The strength of the dollar influences all offshore buying decisions and affects our trade deficit. As the dollar strengthens, imports become more attractive. As the dollar weakens, imports are discouraged. A buyer sourcing from France needs to follow the trend of the franc-to-dollar relationship.

Using the data from his sourcing summary, Michael knows that the payment of either $83,200 or 130,000 marks is due by March 10. Dollars could be put aside to await payment, but there is no need to do that now. Michael probably would feel more comfortable using open credit the same as he does for his domestic buys. However, processing payments across borders ties up seller's capital because of delays, so that isn't always allowed by the offshore seller.

Michael may try to buy in dollars, but the seller may want marks. Eventually, dollars must be used to either pay or *buy* the other currency. The sooner he acts to freeze the value at the time of payment, the better.

The highest translation risk (+ or -) accrues to us when we pay in the supplier's currency. However, by taking the risk, the buyer may sometimes get price concessions. Risk avoidance occurs by buying in dollars in the sense that Michael knows his costs. A buck is a buck is a buck! Paying in dollars is done by 85 percent of offshore buyers. Paying in dollars may not, however, always be desirable or possible. Companies with hard currencies, such as those operating in Germany and Japan, may prefer mark-or yen-denominated contracts. If you insist on buying in dollars, suppliers can raise the product price you pay to cover their translation risk. The supplier might insist on price escalation to cover the same risk.

One factor in contract currency denomination is whether the supplier or the buyer's company can better manage the financial risks. Simply recall that if the dollar is expected to rise versus the relevant currency, buy in their currency. If the dollar is expected to drop, buy in dollars. This decision must be reached *before placing your purchase order!*

WAYS TO MINIMIZE RISK

If your company and the supplier both wish to use their own currency, a swap of currency on the date of PO issuance and reversal at shipment time is possible. This shares any currency fluctuation risk that may occur.

Let's return to our case. How might Michael eliminate the risk of any currency fluctuation against him? He can take steps to:

1. Put a clause into his PO;
2. Use a forward buy; or
3. Hedge through the use of futures or options.

Michael is going to pay in marks. He could wait and pay the rate at time of delivery. However, Michael's management is worried about a rise in the mark's value, and wants assurance that costs won't rise. Michael loses the option of doing nothing and paying when due.

Currency Fluctuation Clause

When buying in the foreign currency, a buyer can try to negotiate a 50/50 currency fluctuation in his or her contract to help maintain long-term relationships. Such risk sharing is used by 55 percent of buyers surveyed recently.

Currency adjustments might be negotiated in advance and inserted as a clause in your purchase order. Such a clause might provide for:

- Gains or losses resulting from exchange rate changes being split equally.
- A band or window set for currency adjustment, "If the exchange translation value varies + or - 5 percent from the price as of the date of this PO, an opposite adjustment of that percentage will be made."
- An adjustment to be made at the time of delivery.
- Adjustments on blanket orders to be made each month, quarter (or whatever).

Using A "Forward Buy" Contract

Michael must eventually use dollars to buy the other currency. The sooner he acts to freeze the value at the time of payment, the better. By using the tactic of making a "forward buy" contract, buyers can protect their foreign currency exposure by buying or selling currency for future delivery. Buys can be made for delivery in 30, 60, 90, and 180 days. Special quotes for longer times can be obtained from your banker.

For example, if the mark is expected to rise, a purchase of marks for future delivery can be made now. If the mark is expected to drop, the marks can be sold now at a set price, for delivery at the time of the exchange of product.

A "buyer's option" is a contract calling for delivery of a foreign currency at a stated future time. The buyer is saying literally, "Sell me the funds today and tell me my costs when I pay." To get forward prices, see Table 11-7. These German currency quotes are taken from the same foreign exchange listing published in the newspapers and used earlier for Table 11-2.

Since Michael wants to *set the price six months ahead,* he must get a special price quote. Upon phoning, his bank informs him that current six-month trading is $.63 and "33—27." The price might be at a premium or discount relative to the spot price. The bank's pricemaker is offering to sell deutsche marks at $.6333, or bidding to buy at $.6327. There is no separate fee charged as the bank's profit is in the price charged.

In summary, a forward contract is used to protect the cost of funds for delivery later. Any risk of exchange rates moving unfavorably (or favorably) for the buyer, between the time the deal is made and the actual delivery date, is gone. Therefore, the buying firm's profit is secure. A buyer can make the deal today and be assured of his or her costs. Through this forward buy, you have locked in the exact product costs with no surprises! Fifteen percent of all buyers use this method.

How a Futures Hedge Works

Another buyer tactic is to use a "futures hedge." How does it work? Buying a currency option is to buy "long" for known future payment obligations due for purchases made. A financial futures contract is a buyer commitment to buy or sell a set amount of that currency at a future time. Contracts are designated for the

TABLE 11-7.   German currency quotes

German Mark	$ U.S. Equiv.	What $ is Worth
Spot	.6387	1.5657
30-day fwd	.6374	1.5688
60-day fwd	.6361	1.5721
90-day fwd	.6349	1.5750

March 10, 1991. *Wall Street Journal, N.Y. Times,* and so on.

months of March, June, September, and December. A futures contract has a closeout expiration date. For example, the September futures contract will close out the first week of that month. The price is free to change with the market until the settlement date on the futures exchange. Though not too predictable in the short range, exchange rates usually move in cycles.

On the job, when the PO is to be issued, check a major paper for the prior day's trades. Table 11-8 shows futures trades made on the International Monetary Market (IMM) of the Chicago Mercantile Exchange. Open interest is the number of contracts that exist for each month and not liquidated by delivery or offsetting contracts. There is a small commission fee paid and margin to be deposited when a futures contract is created. Recall that the forward buy had no separate fee.

Futures for seven major currencies were started in 1972. Of the futures currencies available, each contract size differs as follows:

Australia	100,000 dollars
Canada	100,000 Canadian dollars
France	250,000 francs
Germany	125,000 marks
Japan	12,500,000 yen
Switzerland	125,000 francs
United Kingdom	62,500 pounds

A U.S. dollar index is also available. In our case, 130,000 marks for 2,000 heaters is to be payable in six months. The treasurer believes the dollar will decline (or marks rise). Since each contract is for 125,000 marks, our treasurer would "buy long" now (when the PO is issued), probably for one September contract. Six

TABLE 11-8.   German mark financial futures

German Mark (IMM) March 10, 1991
    125,000 marks; $ per mark

Season High	Low		High	Low	Close	Chg.	Open Interest
.6912	.5820	Mar	.6558	.6367	.6370	-121	52,094
.6870	.6233	Jun	.6522	.6325	.6330	-126	15,895
.6810	.6290	Sep	.6473	.6290	.6296	-128	383
.6770	.6300	Dec	.6385	.6300	.6270	-134	53

Last spot .6378, Off 122
Total open interest 68,425

Note: IMM is the International Monetary Market of the Chicago Mercantile Exchange.

months from the date that payment is due, the treasurer will cancel the obligation to buy by selling one contract (an equal amount of marks originally bought).

The futures prices driven by speculators can go up, down, or in cycles. The author's experience leads to the belief that no one can correctly predict futures trends. Leave that to those expert gamblers. Of all trades in futures, 80 to 90 percent are said to lose money. However, when they win, the rewards are high. Speculators will cover a contract by a financial institution or your company, in hopes of profit. This is a zero sum game. For every winner, there is a loser. This realization causes many companies to shun futures markets as gambling. That's true if your attempt is to make money on futures themselves. That's *not* why a company uses this market. For most companies, the purpose is to hedge.

A critical time arrives when the contract is cancelled by selling it. About 1 percent of contracts expire with the buyer taking possession of the currency. Most will cancel by selling.

A gain or loss results from this financial transaction that will almost exactly cancel the corresponding opposite gain or loss from any exchange rate change in our physical purchase transaction during this six months. Figure 11-1 depicts how the futures action cancels the price change.

In effect, the original profit expected based on the cost of products purchased was insured. The fluctuation of currency was eliminated or hedged as the buyer

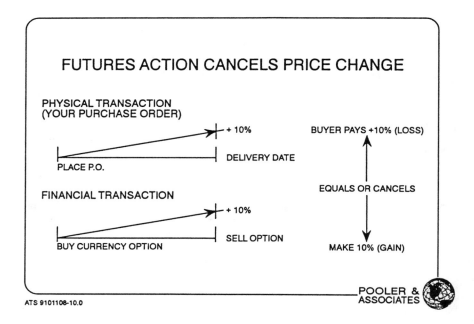

FIGURE 11-1.   Futures action cancels price change.

TABLE 11-9.   Answer to questions asked in Table 11-1.

The correct Foreign Exchange Rates in the Exercise are:

1. a) British Pound   =.5383 x 1000 = 538.3
    b) Canadian $ = 1.1598   1159.80
    c) French Franc   = 5.242   5,242
    d) Mexican Peso   = 2973   2,973,000

2. When you exchange money abroad, you usually get the highest value at: b) bank.
    Taking a trip to Brazil brings into play rampant inflation.
3. Best price from: d. individuals
4. Yes, try to buy with dollars. You may be quoted a far better price.
5. If paying in cruzeiro, make the buy b. as you leave, before boarding the plane if possible.

TABLE 11-10.   Correct data from filling in table 11-3.

	Quote price	$ Equiv.	Unit Price
Germany	65 marks	.6387	41.52
Bulgaria	35.00 $ U.S.	—	35.00
Israel	95 shekels	.4992	47.42

TABLE 11-11.   Correct duty from filling out Table 11-5.

	Ad Valorem[a]	% Dut	Customs $ Pd.	Total P.O. Costs w/o Freight
A. If shipped from German source?	83,040	4	3,322	86, 362
B. Shipped from Bulgarian source?	70,000	45	31,500	101, 500
C. Shipped from Israeli source?	94,840	0	0	94,840

aDenote the value of goods in U.S. dollars only for Customs.

TABLE 11-12.   Exchange conversion and answers for Table 11-6

$$\frac{1162.4 \text{ lira}}{1 \text{ dollar}} \times \frac{0.6387 \text{ dollar}}{1 \text{ DM}} \times \frac{65 \text{ DM}}{1} \times 2{,}000 \text{ heaters} = 96{,}515{,}234 \text{ lira}$$
$$(48{,}257.6 \text{ lira/unit})$$

Answers to questions asked in the case:

1. Not if Michael had reason to ship direct or use a FTZ.
2. Yes, the FTZ or drawback might apply. Refer to Chapter 9.
3. No. Product has to have 50 percent of value added in Canada.

froze the price level at close to the $83,200. The small fee paid ($250) is the insurance cost of eliminating risk.

Of course, had Michael taken no action and the dollar strengthened, he might have come out with an extra gain. That's considered a speculation by many financial types. Recall that the *object is to be certain of costs.*

On large outlays, some firms may choose to hedge on only one-half of the total buy value and accept risk on the other half. A fine line exists between hedging and speculating. When finance begins to delay a move or increase the volume, thus anticipating currency trends, speculation comes into play. It is this enhancing of revenue that, if done well, can be productive. Forecasts of econometric exchange rate data are available from DRI/McGraw Hill and Wharton's Global Exposure Monitor. Some companies may prefer to track their own data.

Companies are divided about the degree of risk to allow. Most Japanese firms will hedge their currency when quoting in dollars. A portion or all the transaction can be hedged, depending on each company's financial policy. A global corporation may act as its own bank and transfer funds within divisions and companies. Reportedly, G.E. and Eastman Kodak will hedge, but others, such as Monsanto, will not.

More complex arrangements, such as the "flexible forward contract" and options on futures limited by "puts and calls," are available. A put gives the right to "put" or sell the currency, while a call gives the right to "call" or buy the currency. All options have both a buyer and a seller. The buyer of a call expects the currency price to rise. The seller doesn't expect the price to reach the option set price.

The main difference between a futures contract and a call is that a futures contract obligates you to buy while a futures "call" gives you the *option* to buy for a small set fee. An option gives the buyer the right to buy (or sell) at a set future price, but he or she doesn't have to! Taking a futures option provides time for your management team to decide whether to buy or not. If you do buy, you know the fixed price. If you don't, you lose only the small option price.

These are sophisticated tactics and should be pursued directly with your finance office and management. Because money can be made or lost in this manner, the person doing the buying must not take the risk alone.

12

Controlling Global Logistics Costs

Intense global competition requires that purchasing, marketing, and transportation work together to achieve cost efficiency without sacrificing service. The American buyer works with the world's most efficient domestic transportation system. Service from and to the United States is also quite sophisticated.

Transportation costs can be a major factor when considering any purchase. More so when using more distant foreign sources whose transportation network may not be properly tied-in with the global logistics pipeline. Logistic costs for offshore buys are a larger percentage of total purchase costs than in the past.

Transportation knowledge about offshore buys is often ignored by purchasing personnel. When the buyer imports into the United States, lack of knowledge can cost fines or unnecessary duties. In some cases, imports can be severely restricted by U.S. Customs. Equally serious are delays that cause friction in supplier relationships. To get better service at the least total cost, buyers should evaluate their possible transportation options before placing their order.

During the 1970s, government regulation was seen as stifling efficiency. No longer is this true. In the early 1980s, the Interstate Commerce Commission's role of protecting carriers and ruling on tariff violations and other "economic abuses" was reduced. This freed carriers to compete in a more open market. Transportation can now be purchased like other services or commodities. Transportation is negotiable. Discounts are available, and a purchaser can negotiate good contract terms, especially when moving frequent or large tonnage.

The main transportation problems facing buyers are the following:

1. Equipment availability and suitability;
2. Time in transit;
3. Control of shipment;

4. Unclear rates and charges;
5. Overcharges (often years after delivery);
6. Slowness in processing loss or damage claims;
7. Prompt proof-of-delivery; and
8. Inconsistent services, such as poor shipment tracing.

The four basic modes of transport are by air, rail and truck (by land), and water. An international shipment is usually a multimodal combination of these, either truck and water or truck and air. The potential of rail for heavy, large, or containerized shipments is clear.

Knowledgeable buyers select preferred routings. The decision of transportation option to use is often a compromise between speed and expense. As they say, time is money. Recall that since you took possession and may already have paid, your goods are inventory being tied up on long ocean voyages. Figure 12-1 depicts a comparison of transit time versus rates.

Backhauls are often the secret to carrier's profits. If a buyer can help secure a full round trip or can fill an otherwise empty "backhaul," this is an excellent way to drop rates. Perhaps a buyer knows of another buyer who has goods shipped in the reverse direction?

Among the factors to consider when deciding the desired method of shipping are:

• Date needed;
• Rates, cost of shipping;
• Cost of insurance;
• Cubic size and weight of shipment;
• Value of products;
• Discharge and destination point;
• Possibility of deterioration;
• Susceptibility to shipping damage;
• Handling requirements during shipment;
• Possibilities of theft;
• Use of containers, type—20-foot, 40-foot, 45-foot, standard or high cube, insulated, refrigerated, controlled atmosphere, and so forth;
• Paperwork required; and
• Carrier's ability to operate in your source country.

AIR SHIPMENT

Frequently, smaller shipments are imported by mail or air. Perishables or delicate instruments often have to be flown. For other goods, when maximum speed is

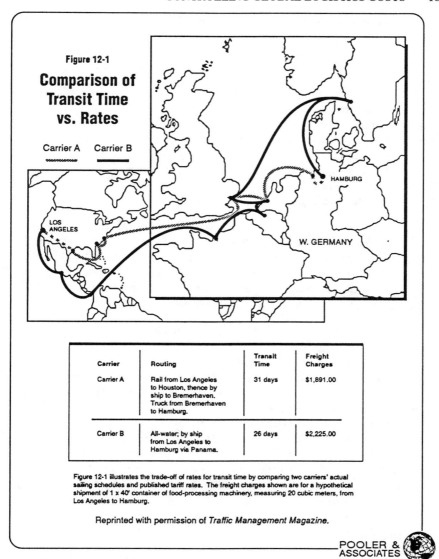

Figure 12-1

Comparison of Transit Time vs. Rates

Carrier A   Carrier B

Carrier	Routing	Transit Time	Freight Charges
Carrier A	Rail from Los Angeles to Houston, thence by ship to Bremerhaven. Truck from Bremerhaven to Hamburg.	31 days	$1,891.00
Carrier B	All-water; by ship from Los Angeles to Hamburg via Panama.	26 days	$2,225.00

Figure 12-1 illustrates the trade-off of rates for transit time by comparing two carriers' actual sailing schedules and published tariff rates. The freight charges shown are for a hypothetical shipment of 1 x 40' container of food-processing machinery, measuring 20 cubic meters, from Los Angeles to Hamburg.

Reprinted with permission of *Traffic Management Magazine.*

POOLER & ASSOCIATES

FIGURE 12-1.   Comparison of transit time versus rates.

needed, full or partial shipment by air is required. Advantages of an air shipment are:

- Speed.
- Insurance is less expensive.
- Cost of warehousing is generally lower.
- Packing needs are less.
- Damage is minimized.
- Loss by theft is reduced (however, major thefts occur at airports if freight is not cleared promptly).
- Quicker transferal to delivery trucks inland after clearance.
- Inventory carrying costs are lower.
- Lead time to procure is less.

While passenger airlines, cargo plane operators, and airfreight forwarders publish rates, remember that most volume shipment rates may still be negotiable. Air freight service is routinely provided by carriers who handle up to 50-, 70-, or 150-pound maximum weight packages. Shipments under 1,500 pounds can now be moved economically by air. Heavier shipments of 2,000 pounds or more usually require special arrangements. Choices available are:

1. Air parcel post (Express mail for two-pound envelopes for next day delivery).
2. Direct airline:
   a. Door to door, such as American Airlines;
   b. Counter to counter, such as Delta, USAIR, United, and others.
3. Overnight Express (Federal Express, UPS, Burlington Air Express, and Airborne Express), which offers:
   a. Overnight freight service with a 100 to 150 pound per carton limit;
   b. Overnight envelope service—up to two pounds; and
   c. Air service for second business day delivery, with possible next morning delivery in major markets, with some weight restrictions.
4. True air freight forwarders, such as Pilor, LEP/Profit, and others that use the lift of scheduled passenger carriers. They often provide lower cost "time definite" delivery for two-, to five-day transit, to support just-in-time needs.
5. Charter flights.

When shipping by air, breaking the shipment down into smaller (50 pound) cartons sometimes allows speedier handling. However, some carriers charge more for multiple piece shipments. For example, 100-pound packages have lower rates than 250-pound ones. Also, some carriers have different "cube" rules. For example, "166 cubic inches are equal to a pound of chargeable weight." Some aircraft operators will waive these cube rules. So you should check the specific services and rates available before specifying packaging.

MOTOR TRANSPORT

Motor carriage is the most popular mode for domestic transport. An old saying, "If you have it, a truck brought it" is true today even when the shipment is made by sea. In choosing a trucking company, consider how many break-bulk (sorting) terminals your shipment will pass through. Fewer "breaks" means faster transit and less damage. Also, single-line carriers are better than joint arrangements, for better tracing and lower damage.

Common carriers are readily available. They may operate over regular or irregular routes. Most less-than-truckload (LTL) carriers operate regular schedules, while truckload carriers schedule to meet your specific needs.

General freight carriers haul a variety of commodities, differing in size, weight, and bulk. They combine different classifications of freight into truckloads, to reduce line haul costs. Consolidated Freightways is an example of a national carrier, with virtually 48 state coverage. Another is Central Transport, with 200 terminals operating primarily in the central and eastern half of the United States.

Motor carriers provide a wide variety of services. Specialized freight carriers usually carry only one, perhaps two, types of commodities. For example, a tank truck can normally not carry both food and nonfood cargoes.

"T.O.F.C.", trailer-on-flat-car (formerly called "piggy-back"), is when the motor carrier puts a container or truck chassis on a flatcar for rail transport. Upon arriving at a rail yard, a driver attaches his truck cab to the trailer and takes the shipment directly to its final destination.

Carriers determine the location of shipments quite readily when computers are used to expedite freight handling and some in-transit information through satellite trucking and communication with individual units. You can take advantage of the transportation industries' free floppy disks for service, rate, and other information. Disks are available upon request from many truckers. Their EDI systems can give you rates, manifests, rated shipping orders, shipment location, and detailed shipping reports.

Freight Consolidation

Smaller volume users may have trouble getting a less-than-truckload (LTL) shipment moved promptly. LTL rates are always higher per hundred weight (cwt) than full truck or bulk rates. You can make your shipment more economical by combining shipments of a variety of items into a single LTL shipment, and pay a lower price per cwt. However, packing is simpler when shipments contain only one kind of package.

While each item has its own rate of duty, commingling of goods with different duties may cause Customs to charge all items at the higher duty if they can't inspect—that is, unless you can show the items are a set and can't be segregated or that costs would be prohibitive. Should Customs insist on segregation, you must pay the expense.

Through a freight forwarder or consolidator, your shipment might be combined with other firms to get lower rates. It pays to combine tonnage of both export and import volume. Laws, rules, and regulations about contract carriage are in the ICC regulations within Title 49, Code of Federal Regulations (parts 1000 to end). These regulations specify obligations of the carrier, shipper, and receiver. They cover routing permits, contract filing, and other services. Since 1978, many regulations have been relaxed or dropped. However, there is still the ICC, with the responsibility to regulate interstate commerce contract carriage.

In addition to transport by ocean, many shipments are interstate or intrastate movements in nature. State economic regulators vary from those with none (Florida, New Jersey) to those considered tighter than the ICC before 1980 (Ohio, Georgia, etc.)

OCEAN CARRIAGE

There are three types of ocean carrier: 1. conference carrier, 2. independent steamship line, and 3. tramp or special charter service.

1. An ocean conference carrier is a member of a legal association of carriers joined to set common freight rates and shipping schedules. By signing a contract with the conference, lower rates are available. Rates are equal on all vessels in the conference. Buyers regularly contracting get good service. The conference operates on a nonprofit basis for the benefit of its carrier members.
2. Independent steamship lines quote rates individually and may be lower by as much as 10 percent, depending on:
   a. Space allocated upon availability;
   b. All ports may not be covered; and
   c. Changes in destination may occur.
3. Tramp vessels usually carry only bulk cargo and have irregular sailing schedules. Charter rates vary widely.

A Conference Carrier must stop at each scheduled port. Most regular trade lanes (United States-Japan, United States-Australia, United States-Hong Kong, United States-Northern Europe) have regular conference schedules. A nonconference carrier may skip and land at an alternative port, depending on the volume of business and trade available.

About 20 percent of ocean vessels are tankers, 25 percent carry dry bulk, 12 percent are combined carriers, and 20 percent carry a mix of containers and break bulk. The balance carry solely containers or are general cargo vessels. To select a carrier, you can look in the daily "shipcards" section of the Journal of Commerce

Shipper's Digest. Find ship schedules of types of carriers going to your destination port for the month of your shipment. A reference for further study is *Service Guide—Ship Your Cargo on U.S. Flag Ships*. It's available from the U.S. Department of Commerce, Maritime Administration, Office of Public Affairs, Washington, D.C. 20230. This gives lists of U.S. lines, foreign trade routes served, and types of services provided.

Also, consider the influence that certain carriers have in the destination port. A carrier handling many shipments to Jamaica may own its own dock there. Therefore, their cargo is the quickest to get unloaded and passed through local customs.

Shipping by ocean carriage enjoys the advantage of being the most economical method of transportation, especially for bulky products. Ocean shipments often use containers that are packed at the factory and sealed to prevent pilferage and contamination.

Some of the disadvantages of ocean carriage are:

• Length of transport time.
• Goods are more susceptible to deterioration because of long transit time and exposure to salt air and water, as well as ship motions.
• Exposure to theft in dock areas.
• Occasional longshoremen strikes can tie up goods. Sometimes, several U.S. ports will be struck simultaneously in a labor dispute. Usually, foreign ports are struck singly, and alternates can be used.
• Congested ports (includes airports) often cause slow unloading.
• Handling at ports can produce damages.

Non-Vessel Operating Common Carriers (NVOCC)

Independent carriers of a special class are NVOCCs. They contract for shipments as a carrier although they don't own equipment, nor operate any ship. About 1,500 companies issue their own NVOCC bills-of-lading, using ships of regular carriers.

NVOCCs are sometimes confused with ocean freight forwarders, as the services do overlap. Also, some large forwarders do operate as NVOCCs. The NVOCC or forwarder buys container space from the steamship at wholesale rates. Two or more may combine their items to share a container that makes for more frequent departures. In such cases, the ocean bill must show the co-loading NVOCC or forwarder.

A new procedure requires the freight forwarder to submit transport documents as FIATA Combined Transport Bill of Lading approved by the ICC, or indicate that documents are issued by an agent of a named carrier. Otherwise, banks will reject papers (per the ICC's UCP 400, Article 25).

Volume purchase of transportation allows the sale of quality transportation at lower cost. This is particularly true for small consolidated shipments. The NVOCC sells contracted space at a discounted retail pricing level that allows a profit to the operator. Even after absorbing the extra costs of trucking, warehousing, and shipping, the NVOCC is able to save buyers up to 15 percent of normal steamship charges. Another savings is reportedly the reduction of damage claims through reduced handling.

Marine Insurance

Laws that apply to Marine Cargo Insurance are listed in the Carriage of Goods by Sea Act (COGSA), for anyone wishing to study them.

This following insurance scenario makes a point. By phone, buyer David tells his freight forwarder, "Take care of all the details. You get our insurance, too. I want the material delivered to my receiving dock." Later, David issues his order along with the required letter of credit, spelling out "FOB: C&F, Delivered."

One week out of port, David hears rumors that the ocean carrier's ship was disabled at sea in severe weather. He feared his cloth materials could get badly soaked on the ship deck. Though loaded in containers, salt water had leaked in during a heavy storm once before.

David instructed his broker to collect on the insurance, as he had to pay for the replacement shipment at once. David is surprised to be told, "That's your responsibility. We just did what you told us in your letter of credit. It's even worse than you think. After I talked with them today, the steamship company said their ship sank last night. You owe them 1/100th the value of their ship. I hope you got the proper marine insurance."

Under the long-standing Admiralty Law, if a ship is in a collision or sinks (a rare occasion), you as owners of the cargo are liable for the loss based on your portion of ship's capacity taken by your cargo. This is a classic, though extreme case of "Who must file a claim?" Note that David failed to use a standard INCOTERM. Of more importance, he failed to take out insurance coverage that under C&F was his responsibility.

Marine insurance is important, yet sometimes difficult to buy at any price. This is why insurance is so vital for offshore procurement. The buyer has to be on guard and *be certain that insurance exists.* And you must make sure it covers all your risks.

Two varieties of marine insurance exist—one is "open" blanket cargo and the other is "special." The "open" or blanket cargo policy is in continuous effect for all shipments. Rates can be lower because of a large volume. For occasional importers, the "special" one-time cargo policy for a single shipment is adequate.

You should put in your purchase order (and letter of credit, as explained under credits) that *either a policy, or a certificate of insurance* (Fig. 12-2.) is required as part of the documentation. This assures that insurance is in force, or relieves the buyer from responsibility to pay.

INSURANCE CERTIFICATE

EXPORTER (Principal or seller-licensee and address including ZIP Code)	DOCUMENT NUMBER	B'L OR AWB NUMBER
	EXPORT REFERENCES	
ZIP CODE		
CONSIGNED TO	FORWARDING AGENT (Name and address—references)	
	POINT (STATE) OF ORIGIN OR FTZ NUMBER	
NOTIFY PARTY/INTERMEDIATE CONSIGNEE (Name and address)	DOMESTIC ROUTING/EXPORT INSTRUCTIONS	

PRE-CARRIAGE BY	PLACE OF RECEIPT BY PRE-CARRIER	
EXPORTING CARRIER	PORT OF LOADING EXPORT	LOADING PIER/TERMINAL
FOREIGN PORT OF UNLOADING (Vessel and air only)	PLACE OF DELIVERY BY ON-CARRIER	TYPE OF MOVE	CONTAINERIZED (Vessel only) ☐ Yes ☐ No

MARKS AND NUMBERS	NUMBER OF PACKAGES	DESCRIPTION OF COMMODITIES in Schedule B detail	GROSS WEIGHT (Kilos)	MEASUREMENT	D OR F

DATE OF POLICY	SUM INSURED $	AMOUNT IN WORDS		DOLLARS

SPECIAL TERMS AND CONDITIONS: SHIPMENTS ON DECK or AIR CARGO when Insured Under this Policy are subject to terms and conditions specified on the reverse side hereof. SHIPMENTS SUBJECT TO AN "UNDER DECK" BILL OF LADING are Insured:-

THIS INSURANCE IS ALSO SUBJECT TO THE FOLLOWING AMERICAN INSTITUTE CLAUSES CURRENT ON THE DATE OF ISSUANCE OF THIS POLICY: MARINE EXTENSION CLAUSES S.R. & C.C. ENDORSEMENT WAR RISK INSURANCE	WHEN GOODS ARE SO DESTINED THIS INSURANCE IS SUBJECT TO:- SOUTH AMERICAN 60 DAY CLAUSE

This Policy not transferable unless countersigned by an authorized representative of this Company or the Assured. Countersigned:

IN WITNESS WHEREOF, this Company has executed and attested these presents.

_____

Secretary   President

Form 80-340 Printed and Sold by UNZ&CO. 190 Baldwin Ave., Jersey City, NJ 07306 • (800) 631-3098 • (201) 795-5400

FIGURE 12-2.   Certificate of insurance. Reprinted with permission of Unz & Co., 190 Boldwin Avenue, Jersey City, NJ 07306

Buyers should require "ocean marine" cargo insurance that includes standard *warehouse to warehouse* coverage. This applies to both land and air transport, as well as traditional ocean shipments. It reimburses for loss or damage while in transit from origin to final destination.

Of paramount concern are exclusion clauses defining limitations of coverage. Examples are nuclear exclusion, wars (war risk policy is special), strikes, riot and civil commotions, delay clause, nationalized insurance restrictions, "all-risk"—definition of risk, and explosion clause. Other insurance clauses buyers may encounter include water act and fire statutes, letters of indemnity, subrogation, time of suit clause, perils added, insurable interest, warranties, and guarantee of collectability. The above are listed to show the extent of complexity and the need for specialized help when delving into insurance matters.

For those that import regularly and don't want to carry their own insurance, coverage can be under the freight forwarder's blanket policy. Such an arrangement means that your goods are usually covered by "warehouse-to-warehouse" insurance.

For a large volume of goods, it may pay to buy your own insurance. Only the end-user or buyer knows exactly what's required. More importantly, when claims are settled, the buyer is better off working with the company that he or she pays for insurance.

Insurance rates depend on factors such as product, destination, shipping method, volume, and contractual relationships. The value of the cargo is computed as cost plus 10 percent for contingencies. For estimating purposes only, the insurance premium for a shipment from Japan could run from 30 to 50 cents per $100 of shipment value. You have to get a specific quotation for each shipment.

Proper planning for loss prevention is the best insurance! Are special risks covered where required? Is insurance coverage in effect throughout the journey? Make sure you have enough. Certain insurance companies specialize in marine insurance. More information may be gotten by writing to the American Institute of Marine Underwriters, 14 Wall Street, New York, NY 10005.

Major Ports

About 400 entry points exist in North America, but only about 37 are major ocean vessel ports that serve the United States. Some of the major ports on the East Coast that handle European trade are Boston, Baltimore, Detroit, New York (including Newark and Port Elizabeth, which handle more than 5,000 ships annually), Newport News, Philadelphia, Baltimore, Miami, Charleston, Tampa, Savannah, Jacksonville, Halifax, and Montreal.

The West Coast ports were the world's fastest growing through the 1980s. The ports of Los Angeles/Long Beach combined rank second in volume only to the Port Authority of New York and New Jersey. Other key ports in the West are San

Francisco, Oakland, Portland, Oregon, Seattle, Tacoma, and Vancouver. All are bustling with traffic in both directions, handling a large amount of container cargo. They are convenient for American trading partners Japan, Taiwan, South Korea, and Hong Kong.

In the Gulf, Southern Louisiana, which includes the ports of New Orleans and Baton Rouge, is a leader in tonnage. They hope to improve their barge-to-ship capabilities. The Port of New Orleans handles the Mississippi traffic, and has large load equipment.

Possible use of T.O.F.C. "land bridge" shipments will save transit time. It takes about ten days longer for a ship to sail to the eastern United States from the Orient through the Panama Canal than if a land bridge (railroad) moved the containers across the United States.

Buyers have to decide the advantages that a port's location provides to them, and how extensive their cargo handling and storage facilities are. Typical services listed are number of piers available, 25- to 180-ton gantries and container cranes, capacity of terminals, and square footage of enclosed or outdoor storage space available. RORO facilities denotes capability to allow roll-on and roll-off capability.

In 1986, Congress passed the Harbor Maintenance Revenue Act, to raise funds to pay the Army Corps of Engineers for its harbor repair work. In 1987, U.S. Customs began collecting a Port Use Tax on all waterborne trade. The tax rate is 0.04 percent of the cargo value.[1] Importers pay the tax at time of entry. This imposes extra papers on Customs brokers, and could result in a small handling fee. Though a small cost, this is a negotiable item to get the offshore exporter to deduct this charge from his product pricing.

Some of the great foreign ports in Europe are Rotterdam, called the "gateway to Europe," which handles about 40 percent of the European distribution through the Netherlands. Bremerhaven is the dominant German port for North American shipping. Handling more than 30 million tons each year, it is one of Europe's largest container ports. Hamburg is a "window to the east," handling much of Czechoslovakian goods and shipping to U.S. and Scandinavia destinations. Other Eastern European countries are expected to increase Hamburg's traffic.

LeHavre on the Normandy coast of France grants easy access to trans-Atlantic shipping. It is the fifth largest port in Europe. Northeast of London is the Port of Felixstowe, the prime container port of the United Kingdom.

TRANSPORTATION CONTRACTS

An "FOB" term in the purchase order spells out the division of responsibilities for transportation and passage of title. The goods are delivered by seller to buyer at a point as explained under INCOTERMS in Chapter 7. In some cases, the risk of loss

---

[1] 1987. *Traffic Management*. April p. 15.

may have already passed to you, though the seller has paid for and is controlling the shipment.

The Motor Carrier Act of 1980 brought about a high degree of deregulation to truckers. Also, the 1980 Staggers Rail Act is credited with creating more competition by reviving the railroad system. These two important acts gave domestic shippers and carriers the freedom to negotiate contracts without heavy-handed government bureaucratic involvement.

Factors to consider when drafting a transportation agreement:
- Determining your company's risks and exposures.
- Determining carrier's liability (common?, $/pound?, or other?).
- Escape clauses with minimum notice times.
- Are the provisions (such as "most favored rates") enforceable?
- Choosing proper insurance coverage (including analyzing premium and loss statistics).
- Choosing a venue to settle disputes.
- Awareness of available carrier resources.

Carrier financial instability is always of concern. Are finances (i.e., debt, cash flow, and capital) strong enough to assure long-term survival? Motor carrier operating ratios are one index of financial health. A carrier consistently above 100 is not covering operating costs.

When global buying, use terms that are familiar to your offshore supplier. You must tie down the freight bill, who assumes the risk of loss or damage, who arranges insurance, and so forth.

Ask yourself (and answer) these questions:

1. What is the lowest possible classification of the goods to be transported?
2. What is the frequency of shipment?
3. How about time/volume rates?
4. What service levels are truly needed?
5. Can we repackage to reduce theft, damage, cube weight, or other cost factors?

The rate will depend on the following:

- Description of the item shipped
- Type of material used to make the product, such as aluminum, plastic, or sheet steel.
- Whether it is assembled or knocked down, folded or nested, packaged in crates, in packages or on skids. All the above can affect costs. So can the next item.
- The density (weight/cubic foot) and length of the item.
- Whether it's new, used, reconditioned, or scrap.
- A liquid or solid.

- Finished or rough form.
- Hazardous, dangerous, or "reportable" as such.

The next step is to negotiate for a better deal. This type of negotiation is similar to buying goods or services. Before negotiating, give thought to the proper description and classification of your items.

Motor Carriage Contracts

Interstate motor carrier contracts are regulated by the Interstate Commerce Commission. While contracts are no longer filed with the ICC, they must be in writing and conform with rules governing contracts. If not, the contract can be declared invalid, and higher price class rates apply (even retroactively).

The National Motor Freight Classification (NMFC) and the intra New England Coordinated Freight Classification (CFC) contain descriptions for all commodities that move by motor carrier. The proper description for your item will assign a specific NMFC number to it, and a "class" that correlates to the economic value. For example, umbrellas (folded) in boxes are NMFC #18800, sub 1, and are rated class 100. Umbrellas (other than folded) are NMFC #18800, sub 2, and are assigned class 400. Open umbrellas will cost about four times more than folded ones to transport by truck.

There are now four key freight characteristics used to set classification (reduced from 15 before deregulation). They are:

1. Density (weight per cubic foot);
2. Stowability;
3. Ease or difficulty of handling;
4. Liability (including value per pound, susceptibility to theft, damage, perishability, propensity to damage other commodities with which it is transported, and propensity for spontaneous combustion or explosion).[2]

While there is no exact weight given to these characteristics, density has been evolving as the major characteristic in new and reconsidered classifications.

Negotiation of point-to-point LTL rates, along with discounts ranging from 20 to 50 percent are possible.[3] This is confirmed by a trucking survey that, "Three out of four discounts gotten by buyers are in the 30 to 50 percent range." Most discounts for domestic carriers were in the 10- to 50-percent range, and 10 percent were higher than 50 percent.

---

[2]Bohman, R. 1989. Characteristics that determine freight classification ratings. *Traffic Management.* May p. 25.

[3]1987. *Purchasing.* April 23 p. 56.

Cost Analysis

It is smart to break down transportation costs as much as possible. Rates are set on a time, weight, or volume basis. For the best results, buyers must work closely with their traffic specialists. Lacking such a specialist, the buyer must learn transportation or seek outside guidance. Outside expertise comes from consultants, third party transportation providers, and often the carriers themselves.

Cost analysis of land transportation services can be broken down into four groupings:

1. Cost/mile of moving materials or goods
   Usually, this is the hourly cost of vehicle operation divided by the number of miles travelled in one hour. Costs include labor, fuel, tolls, vehicle depreciation, and fuel consumed. Also included are costs related to maintenance, wear on tires, and taxes. The total cost is usually standardized for terminal-to-terminal travel.
2. Costs of billing
   These are the costs to set charges, correctly rate and bill, and collect undercharges.
3. Terminal Costs
   These include costs that result from picking up goods from various customers, moving for consolidation, and so forth. Upon delivering, there is a reverse cycle of distributing. Such costs include forklift handling, and so forth, but is heavily labor-intensive.
4. Carrier overhead costs
   Like any business, this item includes the cost of management, overhead, and those costs not directly connected to individual shipments. Lumped in are costs for vehicle registration fees, insurance, and depreciation of the buildings.

As in any buy, the detailed information known by the buyer is invaluable in seeking better carrier rates. Item 4, overhead cost, is an area that most truckers will remove, rather than lose the business. So this is the first area to negotiate. Buyers can see that loading the vehicle, volume of shipment, and so on, all impact the carrier's costs. Buyers can reduce costs from the contract by changing packaging, loading skids, and shrink-wrapping.

Trends in domestic transportation costs are published by Traffic Management magazine. A "Logistics Cost Index" tracks two years of historical data. The base is computed as of 1985 equal to 100. Forecasts are made for various methods of shipping, such as truckload, LTL, rail, and air cargo, projecting cost levels ahead though the next four quarters. Also, warehousing and total inventory carrying costs are tracked. This is an excellent reference comparison with your experience.

Ocean Carriage Contracts

Negotiating rates with deregulated ocean carriers will reduce shipping costs. The marketplace now determines more issues, allowing more flexibility. With deregulation, more contracts are now signed. Instead of a single haul agreement, a contract can cover various items and routes, at an agreed rate. You request special service as needed.

The Shipping Act of 1916 set conference regulations enforced by the Federal Maritime Commission (FMC). Until the Shipping Act of 1984, a U.S. shipper could not enter into long-term contracts with ocean carriers. Now the shipper has an option to move cargo under the regular liner rates or to negotiate service contracts.

The ocean bill of lading formerly covered each shipment as an individual carriage contract. Buyers can now commit their total volume, and negotiate lower fixed rates in broader ocean carrier contracts (in exchange for "take or pay" provisions).

Public Law 98-237 defined a service contract as one between a shipper and an ocean common carrier or conference. Service contracts are filed with the FMC, as are liner tariffs. The contract terms are public, and "me too" similar arrangement applications can be requested by other "similarly situated" shippers with a 30-day window.

Service contracts require that the shipper commits to provide a minimum quantity of cargo over a fixed time period. The carrier commits to a certain rate schedule, and defines the assured space, time in transit, port rotation, or similar service features. Penalties for failure to produce the committed cargo volume is normally spelled out in the contract. Rerating tariff rates is usually done on a fixed dollar amount per container shy of the agreed volume.

Deregulation has forced carriers to be more attuned to customers' needs. While deregulation made special agreements possible, they still must be filed with the FMC. Because a contract filed with the commission cannot be amended, you must use specific terms that are well thought through. For example, such terms as length of agreement, the exact transport work wanted, the amount to pay, and shortfall penalties.

For those desiring added rate information, *Ocean Freight Rate Guidelines for Shippers* is published by the Superintendent of Documents, U.S. Government Printing Office. It describes basic procedures for transporting overseas goods.

Contract Clauses

The agreement names the shipper/consignee and carrier, giving all addresses. Both carrier and shipper should sign.

Terms used in a contract are:

• Transport—Carrier transports in compliance with all laws and regulations. Assumes responsibility and control of goods until turned over properly to either next carrier or owner.

- Tender—Shipper/consignee agrees to tender identified specific volume of material at place of pick up. Trucker agrees to transport along a set routing.
- Receipt—Carrier issues bill of lading as receipt for each shipment and will get proof of delivery.
- Compensation—Rate quoted as per item, pound, ton, mile, containerload, and so forth.
- Billing—Carrier submits invoices, and shipper to pay as noted.
- Liability—Insurance is maintained, keeping shipper harmless from carrier's actions.
- Loss and damage—Relief from liability of carrier for shipment while within its control.
- Transfer—Unless specifically stated, control is not transferrable by either party.
- Time—Duration and length of contract, and termination notice.

The contract for transportation is basically similar to other buying agreements. Here are some key clauses to use:

1. Scope of the work clause
2. Dispute clause
3. Replacement of prior agreements clause
4. "Most favored shipper" clause
5. Force majeure clause

Scope of the work clause is an exacting section that must explicitly specify the work required and by whom. Spell out any special handling instructions or expected perils.

Dispute clause is similar to the arbitration clause reviewed in Chapter 7. Replacement of prior agreements clause means that this new contract replaces any older or prior agreement.

"Most favored shipper" clause is similar to "most favored buyer" clauses inserted in purchase orders by buyers. The essence is that the shipper agrees that he or she will extend any lower rate that he or she gives anyone else for comparable volume and commodity. Shipper discrimination is prohibited. Lower rates that are extended to one shipper must be given to another with similar volume. Or providing equipment, free loading or unloading to another shipper means that these concessions must be given to the most favored shipper also.

Force majeure clause is well known to buyers as an "act of God" clause. It provides for temporary relief from contractual terms should events occur beyond the control of the parties. Shipping examples are work stoppage, dock strike, sinking of a ship, or storm-induced damage to goods in transit.

PACKAGING AND LABELLING FOR
OVERSEAS TRANSPORT

Goods have to be packaged so that customs officers can examine, weigh, or measure before they release the goods. U.S. Customs requires you to have suppliers show exact quantity within each box or package. The marks and numbers are put on each package, and listed on the invoice.

Common markings are the shipper's mark, country of origin, and gross and net weights (in pounds and kilograms). Labels must be understood by overseas handlers who may know only a little English. Such markings allow identification without the need to shove the container or package around to read labels.

Markings must be in English, and may also be in the supplier's language. The port of destination should be specified. Customer identification, with the buyer's name, address, and order number, should be visible. A package should be marked on at least two sides and the top (three sides). Two-inch high stencil lettering in black waterproof ink allows easier reading. Instruct your supplier not to use product names or trade names of commercial goods on the outside of their packages. The anonymous shipment is less tempting for thieves.

Use standardized international shipping and handling symbols adopted by the International Organization for Standardization. Typical symbols are an umbrella and the words "Keep Dry," a picture of a hook with an "X" marked over with the words, "Use No Hooks." Others are a penguin with slash lines and "Do Not Freeze," "This Side Up," and so on. Cautionary labels depend on your items. Hazardous materials require universal symbols adapted by the Inter-Governmental Maritime Consultive Organization.

In worldwide transportation, many people who handle containers often don't read any language, so shippers use pictures called pictographs. Yet some symbols may be confusing because of a cultural bias. "Fragile" is often depicted by the broken goblet, but longshoremen at East African ports, thinking it meant broken glass, reportedly tossed the boxes around.

Excessive packing will needlessly raise the cost of transportation. Packing should assure that the product arrives in safe condition, as economically as possible. A prime concern in designing packing and packaging is to maintain the purchased quality.

Packing and packaging costs are part of the total landed cost of imports. The supplier usually provides packing, using what he or she believes is appropriate. Poor results affect the condition of your goods upon arrival. Dented, marred, or rusty products, with torn parts, can hurt visual appearance, influence sales, and lead to customer rejection. So it is up to you to specify how goods are packed and labelled.

There is a trade-off between light packing, higher transportation costs, and product damage. Damage occurs in a variety of ways. If your goods are not preloaded in a container, a shipment on an ocean freighter will either be loaded into a container with other goods or be hoisted on board with a net sling.

Packing that is satisfactory on an aircraft often can't take the "pitch and yaw" stress in a ship's hold on the tossing sea. Salt water or salt air can ruin shipments easily. Moisture can also be a problem because of condensation. Also, cargo unloaded in the rain can be subject to heavy moisture. A waterproof inner liner with rust-inhibiting coatings and greases often helps.

Shrink-packaging used along with moisture absorbent silica gel absorb small amounts of moisture that could damage items such as motors and machinery. Strapping or "see through" shrink-wrap is an excellent way to prevent load shifting, and also makes it more difficult to steal.

Forklift trucks, as well as conveyers, all can damage poorly packaged products. Overseas ports often don't have the same quality equipment as U.S. ports. Items may be pushed, shoved, rolled, or even dropped during movement.

Crates and skids allow forklifts to move easily. Also, they keep the cargo off the floor, above small puddles. Unitizing the pallet load by strapping or banding keeps it compact and tight. However, some countries, such as Australia, dislike the use of wooden pallets, and you must fumigate them at high cost! In the United States, if insects are seen dropping from the crates, they and their contents have to be fumigated prior to release by Customs. So, for certain types of goods fumigated wood should be used to build the packing crate. It is cheaper in the long run.

Containerization

Within the last 20 years, containers have become the prime method for international ocean and air shipment. Containerization on water allows for the use of fast, modern containerships that use deck-stack loading. Containers come in various sizes, materials, and construction. The FEU (40-foot equivalent unit) is the most common size in use. It is equal to two TEUs (20-foot equivalent units), the original standard.

Special containers may have air conditioning equipment when the shipment warrants its use. They reduce product damage due to excessive moisture. If the product can shift inside, the container should be internally braced.

Containers are often truck bodies, lifted off their wheels and placed on the vessel. Getting a new set of wheels at the import terminal eases inland shipment. For rail shipment, this is known as a C.O.F.C. (container on flat car) shipment. The term "fishyback" was sometimes used to describe this type of ocean shipment.

"House-to-house container" means that the goods are placed in the container at the factory before going out for shipment, and the goods are delivered in the receiving country at the consignees door. House-to-pier means that the goods are loaded at the factory, unloaded at the incoming pier, and delivered as loose freight. Pier-to-house is the reverse, where goods are loaded into the container at the export pier and delivered as a full container at the consignee's door.

Most containers are steamship company-owned and a rental fee is not charged. If a rental is used, and the container is unused on its return trip, the container rental company increases its container use fee. "Ports of the World," available from Insurance Company of North America, describes the type of container services used in overseas shipping. Containers for rent are in the Yellow Pages.

USE OF A FREIGHT FORWARDER

For new importers, there is a tendency to rely on the foreign manufacturer or a foreign freight forwarder to get the product out of the foreign country. Through training and experience, buyers know that in the United States manufacturers handle everything. Why not when we source offshore?

Often, the new importing buyer is dealing with a new foreign exporting company. Neither may have the experience to make transportation work smoothly. It can be dangerous to allow a little-known seller to handle shipping arrangements. The offshore supplier may use a "buddy" who charges excessively. Reportedly, some foreigners with a cozy relationship can rebate part of their charge to those who hire them. Relying on the foreign supplier to monitor your costs and interests could be a costly bad judgement call.

Freight forwarders normally help exporters. Custom brokers help buyers and importers enter goods into the United States. Larger forwarders sometimes wear both hats and act as customs brokers. When the same house is both a forwarder and customs broker, the two roles merge somewhat and appear interchangeable. The two roles are distinctly defined and must be kept separate, as mandated by the Shipping Act of 1984.

Freight forwarders' licenses were authorized by the Shipping Act of 1916. There are more than 1,500 licensed by the FMC today. A "house" will range from 1 or 2 people working out of their home to large multiservice organizations with more than 1,000 employees.

A buyer might hire a freight forwarder if he or she has the responsibility for controlling the shipment. Because of their daily shipping experience, contacts, and knowledge of what works, forwarders act as counselors. As their name implies, a freight forwarder routes and follows the shipment of the goods through foreign countries. The freight forwarder may perform the following services:

- Get quotations for shipping and packaging costs;
- Provide advice on transportation modes;
- Arrange for packing, marking, and labeling;
- Reserve cargo space, and get marine insurance;
- Arrange consolidation of cargo with that of other importers, to reduce costs by lowering cargo rates;

- Expedite shipment through ports, moving goods from ship to rail, truck, or plane; Monitor the shipment to take steps to correct problems as they occur; and
- Telex the buyer with shipment details (important on urgent shipments or if trouble arises).

Typically, a forwarder buys space on common, frequent air flights to major cities, or arranges space aboard an ocean vessel. Also, forwarders get the B/L, shipper's export declaration number and certificate of origin. The forwarder prepares or provides a dock receipt or any special papers to the next transportation carrier.

International freight forwarders watch for important shipments. They may reroute or do whatever is necessary to secure prompt handling. They check paperwork for completeness, to see that everything is in order. Forwarders look for the name of vessel to carry the goods, both ports of loading and discharge filled in, number and type of packages, description of merchandise, weight, size, and cubic measurement along with the proper marks.

A good forwarder will help you avoid problems, or solve unexpected problems that pop up. For example, say that a ship heading for Houston is rerouted to Savannah. Such changes are common practice by certain ship lines, with certain commodities on board. The forwarder, with the consent of the shipper, will steer clear of these type of risks, or make fast alternate arrangements when the material arrives in the new port.

They can advise you on any port charges, consular fees, and insurance costs. Most forwarders have to be competitive, but it's well to get several prices to compare cost of service.

A forwarder charges about $100 per shipment, depending on services. Sometimes a small air shipment is handled for as little as as $40.

Because of low fees, recovery for consequential damages, such as loss of production time due to late delivery, spoilage, and so on, is difficult to collect. Liability for demurrage, detention, and storage are negotiable only if clear arrangements are spelled out in advance. If the delay is the fault of the forwarders, some forwarders carry "Errors & Omissions" insurance to protect themselves, so the buyer should try to get restitution.

DOCUMENTS USED FOR TRANSPORTATION

The sequence of loading a ship is planned. Failure to have the right documents or goods on time means delays and possibly missing a sailing date.

The bill of lading (B/L), shown in Figure 12-3, is a legally binding title contract document that shows ownership. An "on board" stamp shows that the shipment is loaded. The B/L is a receipt for your cargo, and it also is the contract for transportation between shipper and carrier.

STRAIGHT BILL OF LADING—SHORT FORM—ORIGINAL—NOT NEGOTIABLE

RECEIVED, subject to the classifications and tariffs in effect on the date of the issue of this Bill of Lading, the property described above in apparent good order, except as noted (contents and condition of contents of packages unknown), marked, consigned, and destined as indicated above which said carrier (the word carrier being understood throughout this contract as meaning any person or corporation in possession of the property under the contract) agrees to carry to its usual place of delivery at said destination, if on its route, otherwise to deliver to another carrier on the route to said destination. It is mutually agreed as to each

carrier of all or any of said property over all or any portion of said route to destination and as to each party at any time interested in all or any said property, that every service to be performed hereunder shall be subject to all the bill of lading terms and conditions in the governing classification on the date of shipment.

Shipper hereby certifies that he is familiar with all the bill of lading terms and conditions in the governing classification and the said terms and conditions are hereby agreed to by the shipper and accepted for himself and his assigns.

From _____

At _____ 19 ____ DESIGNATE WITH AN (X) BY TRUCK ☐ FREIGHT ☐ Shipper's No. _____

Carrier _____ Agent's No. _____

Consigned to _____

(Mail or street address of consignee—For purposes of notification only.)

Destination _____ State of _____ County of _____

Route _____

Delivering Carrier _____ Vehicle or Car Initial _____ No. _____

No. Packages	HM	Kind of Package, Description of Articles, Special Marks, and Exceptions	UN# or NA#	*Weight (Sub. to Cor.)	Class or Rate	Check Column	

Subject to Section 7 of conditions of applicable bill of lading, if this shipment is to be delivered to the consignee without recourse on the consignor, the consignor shall sign the following statement.

The carrier shall not make delivery of this shipment without payment of freight and all other lawful charges.

Per _____ (Signature of Consignor)

If charges are to be prepaid, write or stamp here. "To be Prepaid."

Received $ _____ to apply in prepayment of the charges on the property described hereon.

Agent or Cashier

Per _____ (The signature here acknowledges only the amount prepaid.)

Charges Advanced

$ _____

C.O.D. SHIPMENT
Prepaid ☐
Collect ☐ $ _____
Collection Fee _____
Total Charges _____

"If the shipment moves between two ports by a carrier by water, the law requires that the bill of lading shall state whether it is "Carrier's or Shipper's weight."

†Shipper's imprint in lieu of stamp; not a part of bill of lading approved by the Department of Transportation.

NOTE—Where the rate is dependent on value, shippers are required to state specifically in writing the agreed or declared value of the property.

THIS SHIPMENT IS CORRECTLY DESCRIBED. CORRECT WEIGHT IS

_____ LBS.

Subject to verification by the Respective Weighing and Inspection Bureau According to Agreement.

Per _____

TOTAL PIECES

† The fibre containers used for this shipment conform to the specifications set forth in the box maker's certificate thereon, and all other requirements of Rule 41 of the Uniform Freight Classification and Rule 5 of the National Motor Freight Classification' †Shipper's imprint in lieu of stamp, not a part of bill of lading approved by the Interstate Commerce Commission.

If lower charges result, the agreed or declared value of the within described containers is hereby specifically stated to be not exceeding 50 cents per pound per article.

This is to certify that the above-named materials are properly classified, described, packaged, marked and labeled and are in proper condition for transportation according to the applicable regulations of the Department of Transportation.

_____ SIGNATURE

_____ Shipper, Per _____

_____ Agent, Per _____

Permanent post-office address of shipper:

FIGURE 12-3. The bill of lading. Reprinted with permission of Unz & Co., 190 Boldwin Avenue, Jersey City, NJ 07306

The bill usually has three original and many unoriginal copies, and lists contents of various packaging units and the description of items shipped. In it the shipper specifies the origin, desired routing, destination point, and rates that apply. Charges are based on gross weight or cubic volume.

Bills of lading are known by the mode of carriage used, such as an "Ocean Bill of Lading," "Railbill," "Air Waybill," or a trucking "B/L" or "Pro." Domestically, when a "short B/L" is used, the detailed printed contract terms and conditions of the regular bill apply though they are omitted.

A "clean" B/L, when signed by the carrier, acknowledges possession of goods in good condition. An "unclean" or "foul" bill means that the goods are damaged or the packaging is broken. Any defect is noted by inserted writing by the carrier, such as "damaged boxes." Carriers may reject shipments that do not meet packaging requirements. A straight bill provides for delivery only to the named party. A "To order" bill is a negotiable instrument and is delivered to anyone endorsed on the bill.

When tracing shipments by phone, ask for the shipper's "pro," or waybill number, which you'll need to trace with the carrier. The bill protects the shipper dollar-wise by declaring exact payment charges. When signed upon receipt, the B/L is important for supporting loss and damage claims. Exceptions noted on the delivery receipt make claims easier to pursue. Concealed damage is difficult to prove.

The shipper places the packing list in a waterproof envelope that is included in or attached to one of the packages. The envelope is marked, "Packing List Enclosed." A transmittal letter covers the list of documents sent along with any special instructions. Forwarding instructions to the inland carrier tell the forwarder to deliver to a particular pier or ship. A short form, Shipper's Letter of Instructions, is commonly in use. Customs officials normally use this packing list document, attached to the customs entry, to check the cargo. Your company will use it to receive and inventory the merchandise.

The dock receipt transfers responsibility for the cargo between seller's carriers and the ocean terminal. Prepared by the shipper or forwarder, the ocean carrier signs and returns the receipt to the inland carrier. It shows possession of the cargo and its condition at time of receipt.

To take possession of your goods after you've cleared Customs, a "delivery order" is issued by the buyer or his or her customs broker to the ocean carrier, giving authority to release the cargo to the inland carrier. It is often called the "Pier Release." This release is forwarded to the selected motor carrier, and authorizes the motor carrier to pick up the imported cargo. If your shipment arrives on the dock minus the required documents, a "steamship guarantee" ("airway release" for an airport) can free goods for use.

As a courtesy, the steamship company will normally notify the consignee by an "arrival notice" two days in advance, with the ship's estimated arrival date. They will provide a "freight release" to the terminal operator, who will call for a driver for unloading. They will assign checkers and an unloading spot where the goods will be kept. The checker's function is to record the number of packages being delivered and to note any exceptions and shortages.

Claims For Shipment Damage

Settlement of loss-and-damage due to rejected goods must be made, costs controlled, and replacements made. Overcharge claims should be processed, and settlement should be received for all losses and damage occurring during transit. Action taken to recover the costs resulting from a casualty is taken under the sue and labor clause by the ships master against the underwriters.

Settling shipping claims is a problem for most buyers. Take an example where a shipment is four cases short. You must reorder, pay for the goods again, and place a claim with the carrier.

The bill of lading is important in settling loss and damage claims. Claims fall into categories known as: a. known loss, b. concealed loss, c. known damage, d. concealed damage, and e. loss or damage due to delay.

"Known loss" refers to a loss that the carrier acknowledges up front. It is the simplest claim to settle. Known damage is noticed and acknowledged by the carrier when delivered. Such information should be noted on the receipt for goods *before signing for receipt.* The receiver must legally receive the goods, but this does not prevent a legitimate claim against the carrier for restitution.

A "concealed loss" is not apparent when delivered, but discovered later. The shipment is in apparent good order and receipt is given. Perhaps the material doesn't agree with the quantity, implying an error in loading. Or someone has stolen part of the contents. Because the carrier did not have the chance to inspect and acknowledge until later, this is a tougher claim to clear.

Losses or damage due to delay in transit are determined by comparing the actual time versus the normal length of time in transit. The carrier has to deliver within a "reasonable time." If the carrier can be shown to be negligent, a claim can be made. However, unless a statement is made on the B/L about the urgency of delivery, a claim is almost impossible to collect.

Claims can be controversial and take much time and expense to settle. Claims can be taken to the Transportation Arbitration Board, made up of shippers, carriers, and attorneys. Any final recourse to a carrier for failure to settle your claim can only be taken by court action.

Cargo loss is subject to investigation and adjustment. Surveyors, adjustors, and settling agents make the settlements for the insurer. This area covers particular charges recoverable, including sue and labor expenses and the various salvage adjustment methods. You will be guided by these people at time of a claim.

In case of loss, claims are made after a reasonable time for delivery has elapsed.

Many transport carriers state that any carriage claims must be filed within 15 days of delivery. This is unenforceable. All claims must be filed in writing within nine months from date of delivery. Standard legal forms are available for claims submission. Set a minimum claim to file, such as $100. It is not worth your time going after less.

Audits

Transportation audits verify the classification used, weights billed, and extensions of total dollars. Maintain records of demurrage charges, to reduce such type losses.

Five types of clerical errors can cause an over-or-under charge claim. These errors are found in:

1. Rate;
2. Weight;
3. Commodity description;
4. Tariff interpretation; and
5. Company identified as payor of freight charges.

You have three years to audit the freight bills. Experience shows that audits can result in savings.

Today, just-in-time delivery advocates favor shipping smaller lots more frequently to keep inventory to a minimum. Balance this versus the higher cost of acquisition, effect on material purchase price, and transportation costs. Then you can evaluate total delivered costs.

13

Supplier Relationships

Ethical issues affect supplier relationships. Buyers are custodians of their company's reputation, and need to resist any impropriety. The buyer must distinguish between what is considered acceptable from what is not. This is not so simple when working with different cultures.

- You can't meet or visit foreigners without being given an occasional small gift. It is difficult to refuse, especially in Korea. Make sure it's of minimal value, and reciprocate. For example, make a substitution. Unlike Americans, Orientals like to give and get small token gifts. They're not bribes. An occasional token gift can enhance the business relationship.
- You're invited to a home and learn he's wealthy. What gift might you give to please your host yet not appear excessive?

Relationships with key supplier personnel deserve special consideration. It is tempting to play hardball with a supplier, especially in times of a "buyer's market." The experienced buyer learns that, every so often, a special favor or extra help is needed. Being unreasonable or discourteous often hurts the buyer in the long term. Anything that causes needless friction lessens buying effectiveness.

ETHICAL STANDARDS CHANGE WHEN
BUYING OFFSHORE

Tact is needed! Openness and friendliness cost little, and will pay off in maintaining a sound relationship. As one experienced purchasing manager said, "The supplier only offers deals to those they like!" He's convinced that it pays to be friendly while he shops around.

In the United States and the United Kingdom, we have an "old boy network." In India, they have members of the same caste. Individuals in developing nations

211

usually classify others as "Ins" or "Outs." In China, members of a dialect group are "Ins." Those outside the circle are the "Outs." "Ins" are considered part of the group or tribe. The author recalls an African asking during a dinner in India, "Are you from the English or American tribe?" "Family" is another way of thinking that members of their group are brothers or sisters. When one does business by concluding a contract, one becomes an "In."

In some societies there is an obligation to repay a favor. And obligations remain until repaid. If someone has given a favor, such as a contract, the next favor must come from the receiver. This is one basis for conducting business on a personal level. Some foreign businesspeople explain that such practices sweeten their enjoyment of doing business.

Gift giving in non-Western cultures has developed into a modern business tool intended to create obligation as well as genuine affection. Westerners seek to discharge obligations, but the Easterner enjoys creating the obligation.

Gift giving intends to create both short-term pleasure and long-term bonds of friendship and loyalty. This is common in Moslem areas of Africa and Asia. The seller succeeds in honoring the buyer, and placing him under future obligation. Gifts trigger future favors and have long-range implications for the friendship. Some American companies make a habit of giving small token gifts when visiting overseas. A Hawaiian company's people take macadamia nuts with them and share part of their company culture with their customers.

U.S. gift giving is down dramatically as economic times have cut down on these type of expenditures. Also, there is the question of ethics. Often, management will exhibit a double standard by offering gifts to their own customers, while looking with a questioning eye at anything received by their buyers.

The buyer uses a company's money to buy products and materials and services he or she doesn't use himself. So is it any wonder that the buyer is under the scrutiny of the supervisor, subordinates, and suppliers, as well as the consumer? For these reasons, professional American buyers have long tried to stop the practice of gift giving, to remove suspicion. When someone is in a decision-making job, such as buying, appearances may be far more important than the actual event.

Fortunate is the buyer whose management states an outright policy against giving and receiving gifts. It's no longer an individual decision. If no policy exists, it is in the buyer's interest to adopt this as his or her own policy. However, the buyer will find there will be international practices that run contrary to domestic ethical norms.

"Payoffs" may on occasion be expected in developing nations. Traditions form the background for payoffs abroad. Practices in some regions have endured for many centuries. For example, in an African tribe, upon concluding an agreement, tradition requires money to be given for a feast in the buyer's honor. It is to mark the beginning of a helpful reciprocal relationship.

Surely, this is an area of cultural exchange that needs to be bridged. While many

Americans rightly espouse a puritanical ethical approach to business as the ideal, other cultures embrace differing ethical values. We need to understand cultural differences to better manage foreign relationships when we travel on their turf. Americans are often oblivious to the importance of acting in ways that win respect.

Typical of the American ego, we sometimes brand these people as corrupt. In their eyes, they're not corrupt, though they are culturally different. Do we have the right to impose our sense of moral righteousness and ethics on other cultures? What makes it okay for foreign sellers to engage in practices that the U.S. government declares illegal?

Achieving good relationships isn't simply avoiding conflicts. While it is mandatory for American buyers to follow the law, we cannot dictate the world's moral or ethical posture. The idea is to use the inherent power in the buying job tactfully and ethically. We can, however, set a good example.

Not All Buying Practices Are Good

The buyer is sometimes under suspicion because of some tactics used that are called "sharp practices." Some sharp practices that are easily avoided are:

1. Not giving a reason for no business;
2. Divulging competitive prices to others;
3. Taking quotes freely, without intention to buy;
4. Giving false information to mislead the seller; and
5. Dropping a long term seller without an adequate explanation.

An example of sharp practice is where a buyer gets supplier A to go below supplier B's price. Then the buyer asks B to do better. This auction keeps up for some time. As one salesman said, "I don't mind auctions, just so long as I get the last chance to bid!" Any salesman who asks for a last look, or buyer who gives it to him, should be shown the door!

In the above auction situation, or when there is reason to feel that the prices are out of line, a good tactic is to *give all suppliers the same equal opportunity* to price again. Buyers should always try to get a supplier's lowest price the first time.

Certainly, buyers accepting money is bribery and unlawful. There is little question about that. But then there are those in-between areas that are of concern in everyday business. Ethical questions center around distinguishing between legitimate sales promotion and inducements meant to influence your buying decisions. Like it or not, this is a potential problem area for anyone engaged in the buying profession. Ideally, decisions should be made on price, value, and service considerations, with freedom from outside influences.

Ethics, simply put, is a standard of how you will act in certain circumstances—"basic principles of right action!" How you react to foreign cultural situations depends on your awareness of their ethical standards. Let's now give thought to several important strategies that impact supplier relationships.

DEVELOP SUPPLIER PARTNERING PRODUCTIVITY

"Strategic partnering" is being practiced where former competitors blend their efforts—hopefully the strength of one partner compliments weaknesses of the partner. A good example is that, with five or six companies able to make a personal computer competitively, the edge may go to the one who ties in the better software producer.

In a similar way, the suppliers are viewed as an integral part of production. There is a need to develop greater cooperation between buying and selling companies. Supplier partnering is a help in meeting foreign competition.

Our era is one of extreme cost competition. Buyers have long-range concern about the availability of materials. A contrasting viewpoint has been an antagonistic approach based on reward or punishment. Unfortunately, to date, many companies have performed better when threatened.

Partnering is not just meeting a buyer's requirements. It is providing new products, methods, and materials to improve quality and keep costs low. Use suppliers' product development and research to improve supplier productivity. One way is to invite key suppliers to a series of meetings where competitive parts or items are scrutinized. The aim is to mutually identify cost reductions or quality improvements. Perhaps there will be more joint design efforts. Remember though, the ability to reward or punish a supplier by using your economic leverage is a powerful motivator.

What is it that PMs are doing now to keep their companies competitive? A 1985 *Purchasing* magazine survey revealed how PMs spend their time, with the percentage reporting in parentheses:

1. Bringing suppliers in for candid discussion of needs (93%);
2. Reducing the number of suppliers (88%);
3. Ask for suppliers' value analysis help (85%);
4. Sourcing overseas more extensively (85%);
5. Refining supplier rating plans (70%);
6. Encouraging sole-sourcing (58%);
7. Training suppliers in SPC and other quality techniques (58%);
8. Training suppliers in JIT (58%);
9. Cutting back on sole-sources (38%);

10. Buying at higher assembly levels (35%); and
11. Putting suppliers on formal VA teams (28%).

Notice numbers 2, 6, and 9. Is there some contradiction?

Integrate with Your Managements Goals

Several key needs of American management are:

- Cost control to achieve product price leadership;
- Coordinated effort to achieve quality of suppliers' items; and
- Global competition in the marketplace, with global vision.

Outstanding performance can be rewarded with certified supplier status, increased business, and a preferred position over competitors. Such certified suppliers should invest to keep up with the state of the art, with assurance their partners will not drop them without good cause.

A review of supplier productivity improvement activities to develop strong cross function ties is helpful. Coordinate supplier's talents with engineering, materials, and quality to support your company manufacturing goals. Of course, this is more difficult to do with an offshore supplier. Domestic firms have an advantage.

A type of partnering agreement for MRO items is the systems contract. It is an agreement to supply all of a family of goods, at a level of price. The goal is to save purchasing time and paperwork, reduce inventory, improve flow of goods, and still achieve best pricing.

Just-in-time (JIT) deliveries are sometimes pushed by the distributor. The buyer makes an advance commitment at a predetermined price to buy all of his or her needs of a family of products as needed.

Users listed the advantages of partnering:[1]

1. Inventory reduction;
2. Reduced paperwork;
3. Reduced acquisition costs;
4. Provides standardized prices for longer term decisions; and
5. Improved quality.

Advantages to the seller:
1. Increased business;
2. Increased efficiencies within the seller with higher sales;
3. Better inventory turns with better planning; and
4. More stable customer relationships, which are renewed and reenforced.

---

[1] 1988. Partners for profit. *Purchasing*. April 28 p. 63.

As expected, there are some problem areas that both partners report:

- Failure to treat partnering type agreements any different from other deals; and
- Failure to study the needs of the other party, and how each will change to help the partner.

Strategic supplier partnering provides a competitive edge to improve not simply supplier relations, but the broader shared responsibility to meet your company's needs.

USING BUYING TEAMS AND COUNCILS

Before starting team buying, we need background about "long-range" versus "day-to-day" buying. We might compare management to building a two-story building. The lower floor plan will contain the functions of the business—that is, engineering, sales, production, finance, and purchasing. The second story will mirror the first, and contain the same functions.

Multilevel buying activities can be classified into two classes: 1. strategic long-range buying versus 2. tactical day-to-day buying. Whether you have 2 or 52 plants doesn't matter—it's just more complex. Figure 13-1 depicts how we'll construct our functional view.

The "upper" long-range planning loop is usually the headquarters, division, or corporate operation. The day-to-day "doing" loop is the plant or decentralized

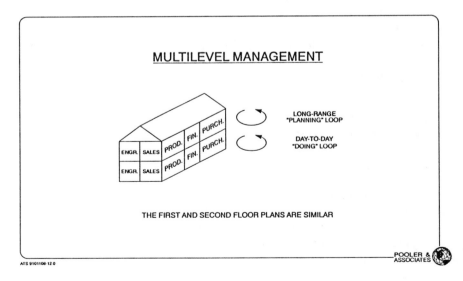

FIGURE 13-1.   Multi-level management "planning" and "doing" loop.

buying. Both loops focus on the same area of operation, but in different ways. The planning loop decides *how* to do the job and makes plans. The doing loop carries out those plans.

Comparing a day-to-day approach to buying versus a strategic long-range approach, the following differences are seen:

Factor	Day-to-Day	Strategic Approach
Time	Short run	One to three years
Channels	Little control	Choice exercised; buying direct when warranted
Resources	Minimal	Best personnel available
Objective	Get goods	Lowest total landed costs to support objectives
New product development	Usual sources	Offshore source advice to engineers
Outlook	Local or regional	Global

Put Theory To Work

How does a practical manager use this theory? Here is an example. A manager explains to the planning loop that they are responsible to see that inventory in the plants is at an agreed level and is kept properly.

The manager reminds the doing loop that *they* are responsible for inventory. He or she tells each plant purchasing manager that they must keep their inventory under control. If it's too high or out of balance, the manager holds them directly responsible. This creates a team effort. The planners monitor and help the doers, while the doers get the job done day-to-day.

The global corporation presents an organizational challenge about how to bring together buying actions. How can buying be centralized despite confusing organizational channels? In organizing to do the job, the classic question is, "Do we buy centralized or decentralized?" We can do both! In dealing with suppliers, a specific item can be bought either solely by a plant or centrally. To enhance productivity, we must act as a team.

Figure 13-2 is the author's suggested vision of a conglomerate, or skyscraper, management. Divisions are acquired, sold, merged, or closed. Like a stack of trays, they are rearranged. Purchasing is one arm of materials management that a company can centralize, no matter what organization structure exists. In multiple operations, centralizing inventory is difficult, globally. However, the buying activity can be controlled for maximum economic leverage, regardless of location of the buyers and suppliers.

The combination central-decentralized approach is highly effective, but takes a

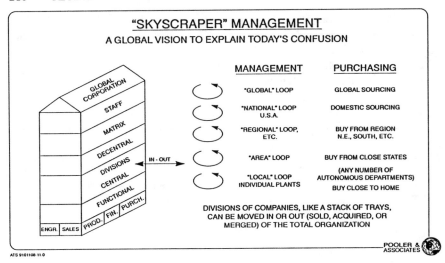

FIGURE 13-2.   Skyscraper management.

high degree of teamwork. The roles of planning and teams need to be defined. Shackling red tape needs to be reduced! There is sometimes friction when a buyer from headquarters tries to coordinate buying with many decentralized buying operations.

Multiple-level buying occurs when the "high and low" of buying attacks problems in the same way. The doing loop hits low and the planning loop high. This results in a multiple attack on the same job, but at different levels.

By understanding how multiple-level team buying operates, it is seen that the more day-to-day activities are placed within each plant or buying section. The longer-range aspects of source of supply, pricing negotiations, and the higher goals may be centralized. This takes a good climate to achieve.

From a purchasing viewpoint, the best of both worlds is to strengthen the autonomy of the decentralized buying, while using maximum volume leverage in negotiations. Most companies achieve the former go-it-alone approach. The latter teamwork requires more strategy planning. The future belongs to those companies that can apply market buying power. They should integrate their decentralized needs at the plant level, while they combine volume leverage.

Focus on the highly repetitive purchases. Every company has potential volume leverage. A global company has many common items and major suppliers. So the opportunity for buying teamwork to pay off is present.

The central buyer must have statesmanship qualities to allow the team captains to perform the job. The team captain negotiates for all, including the headquarter central interests. Through task forces and teams, they strive to support competitively-assessed divisional operating needs.

Many examples of successful teams are known to the author for buying items such as motors, valves, capacitors, fans, and so forth. It takes only about 25 teams for most companies to control more than 90 percent of their production purchases.

Managing Your Suppliers

While following the partnering concept, some PMs believe that the buyer *needs to manage his sources* of supply. Buyers must tell suppliers what is expected. How high is high? How does a buyer manage his or her suppliers? By using available options, such as:

• Increasing or decreasing volume bought;
• Getting local stocking of items, for faster shipments and lower inventory;
• Using competition to get the best package price, leadtime, and quality;
• Giving incentives for better supplier performance;
• Dropping a supplier for poor service;
• Taking legal action (rather drastic);
• Making factual presentations—quality performance data, delivery, and rejection rates; and
• Using persuasion—negotiate, plead, or "give-em-hell."

Written strategy in the form of a procurement plan is controlled by the headquarters-located commodity manager. The plan is agreed to and executed by the team. Once in place, the team is activated by phone. Team members react to impending price increases, product troubles, late deliveries, or whatever the need. When a team endorses a plan, each member promises to carry out a specific negotiation to get company-wide contracts. The result is lowest total landed material cost.

How Buying Teams Work

Experience has shown that:

1. Teams have been highly successful.
2. They are fragile.
3. Communication suffers if leadership is not shared.
4. Team members who endorse a plan will follow it.
5. Team leaders normally are the largest buyer of the item.

Teams are useful when buyers are looking for leverage and want to have a say in controlling their marketplace. If your company is a single plant or company, or decentralized, the seller often can determine the marketplace. That is, they place you in the class they wish.

The suppliers may decide to sell to you as a house account, off the street, or by special arrangement. They may decide to be highly competitive in the East, but get higher prices out West, where they have little competition. In short, you buy in the market that they define. They will negotiate with each buyer in your company that buys from them. That is, unless *you* define the marketplace.

If each buyer is buying at the lowest price he or she can get, what more can you expect with a decentralized organization? What kind of negotiation leverage or power has the buying company got? How do you get anyone to speak for you in a decentralized setup? What is the answer? Through use of buying teams and councils!

The team mobilizes the buyers to present a united front to suppliers. This way, the buyer, and not solely the supplier, is defining the marketing arena and deciding when to negotiate. Whoever can define the global marketplace often can command the pricing situation. By redefining the marketplace to the buyer's advantage, a much better deal often results. The challenge is to break local or regional selling.

To consider teams, we first should think about supplier productivity improvement. Chapter 3 already covered the importance of documented procurement plans to set global sourcing strategies. A strong long-range supplier partnering on local, national and global levels is desirable. Primarily, we should practice long-term buying.

A frequently stated management goal is for the corporation to use its combined purchasing volume leverage when buying! No debating the results desired. The question is, "How do they do it?" Again, the answer is through task forces, teams, and councils.

Table 13-1 shows how an actual team today controls its major motor purchases. This chart depicts combining purchase volume for a typical buying team. At the top are listed the using plants #1, 2, and so on. The suppliers are "A", "B", and so on. Analysis shows that $30 million motors are spent with supplier "A" by buyers in all the plants. Negotiations for $30 million should produce greater savings than each buyer could alone.

If plant #1 centralized its motor buys, it could negotiate $65 million. Plant #2 could negotiate $35 million, and so on. Smaller plants may buy under $1 million. However, what would be the result if all $145 million were collectively negotiated?

If 25 buyers are all buying from the same suppliers, usually three or four buyers will spend the most dollars. The remaining buyers need to all have the same story and approach with the suppliers. The smaller slices of the purchase pie have much to gain. They usually will go along with those with greater leverage, if their input is requested.

TABLE 13-1.   Team combines purchase volume

"Multi-level" approach to buying. Mllions of U.S. dollars.

Supplier	#1	#2	Plants #3	Others	Total
"A"	15	0	10	5	30
"B"	35	5	5	3	48
"C"	0	20	5	1	26
"D"	10	8	2	1	21
All others	5	2	3	10	20
Total	65	35	25	20	$ 145 million

Each buyer does his or her best at competitive day-to-day buying. They negotiate each item, buying from their preferred source. When this activity is enhanced by using total buying leverage, we achieve centralized-decentralized buying. Most buying in larger operations is highly decentralized, so usually the pay off in buying teamwork is high. Buyers can buy centralized when there is a gain; otherwise, they are free to buy independently.

Here is a recap of how buying teams operate:

• All buyers buy each item at the lowest unit price, using normal "day-to-day" purchasing practices.
• The commodity team, under the guidance of its team captain, uses a procurement plan to gather information, and forms the negotiation team.
• All buyers carry out the negotiation strategy of the procurement plan because they were party to its establishment.
• Lower total purchase material costs result from each buyer's individual negotiations, which are enhanced by total volume leverage. This in turn reduces unit price at each plant location.

The task of planning and nurturing teams is the job of the team captain, who most logically, but not always, is the largest user. Some of the most successful teams can be led by that buyer who has the enthusiasm and talent to get the job done.

Here is an example of a successful fan procurement team with purchases of $5.5 million. Throughout the company, 14 individual buyers buy these type fans. Five major buying team members, with concurrence from the others, met before the supplier was invited to negotiate an announced price increase. Exercising leverage, the price increase was cut in half. This amounted to $250,000 cost avoidance through the use of combined buying power. Prices stayed firm for several months while under negotiations.

Purchasing councils are formed by having a representative from each purchasing location meet to plot strategy and check results. Usually, the purchasing manager will fill this function.

OVERSEAS VISITS: AT WHAT POINT NECESSARY?

There is no substitute for first-hand knowledge of the supplier's capabilities. Consider an on-site evaluation of your potential supplier when the homework has been done and the purchase appears desirable. Possibly tie into your routine trip a visit to a trade fair on that continent. The Commerce Department can advise when and where fairs are held. For an initial visit, select firms and determine what to look for *before* you go. Contact other buyers or other reference sources. Timing your visit is a key. Plan your overseas visits carefully. *Visit* suppliers when you have firm leads or quotes and are getting ready to buy. However, don't rush overseas!

A letter of introduction from a bank is helpful if your company isn't known to the supplier. Even global companies may spark little recognition in some countries. Make all contacts well in advance. Let the supplier know your reason for interest and why they should be interested in seeing you.

Provide a brochure about your company and products. Recall the need of the Chinese for much detail about you. Also remember that most offshore suppliers will work better with you as they get to know you. Meet and talk to different levels of supplier management, so they can all share an understanding of the relationship.

Most important, when concluding an important agreement, is home office contact. A critical time to make an overseas visit is to conclude the arrangements when most details are set. This formality should be carefully arranged. For example, a purchasing manager goes to Japan each year to nail down an agreement on prices. He knows what the prices will be before he gets on the airplane. However, he also knows that, until he has face-to-face discussions and concurrence from key managers, these prices are unofficial.

How are women treated when visiting Japan? Culturally, women are not expected to be present. If they are, the Japanese aren't too comfortable with them. However, as American women buyers are perceived to have authority, they have been well received.

Personal Security and Overseas Travel

A buyer from time to time finds that overseas visits are useful. Make use of services available. If an embassy or consulate is advised of your pending visit, they may help with travel itineraries. Most embassies have libraries with information on foreign trade and industry journals. Lists of overseas manufacturers, together with product catalogs, are often available. They may provide aid when you arrive, suggest appointments with potential suppliers, suggest an attorney, and so forth.

While foreign service personnel can't act as legal representatives, they can provide support for a U.S. firm in a trade dispute involving a settlement of more than $500. They will need complete background information to do this.

Visiting American chambers of commerce abroad could help you overcome local barriers, such as language, customs, laws, and regulations. Commercial banks help by telling what they know about the reliability of local manufacturers.

Arrange travel and hotel reservations well in advance and get confirmation in writing to show upon arrival. Make sure there are no local holidays during your planned stay. Holiday information is issued free by the U.S. Department of Commerce.

Suppliers Located In "Hot Spots"

"Hot Spots" that have major political and social upheaval could cause supply disruptions. Areas of recent concern are Afghanistan, Nicaragua, Lebanon, the Philippines, and the former Iraq war zone. In current headlines is the United Nations American-led effort to secure the peace after having thrown back Iraqi takeover of Kuwait's oil fields.

Communist Bloc Changing in Eastern Europe

Now the communistic walls are falling in Eastern Europe. Information on trade can be secured from:

- The U.S./USSR Trade & Economics Board, New York, NY Tel:(212) 644-4559
- USSR Trade Representative, Washington, D.C. (202) 232-5988
- Armtog Trading Corp. (Soviet firm), New York, NY (212) 956-3010
- U.S. Commerce Department, International Trade Administration (ITA):
  Soviet Desk (202) 377-4655
  Polish Desk (202) 377 2645
  Hungarian Desk (202) 377-2645
- Polish Trade Office, New York, NY (212) 370-5300
- Hungarian Trade Office, New York, NY (212) 752-3060
- Eastern European Information Center (EEIC), Washington, D.C.

Trade with the USSR is always tied to political considerations. Grain dominates trade with Russia. The Jackson Amendment tied trade to Russian emigration policies and human rights. Difficulties occur, for example, in squabbling over whether they fulfilled their agreements to buy an agreed minimum tonnage of grain.

As part of Glasnost, Soviet leaders seek to increase joint ventures between their state enterprises and Western companies to modernize their manufacturing. They have to reduce the USSR's chronic shortages of consumer goods.

The USSR wants MFN status. The non-Soviet partner is permitted to own up to 49 percent of the venture. The new venture is guaranteed freedom from confiscation and having to obey Soviet production planning. The capitalist partner may take out their share of profits. The workers can be paid in other than Russian currency. Favorable tax treatment is part of the package.

The Russians become a prime candidate for barter. If they can't barter oil, they may sell gold to get dollars to buy capitalist goods. The Soviet economy needs cash, so they must borrow dollars or get credit.

The former Iron curtain nation's legal system is controversial and based on an adversary system. The result is that their negotiating tactics are alternately to stall and then push for concessions. It is difficult to arbitrate with them.

As former Eastern Bloc countries strongly push use of countertrade, this increases the chances of the buyer having to buy from them. We will do increased business with those countries striving to overcome shackling bureaucratic controls.

The American buyer is free to buy from the USSR. In 1986, they were fifth on the list of trading partners where a surplus favoring the United States exists.

Action Checklist for Travelling Abroad

Safety is an increasing concern for travelers abroad. Robbery is often the worst trip spoiler, so consider bringing a supply of travelers checks. Pickpockets ply their skills on the unwary visitor. Carry some bills and small change of the native currency, but use a money belt, too. Here are a few planning tips.

- Determine the most productive travel time and routing. Consider time zones. Upon arrival, plan rest into your schedule before negotiating. Mistakes occur when you are tired from jet lag.
- Review potential suppliers along your path of travel to prepare list of suppliers you may visit.
- Work with your traffic department or travel bureau for transportation and lodging. AAA or other travel service can be helpful.
- Inform the commercial attache at the U.S. Embassy or the consulate, and request needed services, such as:
  Translators;
  Conference rooms for meetings;
  Current market and local sales patterns;
  Information on local business customs and practices; and
  Possible names and introductions to new suppliers.
- Inform your company's foreign-based sales manager, so he or she is aware of your visit, and can counsel you on details needed.

- U.S. passport is usually mandatory. Is a visa also required?
- Are vaccinations or other inoculations required? "Survival kits" are often available from company first aid for health protection.

Terrorism, while statistically an unlikely event, needs to be prepared for. Most major corporations have alerted their managers to take certain precautions. Terrorism risk forecast newsletters give the latest problems known from monitoring thousands of travellers.

From experience arranging a conference in Brazil, the author learned that robberies occur anywhere. One manager had his pants pocket slashed as he was standing outside his hotel. A bus full of travel agents were stopped and robbed by police (or people dressed as them). Cabs were routinely pulled over by men dressed as police.

Business travel experts say that today's first class flyer is the proverbial sitting duck. With a little common sense and luck, buyers risks can be lessened. Enroute travel advice is:

- Try to book air carriers with good records for security precautions.
- If forced to travel in the Mideast, use politically neutral carriers such as SAS, Swissair, or Quantas.
- Take nonstop routes, if possible.
- Use wide bodied aircraft because it's difficult to maintain terrorist control over a large craft.
- Remove all corporate identification. Tags for baggage can be inserted backwards or partially covered.
- Don't carry papers identifying you as connected with the American government or corporation. Send necessary papers ahead, or print on plain paper.
- Dress casually in tourist clothes, rather than a formal business suit.
- Pack one bag only, so you can move quickly by yourself. Don't let that bag out of your sight.
- Don't carry any electronic device unless unavoidable.
- Check luggage at the airport early. Leave and return close to takeoff time.
- Have outline map of airport to know where to go.
- Don't verbally plan meetings while waiting in various travel lounges.
- Avoid eye contact with strangers.
- Go to the passenger boarding area, the safest place in the airport.
- Avoid aisle seats so that you aren't easily reached during hijackings.
- Have advance boarding passes in hand for all legs of trip.
- Use airline club lounges when possible.
- Terrorists have been irritated by some materials. For example, alcohol and pornographic magazines left in carry-on bags.
- Drink in moderation.

When at your destination:

- Stay clear of baggage claim areas until most baggage is picked up.
- Rent a modest car with an inside hood opener, so the hood can't be easily raised from outside.
- Vary routes taken and your routine, if staying long. Most car victims have been people who are known to take certain routes on schedule.
- When driving, slow down well behind a pulled out car or one suddenly blocking the roadway.
- Stay at first class hotels in a respectable part of city. Ask for a third- to sixth-floor room and know escape routes in case of fire.

Multinationals are also advised to stay out of bars and restaurants known as American hangouts. If you can stay where TV monitors or other similar guarding devices are in the hall, so much the better. Some places may use codes to open doors.

A large company may send a company jet ahead along with agents to check out facilities. However, don't act like Rambo. One manager reported, "It was embarrassing to arrive at the gates of our Italian plant with two men armed with machine guns. The natives must have thought we were crazy."

Security consultants may go overboard. A few advocate soft bullet-resistant body armor (vest) that can be worn under regular clothing. These bulky garments, consisting of up to 23 layers of Kevlar, cause the bullet to be entrapped. While said to be similar to getting a powerful blow, the person will usually survive. Only the highest Government officials, famous people, and police officers might use them.

Not much hampers an American more than getting ill on a trip. It sometimes can't be avoided. All travelers at times have these types of problems. It takes care to avoid the water for even the ice cubes in drinks can cause stomach upset or worse. Teeth can be brushed with beer, if need be.

Be an agreeable guest, and follow your host's suggestions. Slow down and smell the roses or whatever flowers are in that country! Accept something you may not fully understand. Be yourself. Despite all the above, statistically, the most dangerous part of the trip may be from your home by taxi to the local airport.

14

Future Buying Prospects in Global Trade

An analysis of the U.S. international merchandise trade deficit shows recent improvement. From a high of almost $200 billion a few years ago, the deficit dropped to about $100 billion for 1990. While the trade deficit still needs to be reduced, perhaps the major threat to world trade growth is reactive political moves to cut the deficit too quickly. Consider that, in December of 1990, the monthly deficit dropped by almost 30 percent. As of February 1991, that month's deficit was $5.33 billion. So, the deficit is running at a rate of less than $65 billion for this year.

As economic leader of the free world, Americans champion free trade. We deal with 35 major trading countries. The brand of free trade that made America successful was created by dropping state barriers. This was possible under our one government.

CAN GLOBAL "FREE TRADE" SURVIVE?

Hong Kong is on one end of the scale of free-wheeling business, compared to Singapore, which has become over-regulated with heavy controls. U.S. companies are often dealing with foreign governments who must approve the deal and will participate in and shape it. Dealing with governments is more complicated than simpler negotiations with individual companies.

Getting Around Quotas and "Restraints"

Steel imports are about 25 percent of domestic steel consumption. While volume is down from Canada and Japan, it was up 11 percent from the EEC. 67 countries were listed as exporting steel to the United States, though 20 of them (such as

Belize, Fiji, Nigeria, Swaziland, and Thailand) don't make any. While the volume is small, it is feared as another way to beat a quota.

Textiles are a major part of the U.S. trade imbalance. A 54-nation, multi-fiber arrangement put curbs on various fibers. On its own, the United States negotiated in 1990 to limit Taiwan, Hong Kong, and South Korea to no more than 1-percent quantity growth annually. Already, there are reported examples of getting around these quotas. Instead of selling low cost T-shirts, they're selling expensive blouses. "Unisex" T-shirts for women are exported from Taiwan under quotas for men's T-shirts. Hong Kong garment makers are producing in China. Also, they are shifting production to Caribbean basin nations with less restrictive quotas. By leaving off sleeves, the garments are imported as vests. By attaching the sleeves in the United States, Koreans sell them as jackets, which have a smaller quota than vests.

The Textile, Apparel and Footwear Trade Act of 1990 sought to impose global quotas on all products from all countries. It would have allowed only a 1-percent annual growth rate for textiles and apparel, and no growth for footwear imports. Critics pointed out that this bill countered trade liberalizing negotiations, and so it was defeated.

Another end run on quotas is when Brazil ships steel to Panama. There it is converted to pipe that is sent to the United States duty-free as part of the Caribbean Basin Initiative Act.

One way around a closed door policy is to build a factory within that country to be a seller within their economy. As an example, Japan built a highly automated facility in India, where labor is abundant and inexpensive. Although Japanese policy is to keep main production home, they have seen the wisdom of positioning themselves within the potentially large Indian market they will serve.

Some people feel the United States is still not faring well in today's world economy. Protectionism and free trade are the two extremes. These conflicting forces must be balanced somehow to achieve the adopted slogan, "fair trade," but how?

One approach might be to link the volume that a country may sell into the U.S. market according to its volume of purchases. But, that's anathema to the proponents of free trade. And, of course, that is what quotas and trade agreements try to do, though they're not doing the job to their satisfaction. The problem is that conflicting national interests are at work. Foreign trade, viewed as an engine of growth, is often subjected to much political influence. All governments, including the United States, try to provide favorable conditions to win jobs and greater exports.

In the global marketplace, economic development brings into play national self-interests. The United States is trying to keep its top status. However, unfortunately, in a one world economy, it is usually number one who suffers most. Other nations can selectively niche their targets, and avoid the leader's mistakes.

Today, the pendulum is heavily favoring free trade. Yet it's a myth that trade exists in pure form as free trade. Consider other nations' use of countertrade, unfair pricing, and restrictive codes. As pointed out in Chapter 1, the U.S. company is often dealing not with other free companies, but with national managed economies. U.S. buyers are often sent scurrying around the globe trying to figure out what else can be bought from those countries.

In May 1986, a GATT meeting took place, involving international heads of state. Details were to be worked out at the September GATT meeting at Punta del Este, Uruguay. This meeting was considered very crucial at that time. Chances of success were considered slim because there was no agreement on how to solve the large U.S. trade deficit. The "Uruguay Round," as of now, is still unresolved.

The U.S. Senate has long threatened to let loose a flood of protectionist legislation. Holding back these repressive measures have been those moderates who fear trade reprisals that might undermine the world economy. While most trade experts believe in tearing down trading barriers, no international free trade umbrella of law or rules exists. It is sometimes folly for the United States to always champion the free trade philosophy that others sometimes exploit.

BUSINESS AND GOVERNMENT AS PARTNERS?

Many American businesspeople believe that the U.S. government must become still more friendly and supportive towards business. Could a partnership such as Japan, Inc. be forged? Probably not, as business and government have different interests and responsibilities. However, they don't have to be adversaries. They can cooperate and coordinate certain activities, to insure that the United States remains competitive in world markets. National economic goals can be recognized to influence decisions and directives. A priority should be the creation of better industrial efficiency to allow fair economic opportunity for U.S. firms.

Should the United States adopt a trade policy? Proponents for a policy point to the need to protect and created jobs. The various channels to apply antidumping and countertrade measures also causes confusion. Advocates have called for a Department of International Trade at cabinet level to put more teeth into enforcement.

This policy issue raises questions, such as:

• Can we distinguish between products made abroad by U.S.-owned or joint ventures and domestically produced goods that are owned by foreign companies?
• Should we try to discourage Japanese and others from owning U.S. plants here?
• Why can't American companies have U.S. countertrade-type agreements with foreign suppliers when a large trade imbalance exists? Whenever a country is in a surplus position greater than say 20 percent, U.S. buyers could negotiate their purchases to include countertrade measures.
• Should there be a local content requirement, as some foreign governments impose?

Trade barriers, in the form of tariffs, become useless, as foreign companies move into the United States to manufacture. These companies take advantage of all opportunities to protect domestic industries (for example, special concession measures, such as reduced taxes, free trade zones). Thus, tariffs lock the chicken coop to protect the hens, while the fox remains safely inside!

A recent trade dispute shows the strange twists of global competition. Back in 1974, Smith Corona Corporation got relief when it charged rival Japanese manufacturers with dumping typewriters in the United States. Since then, Smith Corona moved manufacturing to Singapore, while the Japanese assembled Brother typewriters in Tennessee.

The Japanese filed charges in April 1991, under U.S. law, alleging that Smith Corona dumps its Asian-made products in America unfairly.[1] Brother Industries claims that prices were cut below costs. Further, Smith Corona shifted from the U.S. largest manufacturer to the largest importer of typewriters. The Japanese said, "While we've been investing in the United States and creating jobs, they've been migrating to Singapore, taking jobs with them."

The goal of achieving trade balances, within a reasonable band, can be achieved if given enough time. Does it matter who provides work? We have an obligation to keep American economic leverage to compete. As other nations put their own economic interest first, so we must strive to keep America the number one economic power.

Competition Can Be Healthy!

The flood of imports has hurt many American companies and cut jobs. However, in the long term it may stimulate America's competitive instincts. America's factories have cut costs, modernized, reduced work forces, and capped pay increases. These companies today are in a better position to compete on world markets.

The pendulum swings. Perhaps Harley Davidson typifies the American success response. Five years ago, H-D almost went bankrupt because of Japanese competition. Today, its workers have been hired back to keep up with demand. They sell out each year. Part of their marketing strategy is to produce only as much as they can sell.

With a philosophy that ideas for improvement come from employees, customers, suppliers, and then management, H-D first pared down as others did. But they built back up lean and dedicated. They are the only survivor of 140 American bike manufacturers. People pay an average of $10,000 for a high-quality bike. Market toward those who can afford, and do it with a mystique. The Harley "Hog" is sold as part of the romance of the road.

---

[1]1991. Typewriter firm tastes its medicine. *Syracuse Herald Journal.* April 19 p. 86.

Purchasing Impact on Profits

Certainly, measurement of purchasing performance is vital. Let those who scoff at measurements recall that we need a reasonable standard to judge anything. Even in our scientific space race, isn't it wonderful that we've got the Russians? Without them, how would we know if we were leading or lagging?

During the 1986 CNN TV broadcast on The Statue of Liberty anniversary, a navy historian said that the definition of a "tall ship" was one that could not go under the Brooklyn Bridge. This is another example that, if there is no standard or sample for comparison, we create one.

To sort out the measurement confusion, TREND was created and first published in May 1966. That's significant, as TREND has withstood the test of time. It's as valid today as the day it was introduced. It is available today as a NAPM video program.[2]

"Total Recognition of Environmental and Numerical Development," TREND, evolved from earlier development of "Indicators of Purchasing Performance," or IPEs. The point to recall is that most numerical measurements are partially indicative of the job being done. All three steps have to be studied. The three distinct steps for measurement are shown in Figure 14-1. If the PM looks at these as three separate yet interdependent areas, it is clear that it's not enough to analyze results only. It doesn't show *how* improvement can be made.

Step 1 is, in effect, "How well has the PM achieved an understanding of efficient purchasing with his buyers, and how well has he studied what makes his buyers want to buy well?"

Next, the PM sees, in Step 2, what his buyers *do!* Is it what they say they'll do, and is it what you believe they should do? Finally, the PM, like all managers, is interested in the third step—results. So he or she tries to measure the end product of performance.

The basic purpose of any standard of measurement is to make an improvement; otherwise, it is wasted effort. TREND, the Three-Step Purchasing Measurement shows that no universal yardstick will ever be the final answer; rather, many areas for improvement will present themselves. All have a good or bad effect on purchasing performance. Emphasis on any one TREND step to the exclusion of the other two can produce only partial understanding.

By studying the department effort in toto, any deficiencies in the three steps that can be corrected *will affect the overall department in some manner.* When the concept or understanding of the buying job's global role is clarified, the results will improve.

Purchasing has considerable leverage on profits and the financial success of any

---

[2]1986. *Measuring Purchasing Efficiency/Trend* (Pal 33 Video for company training). NAPM, Tempe, AZ.

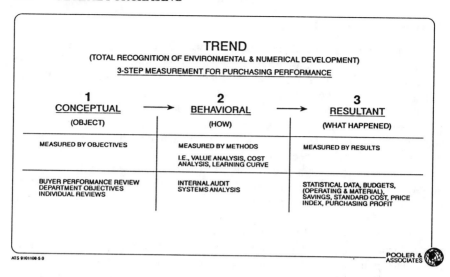

FIGURE 14-1.   Trend measurement system.

company. The impact of purchasing on a company's profit is great. Purchasing can increase profit, but it is not easily achieved! It takes skillful buying by those who understand good purchasing techniques and methods. This leverage on profits increases as profit levels themselves decline in competitive markets. Poor purchasing performance *can* also reduce profits. Purchasing has become an heir to a profit responsibility.

Purchasing's impact on return on investment (ROI) will remain paramount in the future. Figure 14-2 is a blank ROI chart.

Fill out a similar chart for your company's performance, as stated in the company report. Then simply add 2 percent to your cost of purchases and change the original numbers. Also, drop the cost of your purchases by 2 percent and watch those changes. A 2-percent change in purchasing expenditures swings the return on invested capital widely! This proves the strong impact of good or bad buying on your company. Global buying is one way to increase profits.

IMPLICATIONS FOR THE FUTURE

Global buying requires a forward look. Purchasing must *foresee* the shortages. Economic power must be used to contract for and assure supply first, seeking and finding new sources on a global basis. This need to look ahead, to plan, and to manage will continually engage procurement. Fortunately, the purchasing manager is accustomed to dealing in the future. He or she negotiates not for today, but for prices at the time of delivery tomorrow.

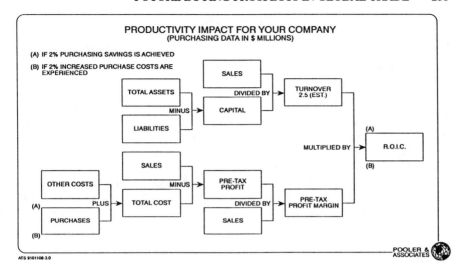

FIGURE 14-2.   ROI productivity impact.

Tactics of buying change, whether a buying or selling market exists. One commodity may be easy to get, while another is in scarce supply. The buyer must often sell to get the goods instead of someone else. A skilled negotiator/buyer may shine in a tough seller's market.

In a seller's market, it may take a more friendly type to be successful—one with better interpersonal skills with the ability to set up trusting relationships. One who is politically adept at being well liked and getting along well. In this market, a tough purchasing manager may be seen as out of touch by his management. So our buyer must shift gears or change his or her style.

Now, the buyer can't, like the chameleon, change colors as every market changes. However, the buyer has to moderate away from extreme positions and be flexible enough to understand his or her cross-cultural environment. Today's buyer must conscientiously seek to expand his or her outlook toward global buying.

Purchasing's role will continually shift as supply and demand forces change. Scarcity of materials will cycle again. Higher prices are needed at times, to reduce consumption as the world's resources are being devoured. The buyer must be knowledgeable about global supply!

Ever-increasing complexity in doing the materials job will require buyers to become ever more knowledgeable about their source's supply capacity. Strategic purchasing planning will include:

- Integrating market and supply strategies;
- Selecting and evaluating vendors and *urging* them to supply;

- Tapping vendor technological innovation first;
- Post purchase liaison—warranty and dispute settlements;
- Negotiating consigned stock to decrease inventory and free funds for growth requirements; and
- Other functions now being performed to varying degrees.

Purchasing will become predictive, rather than reactive. This will require a high degree of planning. Who is exposed to a broader outlook than the global buyer? He deals with other cultures and business practices. He is exposed to greater technology, products, and ways to conduct business, as well as complexity of global transportation and the legalities of international business.

Becoming a global expert offers a purchasing manager a direct shot at joining the company's top planning councils. The opportunity to overview the global economy and understand the financial implications is important. A working knowledge of import regulations, customs tariffs, and so forth, all enhance business acumen.

Within his or her own company, the buyer is exposed to every other department to some degree. Our buyer works with different people with varying temperaments both within and without his company. Daily, potential disputes and supply problems offer a challenge. There is a need to analyze and investigate global supplier capabilities to improve supplier partnering.

An era of cost competition with lower inflation is here. Buyers have long-range concern about supply availability. There is a need to develop greater cooperation between buying and selling companies. Supplier partnering is needed to meet foreign competition.

A buying assignment overseas could be a big plus, providing valuable experience. The global marketplace can be grasped from the buying perspective. In fact, a buyer may work and deal with many countries and different cultures than a salesman who works within an assigned territory!

Ecological regulations affect procurement on issues such as PCB contamination and purity of water effluent. The Environmental Protection Agency (EPA) and the Occupational Safety Hazards Administration (OSHA) sometimes push domestic costs upward, granting advantage to offshore suppliers that are free of those constraints.

Social responsibility is needed as companies bear some accountability to societal needs. Minority supplier and small business buying programs are active. These and other issues effect material supply and increase coordination effort of the purchasing function with others. They all lead to increased demands on the supplier, which *must be enforced through the buyer.*

Some factors that will demand buyer's attention throughout this century are:

1. Growth of the multinational global corporation;
2. Worldwide technical buying and selling that need expanded global skills;

3. Rates of inflation, and currency exchange;
4. Future shortages of materials, along with shorter manufacturing cycles and lower inventories;
5. Profit potential of effective purchasing—the pooling of purchases for negotiation leverage;
6. The need for coordination between central and decentralized materials;
7. Energy availability and cost;
8. The growth of computer use for inventory and buying data;
9. A larger percentage of purchased materials as specialized suppliers develop; and
10. Growth of supplier partnering:
    a. The need for closer ties with supplier's design capabilities; and
    b. Challenge to keep competitive leverage while maximizing mutual goals.

Of the above, the development of global buying is the most significant development affecting the purchasing job today. It's a responsibility of the job to help in keeping the company competitive and in operation. So, we agree—while we will be domestically based buyers, we must have a global outlook. Coupled with our knowledge of the U.S. supply system, we can be unequalled on this earth!

Definition of Purchasing

Purchasing has long been defined as, "Getting the right item, at the right price, at the right quality and quantity, and at the right time, from the right source." While all true, that old definition doesn't cover today's more demanding world, and this multifaceted buying job.

Consider this definition to show the job's scope:

> Purchasing represents internal and end-use consumers in the global buyer/seller relationship. Through authority to commit and control expenditures to suppliers, assurance of supply and profitable operation is secured.

People will make it happen! The challenge is here and now to win the international competition. You, the buyer, are the key player in global sourcing.

What an exciting and challenging future for those with global vision, who are prepared to tackle this demanding task. How well we do our jobs will determine how American companies will survive in the marketplace. Reach for the world of global purchasing!

Appendix A

Organizations Buyers May Contact

Organizations with services of interest to global buyers:

Department of the Treasury, 51615 H Street, NW, Washington, D.C. 20062. (202) 659-6000

U.S. Customs Service, 1301 Constitution Avenue, NW, Washington, D.C. 20229. (202) 566-8195

Dun and Bradstreet, 99 Church Street, New York, NY 10007. (212) 349-3300

Export-Import Bank of the U.S., 811 Vermont Avenue, NW, Washington, D.C. 20571. (800) 424-5201

Federal Trade Commission, Pennsylvania Avenue at Sixth Street, NW, Washington, D.C. 20580. (202) 523-3625

Superintendent of Documents, U.S. Government Printing Office, Washington, D.C. 20402. (202) 783-3238

U.S. International Trade Commission, 701 E Street, NW, Washington, D.C. 20004. (202) 523-0161

Export Trade Services Division, Washington, D.C. 20250. (202) 447-3031

U.S. Superintendent of Commerce, Industry and Trade Administration, Bureau of East West Trade, Washington, D.C. 20230. (202) 377-5500

International Trade Center, UNCTAD/GATT, Palais des Nations, 1211 Geneva - 10, Switzerland

Office of the U.S. Trade Representative, 1800 G Street, NW, Washington, D.C. 20506 (202) 395-4647

U.S. Department of Commerce:
1. International Trade Administration (ITA), 14th Street and Constitution Avenue, Washington, D.C. 20230. (202) 377-3808
2. Maritime Administration, Office of Public Affairs, Room 3895, Washington, D.C. 20230. (202) 377-2746
3. National Technical Information Service, 5285 Port Royal Road, Springfield, VA 22161.
4. District offices in each state. Consult phone directory.

236

U.S. Department of State, Bureau of Economic and Business Affairs, 2201 C Street, NW, Washington, D.C. 20520. (202) 632-0354

Organization for Economic Cooperation and Development, 1750 Pennsylvania Avenue, NW, Washington, D.C. 20006 (202) 724-1857

Small Business Administration Office of International Trade, 1441 L St., Washington, D.C. 20416. (202) 653-6600

UNIPUB (United Nations Publications Headquarters), 245 Park Avenue, South, New York, NY 10010.

World Bank Publications Division, Room A-110, 1818 H Street, NW, Washington, D.C. 20062. (202) 477-2057

International Chamber of Commerce, U.S. Council, 1212 Avenue of the Americas, New York, NY 10026. (212) 354-4480

Chamber of Commerce of the U.S., 1615 H Street, NW, Washington, D.C. 20062. (202) 659-6000 Branches located in most cities. See your Yellow Pages.

World Trade Institute, One World Trade Center, New York, NY 10048. (212) 435-7000

National Association of Purchasing Management (NAPM), 2055 East Centennial Circle, PO Box 22160, Tempe, AZ 85282. (602) 752-6276, Fax (602) 752-7890

International Federation of Purchasing and Materials Management (IFPMM), International Management Institute, PO Box CH—5001 Aarau, Switzerland. (064) 247131, Telex 981293

KEY EMBASSY ADDRESSES

Embassy addresses most likely needed for exporting items required by an American buyer:

Australian Embassy, 1601 Massachusetts Avenue, NW, Washington, D.C. 20036. (202) 797-3000

Brazilian Embassy, 3006 Massachusetts Avenue, NW, Washington, D.C. 20008. (202) 797-0100

Embassy of Canada, 1746 Massachusetts Avenue, NW, Washington, D.C. 20036. (202) 785-1400

Chinese Embassy (People's Republic of China), 2311 Massachusetts Avenue, NW, Washington, D.C. 20008. (202) 667-9000

Embassy of France, 1100 Connecticut Avenue, NW, Washington, D.C. 20006. (202) 223-6710

Embassy of the Federal Republic of Germany, 4645 Reservoir Road, NW, Washington, D.C. 20007. (202) 331-3000

Embassy of Great Britain, 3100 Massachusetts Avenue, NW, Washington, D.C. 20008. (202) 462-1340

Embassy of India, 2107 Massachusetts Avenue, NW, Washington, D.C. 20008. (202) 939-7000

Embassy of Indonesia, 2020 Massachusetts Ave., NW, Washington, D.C. 20036. (202) 775-5200

Embassy of Ireland, 2234 Massachusetts Avenue, NW, Washington, D.C. 20008. (202) 483-7639

Embassy of Israel, 1621 22nd Street, NW, Washington, D.C. 20008. (202) 483-4100

Embassy of Italy, 1601 Fuller Street, NW, Washington, D.C. 20009. (202) 234-1935

Embassy of Japan, 2520 Massachusetts Avenue, NW, Washington, D.C. 20008. (202) 234-2266

Hong Kong Office, (send c/o the Embassy of Great Britain)

Embassy of Mexico, 2829 16th Street, NW, Washington, D.C. 20009. (202) 234-6000

Embassy of the Republic of Singapore, 1824 R Street, NW, Washington, D.C. 20009. (202) 667-7555

Embassy of Spain, 2558 Massachusetts Avenue, NW, Washington, D.C. 20008. (202) 332-4262

Embassy of South Korea, 2320 Massachusetts Avenue, NW, Washington, D.C. 20008. (202) 438-7383

Embassy of Sweden, 600 New Hampshire Avenue, NW, Washington, D.C. 20037. (202) 965-4100

Embassy of Switzerland, 2900 Cathedral Avenue, NW, Washington, D.C. 20008. (202) 462-1811

Appendix B

Existing U.S. Foreign Trade Zones

ZONE #	LOCATION	PHONE #
1	New York, NY	(718) 834-0400
2	New Orleans, LA	(505) 897-0189
3	San Francisco, CA	(415) 391-0176
4	(Open)	
5	Seattle, WA	(208) 382-3257
6	(Open)	
7	Mayaguez, Puerto Rico	(809) 765-2784
8	Toledo, OH	(419) 698-8026
9	Honolulu, HI	(808) 548-5435
10	(Open)	
11	(Open)	
12	McAllen, (San A.) TX	(512) 682-4306
13	(Open)	
14	Little Rock, AR	(501) 490-1468
15	Kansas City, MO	(816) 421-7666
16	Sault Ste. Marie, MI	(906) 635-9131
17	Kansas City, KS	(816) 421-7666
18	San Jose, CA	(408) 277-5823
19	Omaha, NE	(402) 444-5921
20	Suffolk, VA	(804) 623-8080
21	Dorchester Cty, SC	(803) 871-4870
22	Chicago, IL	(312) 646-4400
23	Buffalo, NY	(716) 846-8500
24	Pittston, PA	(717) 655-5581
25	Port Everglades, FL	(305) 523-3404
26	Shenandoah, GA	(404) 656-6338
27	Boston, MA	(617) 973-5500

ZONE #	LOCATION	PHONE #
28	New Bedford, MA	(617) 997-6501
29	Louisville, KY	(502) 935-6024
30	Salt Lake City, UT	(801) 328-3211
31	Granite City, IL	(618) 877-8444
32	Miami, FL	(305) 350-7700
33	Pittsburgh, PA	(412) 471-3939
34	Niagara County, NY	(716) 439-6033
35	Philadelphia, PA	(215) 928-9100
36	Galveston, TX	(409) 766-6112
37	Orange County (Goshen), NY	(914) 564-7700
38	Spartanburg County, SC	(803) 871-4870
39	Dallas/Fort Worth, TX	(214) 574-6720
40	Cleveland, OH	(216) 241-8004
41	Milwaukee, WI	(414) 764-2111
42	Orlando, FL	(305) 859-9485
43	Battle Creek, MI	(616) 989-8197
44	Morris County, NY	(201) 648-3519
45	Portland, OR	(503) 231-5000
46	Cincinnati, OH	(513) 579-9143
47	Campbell County, KY	(513) 579-3143
48	Tucson, AZ	(602) 792-6882
49	Newark/Elizabeth, NJ	(212) 466-7985
50	Long Beach, CA	(213) 437-0041
51	Duluth, MN	(218) 727-8525
52	Suffolk County, NY	(516) 360-4800
53	Rogers County (Tulsa), OK	(918) 266-2291
54	Clinton County, NY	(518) 563-3100
55	Burlington, VT	(802) 862-5726
56	Oakland, CA	(415) 639-7405
57	Mecklenburg County, NC	(704) 588-2868
58	Bangor, ME	(207) 947-0341
59	Lincoln, NE	(402) 476-7511
60	Nogales, AZ	(602) 287-3411
61	San Juan, PR	(809) 721-1273
62	Brownsville, TX	(512) 831-4592
63	Prince George's County, MD	(301) 622-9000
64	Jacksonville, FL	(904) 633-5250
65	Panama City, FL	(904) 763-8471
66	Wilmington, NC	(919) 763-1621
67	Morehead City, NC	(919) 763-1621
68	El Paso, TX	(915) 772-4271
69	(Open)	
70	Detroit, MI	(313) 259-8077
71	Windsor Locks, CT	(203) 623-4919

ZONE #	LOCATION	PHONE #
72	Indianapolis, IN	(317) 236-6246
73	Baltimore/Washington, MD	(301) 859-4449
74	Baltimore, MD	(301) 837-9305
75	Phoenix, AZ	(602) 261-8707
76	Bridgeport, CT	(203) 576-7221
77	Memphis, TN	(901) 528-3307
78	Nashville, TN	(615) 259-5121
79	Tampa, FL	(813) 223-8381
80	San Antonio, TX	(512) 299-8080
81	Portsmouth, NH	(603) 436-8500
82	Mobile, AL	(205) 438-7334
83	Huntsville, AL	(205) 772-9395
84	Harris County, TX	(713) 226-2100
85	Everett, WA	(206) 433-1629
86	Tacoma, WA	(206) 433-1629
87	Lake Charles, LA	(318) 439-3661
88	Great Falls, MT	(406) 761-5036
89	Clark County, NV	(702) 739-8222
90	Onondaga County, NY	(315) 470-1343
91	Newport, VT	(802) 748-5181
92	Harrison County, MS	(601) 982-6606
93	Raleigh/Durham, NC	(919) 549-0551
94	Laredo, TX	(512) 722-0563
95	Starr County, TX	(512) 487-5606
96	Eagle Pass, TX	(512) 773-1111
97	Del Rio, TX	(512) 744-2781
98	Birmingham, AL	(205) 254-2277
99	Wilmington, DE	(302) 736-4271
100	Dayton, OH	(513) 226-1444
101	Clinton County, OH	(513) 382-5591
102	St. Louis, MO	(314) 721-0900
103	Grand Forks, ND	(701) 772-7272
104	Savannah, GA	(912) 964-0904
105	Providence/N. Kingston, RI	(401) 277-2601
106	Oklahoma City, OK	(405) 231-2583
107	Des Moines, IA	(515) 278-9517
108	Valdez, OR	(503) 227-4567
109	Watertown, NY	(315) 785-3226
110	Albuquerque, NM	(505) 842-0088
111	JFK Int'l Airport, NY	(212) 656-4402
112	Colorado Springs, CO	(303) 320-5313
113	Ellis County, TX	(214) 299-6301
114	Peoria, IL	(309) 676-0755
115	Beaumont, TX	(409) 722-7831

ZONE #	LOCATION	PHONE #
116	Port Arthur, TX	(409) 722-7831
117	Orange, TX	(409) 722-7831
118	Ogdensburg (Syracuse), NY	(315) 393-4080
119	Minneapolis/St. Paul, MN	(612) 348-7116
120	Cowlitz County, WA	(206) 423-9921
121	Albany, NY	(518) 272-1414
122	Corpus Christi, TX	(512) 882-5633
123	Denver, CO	(303) 371-2511
124	Grammercy, La Place, LA	(504) 568-6194
125	South Bend, IN	(219) 233-2666
126	Sparks, Reno, NV	(702) 784-3844
127	West Columbia, SC	(803) 794-3427
128	Whatcom County, WA	(206) 734-8180
129	Bellingham, WA	(206) 676-2500
130	Blaine, Bellingham, WA	(206) 676-2500
131	Sumas, Bellingham, WA	(206) 676-2500
132	Coos County, OR	(503) 267-7678
133	Quad-City, IA/IL	(309) 788-7436
134	Chattanooga, TN	(615) 752-4305
135	Palm Beach County, FL	(305) 832-4556
136	Brevard County, FL	(305) 783-7831
137	Wash. Dulles Airport, DC	(703) 661-8040
138	Franklin County, OH	(614) 461-9046
139	Sierra Vista, AZ	(602) 459-6070
140	Flint, MI	(313) 766-8620
141	Monroe County, Rochester, NY	(716) 428-5321
142	Salem, NJ	(609) 935-6380
143	West Sacramento, CA	(916) 371-8000
144	Brunswick, GA	(912) 265-6900
145	Shreveport, LA	(318) 636-7266
146	Lawrence County, IL	(618) 943-5733
147	Reading, PA	(215) 376-6766
148	Knoxville, Maryville, TN	(615) 983-7715
149	Freeport, TX	(409) 233-2667
150	El Paso, TX	(915) 775-1411
151	Findlay, OH	(419) 424-7095
152	Burns Harbor, Portage, IN	(219) 787-8636
153	San Diego, CA	(619) 236-6550
154	Baton Rouge, LA	(504) 387-4207
155	Calhoun/Victoria City TX	(512) 552-3237
156	Weslaco, TX	(512) 968-3181
157	Wyoming, Casper, WY	(307) 472-6688
158	Vicksburg/Jackson, MS	(601) 636-4422
159	St. Paul, AK	(907)546-2331

160	Anchorage, AK	(907) 343-4431
161	Sedgwick County, Wichita, KS	(316) 268-7575
162	North Haven, CT	(203) 787-6735
163	Ponce, PR	(809) 842-0505
164	Muskogee, OK	(918) 687-5459
165	Midland, TX	(915) 563-1460
166	Homestead, FL	(305) 247-7082
167	Brown City, WI	(414) 437-8704
168	Dallas/Ft. Worth, TX	(214) 991-9955
169	Manatee Cty., FL	(813) 722-6621
170	Clark Cty., IN	(317) 232-9200
171	Liberty Cty., TX	(713) 592-3404
172	Oneida Cty., NY	(315) 736-0888
173	Grays Harbor, WA	(206) 533-9528
174	Pima Cty., AZ	(602) 323-9759
175	Cedar Rapids, IA	(319) 362-3131
176	Rockford, IL	(815) 965-8639
177	Evansville, IN	(317) 232-9200
178	Presidio, TX	(915) 229-3724
179	Madawaska, ME	(207) 728-4273

Bibliography

Note: This is a Buyer's Library of International Source Information. Following this alphabetical listing are publications by government agencies and private business organizations. Other addresses are in Appendix A.

Aljian's Purchasing Handbook. 4th ed. 1982. New York: McGraw-Hill.

Cavinato, Joseph. 1989. Duty drawback: an often overlooked cash opportunity. Chilton's *Distribution* 19-25.

Dowst, Somerby. 1986. International buying—the facts and foolishness. *Purchasing* June 25 issue, 52-53.

Dowst, Somerby. 1986. If you can't buy overseas don't answer "Help wanted" ads. *Purchasing* September 11 issue, 66-68.

Dowst, Somerby. 1987. The why, how, and what of overseas purchasing. *Purchasing* 54-55.

Foster, Dean and Ellen Raider. 1988. Bringing cultural sensitivity to the international bargaining table. *Business Age* 50-54.

Monckza, Robert M. and Larry C. Giunipero. 1990. *Purchasing Internationally: Concepts and Principles*. Michigan: Bookcrafters

Pooler, V. H. 1964. *The Purchasing Man and His Job*. New York: American Management Association.

Pooler, V. H. 1964. Developing the negotiation skills of the buyer. American Management Association *AMA Bulletin #50*.

Pooler, V. H. 1966. TREND: Total approach to measuring purchasing performance. *Purchasing* May issue 54-61.

Pooler, V. H. 1967. AMA training recording and manual, *Listen In On Purchasing*. New York.

Pooler, V. H. 1973. Measuring the purchasing man: TREND. *Journal of Purchasing and Materials Management*. Vol. 9, No. 4 November issue, 68-85.

Pooler, Victor H. and Robert Johnson. 1976. *Fundamentals of Effective Purchasing*. Program Instruction Course. New York: Argyle.

Pooler, V. H. 1978. Movie— *TREND: Measuring Purchasing Productivity*. 1987 Revised VHS editions. PAL 30. New York: NAPM.

Pooler, V. H. 1978. Purchasing management. In *Encyclopedia of Professional Management*, ed. Lester R. Bittel, pp 1016-1025. New York: McGraw Hill.

Pooler, V. H. 1970 & 1980. Contributor to *AMA Management Handbook*. Also to McGraw-Hill's *Purchasing Handbook*.

Pooler, V. H. 1985. Purchasing management. In *Handbook for Professional Managers*, ed. Lester R. Bittel and Jackson E. Ramsey, pp 1016-1025. New York: McGraw Hill.

Pooler, V. H. 1986. Ten rules for offshore buys will help get you started. *Purchasing* October issue, 62A21.

Pooler, V. H. 1987. *Purchasing: Balancing Price and Value*. Chicago: American Supply Education Foundation, Inc.

Pooler, V. H. 1987. How to construct a library of valuable information sources. *Purchasing* February 26 issue, 97.

Pooler, V. H. 1987. Understanding the options when you choose a buying channel. *Purchasing* June 11 issue, 130A35.

Pooler, V. H. 1987. More options to fill out the buying channels picture. *Purchasing* September 24 issue, 98A16.

Pooler, V. H. 1988. Know the laws of the lands when you start global sourcing. *Purchasing* January 28 issue, 34B35.

Pooler, V. H. 1988. Standard transportation terms are recognized worldwide. *Purchasing* July 28 issue, 121.

Pooler, V. H. 1988. Customs brokers take big load off importing buyers' shoulders. *Purchasing* November 10 issue, 96C8.

Pooler, V. H. 1988. Don't be backward about starting with a forwarder. *Purchasing* September issue, 96.

Pooler, V. H. 1989. Buyers should know how to make letters of credit work for them. *Purchasing* March 9 issue, 93.

Pooler, V. H. 1989. You can't duck documentation, so you'd better understand it. *Purchasing* March 23, 129.

Pooler, V. H. 1989. Methods of payment deserve close look on offshore buys. *Purchasing* May 4 issue, 96B31.

Pooler, V. H. 1989. You may have to put a different spin on some of the traditional terms. *Purchasing* July 20 issue, P100A9.

Pooler, V. H. 1989. Stateside buying terms can be adapted for use overseas. *Purchasing* July 24 issue, 100A9.

Pooler, V. H. 1990. Watertight contracts keep offshore buys from harm. *Purchasing* April 19 issue, 134.

Pooler, V. H. 1990. Understanding import duties is first step to the best deal. *Purchasing* May 3 issue, 84A12.

Pooler, V. H. and David J. 1981. Purchasing's elusive conceptual home. *Journal of Purchasing and Materials Management*. Summer issue, 13-18.

Quinn, Francis J. 1986. Let's negotiate! (shipping rates). *Traffic Management* 46.

Rosenthal, Thomas M. 1989. Hidden Drawbacks [U.S.—Canada FTA]. *Global Trade* 10-12.

Scraub, Jerome. 1980. *Drawback, a guide to increasing trade profit*. Jersey City: Scott Printing 16 pp.

U.S. GOVERNMENT PRINTING OFFICE

The following are for sale by the Superintendent of Documents, U.S. Government Printing Office (GPO), Washington, D.C. 20402:

Importing into the United States. Describes the customs organization and procedures to follow when importing goods into the United States. It covers clearance, entry of goods, duty assessment, invoices, marking, special laws, and foreign trade zones. Customs publication No. 504 for sale by Department of the Treasury, Bureau of Customs, Washington, D.C. 20229, and GPO.

Guide to the U.S. Generalized System of Preferences. 1988. Office of the President, U.S. Trade Representative, Washington, D.C. GPO, 271 pages.

Harmonized Tariff Schedules of the United States (HTSUSA). 1991 (issued annually) loose-leaf edition of U.S. Customs Regulations. Lists all articles imported into the United States. Published by the U.S. International Trade Commission, Washington, D.C. 20436. It can be purchased from the Superintendent of Documents ($85 Sept. 1989). Can be found in most large public libraries.

Key Officers of Foreign Service Posts Guide for business Representatives: #7877. Listing of all U.S. embassies, key officers, and consulate addresses.

Business Guide to the Near East and North Africa #003-009099255-9. Explains how to do business in these areas and services of the U.S. government available.

East-West Countertrade Practices. Stock # 003-009-0258-3. Ocean freight rate guidelines for shippers. Basic procedures for transporting overseas goods.

U.S.—Canada Free Trade Agreement. Customs #592 covers details of bilateral agreement to remove trade barriers, etc.

Foreign Assembly of U.S. Components (formerly the 807 guide) No. 539. September 1990.

Key Officers of Foreign Service Posts. U.S. Department of State listing of all U.S. embassies and consulates (Refer Appendix A).

Background Notes. U.S. Department of State. Covers individual countries, history, government, economic and political conditions, and foreign relations.

U.S. Department of Commerce's ITA Publications

Foreign Trade Statistics Data Finder. Summary of government publication and trade reports on export and import statistics by the International Trade Association. From U.S. Department of Commerce, or Subscriber Services, Bureau of the Census, Washington, D.C. 20233.

U.S. Commercial Offices and the Foreign Commercial Service Posts. Free upon request from the U.S. Department of Commerce, Publication Distribution Room 1617, Washington, D.C. 20230

Service Guide—Ship your Cargo on U.S. Flag Ships. (U.S. lines serving foreign trade routes, ports of call, and types of services provided.) U.S. Department of Commerce, Maritime Administration, Office of Public Affairs, Washington, D.C. 20230.

World Traders Data Reports (WTDR program provides background on reputation, country/product profiles of foreign firms). U.S. Department of Commerce. Takes 60 to 90 days for $75 each, though banks often give same data to customers quicker and cheaper.

The Agent/Distributor Service. (Agent and distributor services and how representatives help can be found overseas.) U.S. Department of Commerce.

International Chamber of Commerce

The following can be ordered from the ICC Publishing Corp., 156 Fifth Avenue, Suite 820, New York, NY 10010, (212) 206-1150.

ICC Incoterms: International rules for the interpretation of trade terms. 1986. Paris: ICC Services 135 pp.

A simplified Guide to Customs Services. United States imports.

Introduction to ICC Rules on International Contracts. Points to be considered in negotiating international trade contracts.

Standard Forms for Issuing Documentary Credits. Uniform customs practice and banking information. Primarily of use in explaining use of documentary credits. No. 323. Some banks have this available free.

Key Words in International Trade. ISBN 92-842-00234 336 pp.

Guide to Documentary Credit Operations. ISBN 92-842-1021-6 336 pp.

Guide to Arbitration. ISBN number 92-842-1018-6 140 pp.

Arbitration Law in Europe. ISBN 92-842-1014-3 370 pp.

Rules for the ICC Court of Arbitration. (Rules and schedule of conciliation and costs.) No. 291 34 pp.

TRADE DIRECTORIES

Directory of American Firms Operating In Foreign Countries. U.S. firms and the foreign firms they control, with information on officers, products, and services, along with all addresses.

American Register of Exporters and Importers. More than 30,000 firms and products along with export officials, steamship lines, foreign trade associations, etc. 90 West Broadway, New York, NY 10017

International Yellow Pages. By country, city, and product. An 800 number found in your local phone directory brings Yellow Pages and White Pages from anywhere around the world. An example is *Italian Yellow Pages for the U.S.,*

AT&T's annual directory issued in English. Free upon request or by writing to AT&T, 412 Mt. Kemble Ave., Morristown, NJ 07960.

1991 U.S Custom House Guide. (or latest edition). Philadelphia: North American Publishing Company, 401 N. Broad Street, Philadelphia, PA 19108-9988. Cost is somewhat over $300. Contains harmonized code, customs regulations, port cargo-handling capabilities, and other data.

Sourcing Guide for Importers. How-to guide available free upon request. UNZ & Co., P.O. Box 308, Jersey City, NJ Or call (800) 631-3098.

1991 Canadian Trade Index. Database of more than 13,000 manufacturers, their products, trademarks, and brands. Canadian Trade Index, One Yonge St. Suite 1400, Toronto, Ontario M5E 1J9, Canada.

Guide to Hong Kong Products. International Publishing Ltd. 11th floor, Block A, Hung Ho Building, Kings Road 2, North Point, Hong Kong.

Annual Directory of Hong Kong Industries. H.K. Productivity Centre, P.O. Box 99027, Tsimshatsui Post Office, Kowloon, Hong Kong.

Export International Alex Publication. P.O. Box 33918, Sheung Wan Post Office, Hong Kong.

Trade Directories of the World, Croner Publications Inc. Publishes variety of international information. 211-03 Jamaica Avenue, Queens Village, NY 11428.

The Financing of Exports and Imports. Reference guide on financial aspects of both exporting and importing. Morgan Guaranty Trust Co. of New York Wall St., New York 10015.

Ports of the World. Guide to cargo loss control. Marine & Aviation Services Ltd., Insurance Company of North America, P.O. Box 7728, Philadelphia, PA 19106

Standard Trade Index of Japan. Guide to manufacturers, business concerns, and trading companies. International Publication Service, 114 East 32nd St., New York, NY 10016

Directory of Manufactures In Taiwan (two volumes). Covers about 45,000 manufacturers. Tsai-Huang Pi-Fang, No. 86 Wuchan West 6th St., Taichung, Taiwan, R.O.C.

Taiwan Electric/Electronic Products. Company information, indexed both alphabetically and by product. Taiwan Electric Appliance Manufacturers Assn. No. 315-317. Sung Chiang Road, 7th floor, Yu-Fong Building, Taipei, Taiwan, R.O.C.

Singapore Manufacturers Association Directory. Annual directory of manufacturers listed alphabetically and by products. The Singapore Manufacturers Association, Suite 118, First Floor, World Trade Centre, 1 Maritime Square, Telok Blangah Road, Singapore, 4.

Singapore Electronics Buyers Guide (annual). Electronics industry, listing suppliers and products. Association of Electronic Industries in Singapore, 1A, Lorong Rukang Lima, Singapore 2261.

Kelly's Manufacturers And Merchants Directory. Annual listing of companies by product and country. Included are the United Kingdom, Europe, Africa, and the Americas, as well as Asia. Write Neville House, Eden Street, Kingston-upon-Thames, Surrey, KT1 IBY, England.

MAGAZINES AND NEWSPAPERS

Japan Economic Journal, a weekly magazine about economics and business. Nihon Keizai Shimbun, Tokyo International, P.O. Box 5004, Tokyo, Japan.

Korean News Review, a weekly magazine covering political, cultural, social, and economic issues. Korean Herald, Inc., 250 West 54th St. (7th floor), New York, NY 10019

Taiwan Merchandise Overseas Weekly, on business and economic news. China Economic News Service, United Daily News Building, P.O. Box 43-60, Taipei, Taiwan, R.O.C.

Trade Opportunities In Taiwan, a weekly on business and economics that lists various products and companies offering products for sale. Taipei World Trade Center, P.O. Box 81-28, Taipei, Taiwan, R.O.C.

U.S. Custom's Bulletin, issued weekly by the GPO.

China's Foreign Trade (bimonthly). Economic and foreign trade and data on export commodities. China Publications Center, Guoji Shudian, P.O. Box 399, Beijing, China.

Frommer Guides, and also *Fodor Guides*. Issued for many countries, and are excellent for travelling information. They are available in most book stores.

Buying Negotiation Guides. Pooler & Associates, One North Ridge, Syracuse, NY 13214. Available for most (30) major industrial nations. Guides provide customs, culture and business practices, together with economics as a refresher for a buyer about to visit a particular country.

Asian Sources Journals. Issued monthly, for products such as: electronic products, electronic components, sporting goods, toys, and housewares, timepiece, garments and accessories, and hardware. All of above published by Trade Media Lt., P.O. Box 1786, Kowloon Central Post Office, Hong Kong.

Asia business newspapers, English editions, cover Japan, Hong Kong, Malaysia, Philippines, Singapore, South Korea, Thailand, and Sri Lanka. Issued by Worldpaper, 424 World Trade Center, Boston, MA 02210 (617) 439-5400. Telex 6817273.

Business America, The Magazine of International Trade, (biweekly). U.S. Department of Commerce, ITA.

Glossary of Global Purchasing Terms

This glossary of global purchasing terms is intended as a quick reference. For more details, the buyer should read the appropriate chapters. Logistical terms are separately listed below.

Acceptance (Bankers or Trade Acceptance) occurs when a draft is presented to a bank for acceptance for payment. The drawee is the supplier or "acceptor." The buyer writes the word "Accepted" and the date on the face of the draft.

Admission to FTZ (used in place of entry) is physical arrival of goods in the foreign trade zone with the approval of the zone grantee and Customs.

Assembled in the U.S. is used by domestic firms that send parts offshore for working and assembly and then import under Section 807. See Chapter 8.

Assists are drawings, technical instruction, tools, and dies that a U.S. buyer provides to an offshore supplier. Importer must pay duty on value of these "assists" as part of the transaction value.

ATA Carnet "Admission Temporaire—Temporary Admission." See **Carnet**.

Banks:
1. **Issuing bank**—The buyer's domestic bank that issues credits upon request.
2. **Correspondent bank**—One that is a depository for other banks within the correspondent's locality.
3. **Advising bank**—Usually a correspondent bank in the supplier's country to handle L/C by notifying the supplier that the credit is opened in their favor.
4. **Collecting bank**—Can be any involved in the collection process.
5. **Confirming bank**—One that guarantees payment of other banks in an L/C. Confirmation is requested by supplier when the issuing bank's ability to pay is questioned.

Barter is exchange of goods directly without use of money.

Bilateral Trade Agreement is a formal agreement for commerce between two countries. An example is the U.S.—Canada Free Trade Agreement.

Boycott   is a refusal to deal commercially with a person, firm, or country.

Carnet   is an international customs document issued by national chambers of commerce affiliated with the ICC. Carnet permits a holder to carry merchandise *temporarily* into most foreign countries, without paying duties or posting bonds. The goods most commonly are samples and must be returned.

Cartel   is a form of organization whose purpose is to fix prices. It is illegal within the United States. The Organization of Petroleum Exporting Countries OPEC. is the best known example.

Cash Against Documents   (CAD) is payment for goods in cash upon transfer of title documents to the buyer.

Cash in Advance   (CIA) requires payment for goods in full before shipment.

Certificate of Origin   is required by Customs for certifying country where produced. Vital to gain benefits of lowered rates or duty-free under various trade agreements.

Certificate of Survey   (Manufacture, Inspection, Weight, etc.) is a document, often notarized, that certifies about manufacture, accuracy, weight, and so forth.

Chamber of Commerce   is an association that promotes local business interests.

Classification   is set by Customs and determines rates of duty. See *Harmonized Code* (HTSUS)

Clean Draft   is one that has no other documents attached.

Commercial Invoice   is the document requesting payment that is used in commerce listing goods bought and prices to be paid.

Common External Tariff   (CXT) is uniformly applied by a common market such as the European Community to imports from outside the union.

Common Market   allows unrestricted trade among members. Name applied to the European Economic Community (EEC).

Confirmed Letter of Credit   is an L/C that has been "confirmed" by a bank. This means that the bank guarantees the payment. The credit cannot be cancelled without mutual consent of buyer and seller.

Consignment   is delivery of goods from supplier, with title remaining with the owner until consignee has sold or used them.

Consignment   is the physical transfer of goods from supplier (consignor), who retains ownership, to the buyer (consignee). Payment is made later, after resale.

Consular(ized) Invoice   is one signed by a consular official of the offshore supplier's country certifying the value, quantity, and nature of the shipment. Not required by the United States.

Countertrade   is a reciprocal trading arrangement, including barter, counterpurchases, buyback, and offset. Refer to Chapter 1.

Countervailing Duty   is an extra duty imposed to offset foreign government subsidies or unfair pricing (dumping) within the United States.

Country of Origin   is the country that made or produced at least 35 percent of the content value.

Currency   is the medium of exchange, such as coins and bank notes. Hard currency is expected to rise versus the U.S. dollar. Soft currency is expected to drop versus the U.S. dollar.

Customs   is the government's agency designated to collect duties levied on imports. (In the U.S., Customs is part of the Treasury Department.)

Customs Bond   is a signed contract assuring performance imposed by law.

Custom(house) Broker   is an individual, or firm, licensed to enter and clear goods through customs.

Date Draft   is a draft that matures at a specified number of days after the date of issuance.

Demurrage   is charges for excess time taken for loading or unloading a vessel.

Developing Countries,   or Beneficial Developing Countries (BDCs), is a term for countries not yet highly industrialized, and lacking technology. They include more than 130 countries of Africa, Asia, Oceania (except Australia and New Zealand), Latin America, and the Middle East, with exceptions.

Dock Receipt   is signed by a domestic carrier to acknowledge receipt of shipment from an ocean carrier at an international dock.

Documents against Acceptance   (D/A) are instructions given by a shipper to a bank, indicating that documents transferring title to goods should be delivered to the buyer only upon buyer's acceptance of the attached draft.

Documents against Payment   (D/P) indicates to bank that documents transferring title to goods should be delivered to buyer only upon payment of the attached draft.

Draft   (Bill of Exchange) is an unconditional order in writing from the drawer to the drawee, directing the drawee to pay a specified amount to a named payee at a fixed future date.

Variations are **Arrival Draft, Time Draft,** and **Sight Draft. A Clean Draft** has no other documents attached versus the **Documentary Draft,** which does.

Drawback   is a program to get a 99 percent refund of duties already paid on imported goods that can be claimed if later exported.

Drawee   is the individual or firm on whom a draft is drawn, and who owes the amount indicated.

Drawer   is the individual or firm that issues or signs a draft and stands to get payment of the amount from the drawee.

Dumping   is selling merchandise within a country at prices that are below cost and thus harmful to domestic competition.

Duty   is the customs tax levied on certain items upon entering into a country. Rates are based on:

1. **Ad Valorem** ("according to value") is applied as a percentage of the transaction value, and is most commonly used.
2. **Specific,** or per pound, unit, and so on.
3. **Compound** is Ad Valorem and a specific combined rate.

Embargo   is a government order prohibiting shipments to leave or enter its ports.

Exchange Controls   means rationing of foreign currencies, drafts, and obligations by countries seeking to ease balance of payment difficulties. When such measures are imposed, importers must apply for prior authorization to bring in designated amounts and types of goods. These measures restrict imports and are considered nontariff barriers to trade.

Exchange Rate   is the price at which one currency is bought (exchanged) for another.

Excise Tax   is sometimes called a consumption tax on certain goods produced within or imported into, a country.

Export Credits   are used where countertrade is encountered. These credits can be swapped or traded with other companies to fulfill agreed countertrade.

Export Declaration   is required by the exporting government (U.S. Department of Commerce for U.S. export) to control exports, and as a source for export statistics.

Export Management Company   (EMC) is a private firm that exports for several manufacturers or clients for a commission.

Force Majeure   clause exempts the parties for nonfulfillment of obligations resulting from drastic conditions beyond their control (floods, war, earthquakes, fire, etc.).

Foreign Trade Zone   (FTZ) is a designated policed area, often nearby a port, legally outside the customs territory of a country, although located within that country. The FTZ may have "facilities for lading, unlading, handling, storing, manipulating, manufacturing, and exhibiting foods, and for reshipping them by land, water, or air."

Forward Buy   is arranging for a future purchase of another currency from a bank at a quoted value.

Free Trade   is a theoretical concept that assumes international trade unencumbered with government impediments such as tariffs or barriers.

Free Trade Area   (FTA) exists when two or more countries have eliminated most tariffs and nontariff barriers affect trade among themselves. Examples are the European Free Trade Association (EFTA) and the U.S.—Canada Free Trade Agreement.

General Agreement on Tariffs and Trade   (GATT) is a multilateral treaty to promote trade by reducing tariffs.

Generalized System of Preferences   (GSP) is a program allowing duty-free entry for more than 2,800 tariff schedule items from more than 130 Beneficial Developing Countries (BDCs)

Global Buyer   is one who seeks to get the lowest landed costs for his or her buys for each of his or her fellow plants and subsidiaries wherever located in the world. This compares to an **international buyer**, who simply imports something across his or her national border.

Harmonization   is a term for international efforts to uniform customs nomenclatures and procedures.

Harmonized code   (HTSUS, Harmonized Tariff Schedule of the United States) is a code that determines classification for duty rates.

Harmonized Code or System (HTSUS)   is now used for classification of goods. No longer does each country have its own code, so they are "harmonized."

Hedging   is the practice of buying foreign currency futures as a "hedge" to assure that the buyer pays exactly what he or she expects at the time of placing his or her order. Refer to Chapter 11.

Import License   gives evidence of the legal right to import restricted items into a country. It is required by some governments for certain goods.

Imports   are goods brought into one country from another. An importer is the buyer who accepts and pays for goods.

International Chamber of Commerce   (ICC) has standardized and improved ways of conducting global business transactions.

Irrevocable Letter of Credit   is an L/C that can not be cancelled if a supplier complies with its terms and conditions.

Issuing Bank—Refer to Banks.

Joint Venture   is a business partnership with shared ownership and control.

Letter of Credit   (L/C) is a financial document issued by a bank as instructed by the buyer, authorizing the seller to draw a specified sum of money under specified terms.

Licensing   is an arrangement whereby a manufacturer grants permission to others to manufacture that product in return for royalties.

Liquidation   is a customs term that the record of entry is closed and the duty paid is correct.

Merchandise   includes goods and wares of every description that may be imported.

Merchant   is an individual or firm that buys products from manufacturers and then packages and marks goods for resale under their name.

Most Favored Nation   (MFN) is a policy of nondiscrimination in trade, providing equal treatment to all trading partners, that is given to Most Favored Nations. All signers of GATT receive MFN treatment unless denied by the importing country.

Multilateral treaty   is one signed by three or more countries. See **GATT, EEC.**

Open Account   is used domestically when goods are shipped without guarantee of payment. Buyer honors invoice sent by seller.

Phytosanitary Inspection Certificate   is issued by supplier's equivalent of U.S. Department of Agriculture to satisfy import regulations that shipment has been inspected and is free from harmful pests and plant diseases.

Power of Attorney   occurs when the buyer signs agreement that allows others (broker) to act on his or her behalf.

Preliminary Advice   is a teletransmission sent to advising bank giving brief details of L/C being issued.

Pro Forma Invoice   is one provided by supplier (or by buyer) prior to the shipment of goods to secure an L/C. The pro forma gives the kinds (specifications) and quantities to be sent, certifying their dollar value.

Protectionism   is the deliberate use of restrictions on imports to enable relatively inefficient domestic producers to compete with foreign producers.

Purchasing Agent   is a purchaser of goods in his or her country on behalf of foreign importers (government agencies and large private firms).

Quota   is a limit to the quantity of goods of a specific kind that a country permits to be imported without restriction or added duties.

Quotation   is an offer to sell goods at a stated price and under what conditions.

Shipper's Export Declaration   is required by supplier's government. Prepared by shipper, it gives all data about export and is used for statistical purposes.

Tariffs   are technically a "listing of duties," though in practice both terms are used for duty rate.

Temporary Importation Bond   (TIB) is an entry procedure allowing temporary importation of goods that will be exported (or destroyed) at a later date without incurring a duty.

Time Draft   matures either a certain number of days after acceptance or a certain number of days after the date of the draft.

Trading Company   is a firm that purchases goods from many countries and then supplies them to other countries for a small commission.

Transportation and Exportation Entry   is used for shipments that may come into the United States without duty, when they are to be reshipped to another country.

Trigger Price Mechanism   (TPM) is a U.S. system for monitoring imported steel to identify imports that may be "dumped." Imported steel below set prices may "trigger" formal antidumping investigations by the Department of Commerce and the U.S. International Trade Commission. It only affects stainless wire at present.

Unfair Trade Practices   means governmental support such as subsidies, rebates, and credits, that results in competitive advantages against domestic sellers.

United Nations Conference on Trade and Development   (UNCTAD) seeks to focus on economic measure to accelerate Third World development.

World Bank   is the common term for the International Bank for Reconstruction and Development (IBRD) located in Washington, D.C. It sells bonds in world markets, and makes loans for development purposes. Profits are plowed back into capital resources for future loans.

World Intellectual Property Organization   (WIPO) is an agency of the United Nations that promotes cooperation internationally for the protection of intellectual property, literary and artistic works, copyrights, and so forth.

LOGISTIC TERMS

Bill of Lading   (B/L) is a document that sets the terms between shipper and carrier to move goods as specified. It serves as a receipt for the shipper that the carrier accepted the goods listed.

Variations are **Air Waybill, Ocean Bill of Lading, Railbill,** and **Trucking B/L or "Pro."**

A "Short B/L" omits conditions of the regular bill that still apply. "Clean" B/L means goods in good condition. "Unclean" or "foul" bill means that the goods are damaged or the packaging is broken.

"Straight bill" provides for delivery only to the named party. "To order bill" is a negotiable instrument and is delivered to anyone endorsed on the bill.

Booking Request   is a request for space on an ocean vessel.

Bonded Warehouse   is a secured Customs-approved privately owned storage facilities, where goods are stored. No duty is required until imported into the United States.

Break-Bulk   terminals sort shipments for handling ease and reloading. Also, it is the act of combining or breaking down shipment.

C&F   means cost and freight are included.

Charter Rates   are charged by carriers without set routes. These rates are highly negotiable.

CIF   means the same as C&F with addition of insurance.

COFC   stands for Container on Flat Car shipment. Sometimes "Fishyback" was descriptively used for ocean shipments.

Common Carrier   is a transporter such as air carrier, railroad, or trucking, shipping line with set routes.

Conference Rates   are uniform rates set by ocean conference by agreement.

Container Ship   is one that is designed solely to handle containers for ease in loading and unloading.

Delivered at Frontier   means that the supplier's obligations are fulfilled when goods arrive at the frontier, but before passing through the customs border of the importer.

Delivery Order   contains instructions from the customs broker to the ocean carrier as authority to release the cargo to the inland carrier.

Delivery Receipt   is provided by carrier upon arrival and signed by buyer upon receipt of goods. This proves that the goods were delivered.

Dock Receipt   is an acknowledgement that goods are in the harbor master's possession, ready for loading or unloading.

Ex-Dock   (Ex-Quay) signifies that the price quoted applies at the point of origin dock.

FAS Vessel   ("Free Alongside") is a term indicating that the quoted price includes the cost of delivering goods alongside a specific vessel.

"Fishyback"   —See **COFC**.

FOB (Vessel, rail, etc.)   ("Free on Board") indicates that the quoted price includes cost of loading goods for carriage at a specified place. Same as for "Free on Rail" or "Free on Truck" (means railway wagons!), which are both used only for rail shipment.

Foul B/L.   See **B/L**.

General Order Charges   are costs incurred for warehousing goods from the dock. This includes goods not ready for loading or not picked up within time limit.

Gross Weight   is the full weight of a shipment, including goods and packaging.

Incoterms   are (international commercial terms) that were standardized by the ICC. Refer to Chapter 7.

Insurance, All Risk   is the broadest coverage available to a shipper, and covers all in-transit losses.

Insurance Certificate   assures the buyer that insurance is provided to cover loss or damage to the cargo while in transit.

Lighter   is an open or covered barge that is towed by a tugboat, mainly in harbors and inland waterways.

Marine Insurance   covers buyer's loss or damage of goods at sea. Covers losses from fire, shipwreck, piracy, and so forth. However, losses that can be recovered from the carrier are not covered.

Marking   is the use of letters, numbers, and symbols on cargo packages for identification. Also, all imported items must bear identification marking as to country of origin.

NVOCC   is a Non-Vessel Operating Common Carrier that contracts as a carrier, though owning no equipment or ship. See Chapter 12.

Ocean Bill   is a B/L used for exporter to consign a shipment for ocean carriage.

Packing List   shows the number and kinds of items being shipped and provides information for shipment control.

Pier Charge   is a cost of moving though a pier.

"Piggyback"   —See **TOFC**.

RORO   (Roll-on or Roll-off) facilities shows that port can handle a container with wheels. This allows easy movement on or off the ship.

Ship's Manifest   is a written instrument signed by the captain that lists individual shipments onboard the ship.

Steamship Conference   is a group of carriers that operate under mutually agreed terms and freight rates.

Tare Weight   is weight of a container and packing materials, excluding the weight of its contents.

TOFC   (Trailer-on-Flat-Car, formerly called "Piggy-back") is when the motor carrier puts a container or truck chassis on a flatcar for rail transport.

Tramp Steamer   is a ship not operating on regular routes or schedules, and does not belong to a conference.

Transmittal Letter   lists particulars of the shipment and documents being sent, together with instructions for disposition. Special instructions are also included.

W.A.   ("with average") is a marine insurance term denoting partial protection when damage exceeds 3 percent.

Warehouse Receipt   issued by a warehouse operator, lists goods received for storage.

Weight Certificate   —See **Certificate of Survey**.

Wharfage   is a charge assessed by a pier or dock owner for handling incoming or outgoing cargo.

Without Reserve   is a term indicating that a shipper's agent can make decisions and adjustments without prior approval.

Index